Gender, Sex and Status:

Turmoil in America

GENDER, SEX AND STATUS

TURMOIL IN AMERICA

GERHARD FALK

Algora Publishing
New York

Library of Congress Cataloging-in-Publication Data —

Names: Falk, Gerhard, 1924– author.
Title: Gender, Sex and Status: Turmoil in America / Gerhard Falk.
Description: New York : Algora Publishing, [2019] | Includes
    bibliographical references and index. | Summary: "Prof. Falk discusses
    recent evolutions in American society, providing hard data to help
    readers assess the issues objectively. He examines how young people are
    being led astray by today's attitudes toward sex, rampant alcohol and
    drug use, and a focus on rights and privileges"- – Provided by publisher.

Identifiers: LCCN 2019048622 (print) | LCCN 2019048623 (ebook) | ISBN
    9781628944075 (trade paperback) | ISBN 9781628944082 (hardcover) | ISBN
    9781628944099 (pdf)
Subjects: LCSH: Women—United States—Social conditions. | Sex—United
    States. | Social problems—United States. | United States—Social
    conditions—1980–
Classification: LCC HQ1421 .F348 2019 (print) | LCC HQ1421 (ebook) | DDC
    305.40973—dc23
LC record available at https://lccn.loc.gov/2019048622
LC ebook record available at https://lccn.loc.gov/2019048623

Printed in the United States

Acknowledgments

Many thanks to Dr. Ursula Falk, my wife, for proofreading this manuscript, and to my son, Clifford Falk, for proofreading and for improving the endnotes.

TABLE OF CONTENTS

INTRODUCTION

Sex and age are the two criteria which all human societies use to determine status and role or gender within their culture. Gender refers to acquired characteristics such as education, occupation and wealth. Sex refers to the biological differences between women and men.

In nonindustrial cultures, older men hold a higher status than women and young men, and generally speaking men in nonindustrial societies dominate women.

In American society these arrangements were also true until the sexual revolution of the 1960s propelled women into occupations previously reserved entirely to men. The National Opinion Research Council has repeatedly demonstrated that occupation is the most important criterion for determining prestige in America. As more and more women gained a college education in the 1960s and later, women succeeded in entering the professions, such as medicine, law, pharmacy, engineering and academia. Women also became owners of businesses and executives of corporations, so that it is no longer surprising to 21st-century Americans that the chief executive officer of General Motors is a woman.

A review of women's occupations in the early 21st century reveals that women have moved far from the housewife role which, in the 1950s, was about the only status role available to them. Nonetheless, even as late as 2019 the average income of women is still less that the average income of men, due to various factors.

Sociology teaches that status is the sum of our rights and privileges, and role is the sum of our duties and obligations. By attaining more and more education, and therefore more economic independence, American women have proved that the centuries-old subjection of women to men was not rooted in biological differences.

Although the status of American men has been somewhat altered by the achievements of women, it is largely similar to that which it has always been, even as men must accommodate competition from women.

The liberation of women at the end of the 20th century also has led to a sexual revolution which now allows women to express themselves sexually in a manner prohibited in all previous generations.

Consequently divorce, abortion, prostitution and pornography have been liberated from that hidden status in the past and are now openly displayed. This acceptance of sexual behavior is particularly visible among our role models such as politicians, entertainers and sports figures. Undoubtedly, American women and men have benefited from this openness to sexual conduct. It is however also evident that many young adults of college age have been badly served by the promotion of sexual behavior associated with drinking alcohol and using other drugs. This combination of early sexual experiences associated with peer pressure to participate in uncontrolled sex and drinking has led to injury and death among college students at the so-called party schools, which are nothing more than a pretense of higher education.

Efforts to curb the unfortunate consequences of sexual liberation for youngsters have concentrated on sex education. The evidence is, however, that sex education is a failure. Therefore it is incumbent on American adults to curb the excesses of those too young to recognize the painful consequences of their actions.

This book is dedicated to that end, not because we seek the sexual repressions of the past, but because we want to free sexuality from the disasters which so many Americans disregard and which are the consequences of the influence of the American media culture.

CHAPTER 1. WOMEN'S OCCUPATIONS AND INCOME IN THE PROFESSIONS

The most common and universal experience of mankind consists of the relationship of women to men and men to women. Two words are used in the English language to describe this connection. Descriptions or references to the biological differences between women and men are talking about "sex." That word is derived from *segare*, to divide or segregate. On the other hand, the cultural differences between women and men are called gender.

There are three aspects of culture. Material culture consists of all physical objects made by humans, such as an atomic bomb or a nail. Then there are ideological aspects of culture, the things we believe. And finally there is behavioral culture, which consists of what we do. Evidently, women as well as men conduct themselves in a manner which reflects the beliefs common in that culture and supported by the physical objects available. For example, there was a time in American history when birth control and abortion were denounced by Christians and Jews alike. Furthermore, technology in the first half of the 20th century and certainly in the 19th century and before hardly supported efforts at birth control and made abortion both dangerous and difficult.

In the 21st century this has changed. Because of the discovery of The "Pill" as well as the belief that women are entitled to be more than mothers and housewives, both birth control and abortion are popular in the United States although also subject to some controversy.

Most important for understanding the relationship of women and men in the 21st century is recognition that women are in the ascendancy in this country not only because nearly half the American labor force is female but also because approximately 60% of all American college students are women.

As a consequence of these developments, more than half of all medical and law students in the United States are female, even as large numbers of women have become successful in the business world, either by owning their own businesses or by climbing the corporate ladder.

The result of these developments is a certain amount of friction between the sexes, leading to widespread complaints by women concerning male aggression and sexual harassment.

Other consequences of this most recent approach to sexual and gender relations are such phenomena as wives earning more than their husbands; women bosses exercising authority over men; women not only voting but getting elected to such positions as state governor or federal senator or representative. One woman even ran for President of the United States.

Women have recently entered formerly all-male professions such as corporate executive, pharmacist, physician and engineer. In view of all this, it is the purpose of this book to feature and explain many of the recent developments in gender relations with a view of making at least some contribution to the alleviation of so many difficulties concerning gender and sex.

Recently the United States Census reported that there were 163.2 million women in the United States. The number of men was 158.2 million in July 2015. This discrepancy is principally the result of longevity, as women age 85 and older outnumbered men in 2015 4.1 million to 2.1 million.[1]

Anyone who has ever visited a nursing home could see at once that women residents outnumber men considerably. There are several reasons for this discrepancy. First is "toxic testosterone." As early as years 15 to 24 the male to female mortality rate increases for males at the onset of puberty. During this period, men are three times more likely to die than is true of women, as most of these male fatalities are caused by reckless behavior and violence. The most common causes of death for young men are motorcycle accidents, followed by homicide, suicide, cancer, and drowning. Until late middle age, male and female mortality declines. Yet, behavior related fatalities continue to be the most common cause of death of men aged 50 to 64. Men in that age are twice as likely as women to die in auto accidents and four times as likely to kill themselves.[2]

Another factor contributing to the presence of a majority of women in the United States is that although 104 boys are born for every 100 girls, stillbirths, spontaneous abortions, and miscarriages are more common for male fetuses than for female fetuses. More boys die in infancy and mortality rates for males exceed those for females at each year, so that women are in the majority by age 25.[3] Women are also the majority of college graduates and have therefore increased female income since 1970.

Industrial and Business Executives

Fortune magazine reports that in 2017, 6.4% or 32 of the Fortune 500 list of US companies were run by women. Women CEOs are still a tiny minority, and yet the number of women on the Fortune 500 list for 2017 was the longest ever.

Included in that list is Margaret Whitman, the president and chief executive officer of the Hewlett-Packard enterprise. Hewlett-Packard makes computers and other electronic devices. In the fiscal year 2016 Whitman was paid $35.6 million, consisting of $1.5 million in base pay, over $3 million in a bonus, $19 million in stock awards, and another $11,000,700 as an option award as well a category called "total other" consisting of $283,500.

The Chief Executive Officer of General Motors, Mary T. Barra, was paid $22.4 million in 2016, with a base pay of $2 million and additional bonuses, stock awards, and other options.

Likewise, the chief executive officer of Pepsico, Indra Nooyi, was paid $25,200,000 in 2016, with a base pay of $1,725,000. Marilyn Hewson is the CEO of Lockheed Martin, an airplane manufacturing company. In 2016, she was paid $19,400,000 from various sources, and Safra Catz, CEO of Oracle Corporation was paid $40,700,000 in 2016. Oracle Corporation makes software and database components.

While female top executives in industry are still a rarity, it is certain that the ever increasing number of women college graduates will ensure the continued growth of a female contingent in the ranks of American chief executives.[4]

Physicians

For centuries, women have depended on men for their livelihoods. In the 21st century in the United States and partially elsewhere, women have attained a degree of economic independence not known before. Women now comprise over 76 million workers, or 48% of the American civilian labor force. The Bureau of Labor Statistics has published a long list of occupations showing the total number employed and displayed by gender, race and ethnicity. These statistics reveal that some changes in favor of employed women have indeed occurred during the seven years 2010 to 2016. For example, in 2010, when there were 850,000 physicians in the United States, 29.7% were women. In 2016, when there were 954,000 physicians in the United States, 33.5% were women. This means that in 2016 there were 295 physicians in the United States for every 100,000 in the population. According to the Medical Group Management Association, the average median income of American physicians is $251,578. Anesthesiologists earn a median of $453,687 and family physicians earned a median of $230,456, and other specialists earn a medium between these two extremes.[5]

In 2016, female physicians earned less than male physicians. Male primary care physicians earned $225,000 and women in the same occupation were paid $192,000. Male specialists were earning $324,000 while female specialists earn $242,000. It is encouraging that between 2012 and 2016 women's earnings increased 36% while men's income increased only 29%. The principal reason for a lesser income is the need of women to take care of children. Therefore there are biological reasons for income inequality between women and men.[6]

A number of historical conditions have segregated dentistry from the other medical specialties. Nevertheless, dentistry is a form of surgery. In 2016 the total number of dentists in the United States was 139, 41. The average salary for men in dentistry was $184,031, and for women dentists the average salary was $128,726. In 2016 about 79% of dentists were men and 21% were women.[7]

Work Experiences of Women in the Professions

Although women have made considerable progress entering professions which were once the province of men alone, there are still many Americans who have not accepted the entry of women into medicine, dentistry, law, pharmacy, engineering, and other occupations. Expecting that only men are engaged in the professions, patients of medical clinics will ask a woman doctor who has just introduced herself: "When is the doctor coming?" This kind of dismissive behavior may well be related to "selective perception," which allows the subject to see only what he expected while ignoring the evidence. Undoubtedly, such experiences are painful reminders of status discrimination directed at women. Such comments assault the targets' sense of self-worth. People whose judgment is questioned will doubt their own self-worth and wonder whether their own opinion is worth anything. All this continues, although in 2016 47% of medical students were women and 30% of all physicians now practicing are women.

Many professional women have numerous difficulties which do not affect men. First is the production and raising of children. It is quite common for professional women to be pregnant for the first time even as they need to learn the requirements of a new job. That job may well consist of teaching in a medical school, as about one third of all medical professors are women and 16% of deans of a medical school are women.[8]

The Physician Work Life Study included 5,704 physicians who were surveyed concerning 150 items regarding career satisfaction. This resulted In the finding that female physicians were more satisfied with patient and colleague relationships than was true of men, despite the fact that mean income for women doctors is approximately $22,000 less than that of men.[9]

Gender differences exist in both the experience and satisfaction with medical practice.

Pharmacists

According to the Bureau of Labor Statistics, there were 940,000 pharmacists in the United States in 2016. Of these, 63.4% were women, earning $1839 a week. This is approximately $98,000 a year. Since 2014, more than 60% of pharmacy students were female, so that by now in 2018 the majority of licensed pharmacists are women. The Bureau of Labor Statistics also reports that more than three quarters of health workers are women. This includes nurses, physician's assistants, doctors, dentists and pharmacists.

Although most doctors are men and most nurses are women, this is not true among pharmacists. The sex ratio in the pharmacy profession is about 50%–50% (about 9% of licensed women pharmacists do not work because they have children). If part-timers are included, than women outnumber men 55% to 45%. Pharmacy appears to be the most egalitarian of the professions. 50 years ago, women were only 8% of all pharmacists. This was true because pharmacies were mostly privately owned, and the owners were men who worked as much as 12 hours a day, which women could not do because of their family obligations. Today, most pharmacies are owned by drug store chains such as Walgreens, CVS, and Rite Aid. These large chains allow pharmacists to work shorter hours and even part time. In 1979, The American Pharmacists Association elected its first female president.

Today the pharmacy degree is a six year professional doctor degree which can be entered directly from high school. Pharmacy has been growing since the early 2000s. The Labor Department expects another 25% growth adding 225,000 jobs by 2020.[10]

Lawyers

According to the Bureau of Labor Statistics there were 745,000 American lawyers in 2016. Of these, 299,000 were women, earning an average of $96,514. Male lawyers earned $118,160 annually. There are lawyers who earned a great deal more than the average here shown. Moreover, there are considerable differences in the income of all Americans, because the cost of living differs considerably from state to state and from region to region. Indeed, income on the East Coast and on the West Coast appears much larger than what is earned in other regions of the country. However, expenses for housing and other necessities are far greater in New York and California then in the Dakotas or in Iowa. This is true for lawyers and all other employees.

There are some lawyers who work in large law firms which may have a large contingent of lawyers while other lawyers work alone. Therefore the experiences of lawyers differ considerably. Many lawyers work for governments, such as local, state and federal agencies. Surely lawyers who act as public defenders are poor.

Women working in the law have published a number of journal articles complaining that they were treated unfairly and that they were the subject and victim of extreme sexism. According to The National Association For Law Placement, women have made little progress at big law firms. In fact, The National Association of Women Lawyers reports that the gender wage gap has actually grown. The typical female partner earns about 80% of what the typical male partner earns. Women lawyers also claim that they are treated abominably in large law firms. Examples are numerous. A woman lawyer claimed she was told to shut up and sit down by opposing counsel during a jury trial. Women also complained that they were interrupted in their legal work by being forced to perform office tasks. Other women lawyers complained that some men make remarks concerning the length of a woman's skirt or have to listen to remarks concerning their looks. Numerous women lawyers are assumed to be secretaries and are asked to bring male lawyers coffee. There are also lawyers who seek to date lady lawyers in the middle of a court proceeding. Adult women lawyers are labeled sweetie, honey, or dear, but never attorney, even by judges, other attorneys and clients. Some men even hint or are blatant asking for sex. Some law firms find that there are clients who say they don't want a woman lawyer assigned to their case.[11]

Joan M Hall was admitted to membership in the American College Of Trial Lawyers in 1982. She was only the fourth woman among 3600 members. Receiving a plaque of admission to the American College of Trial Lawyers, she noticed that the legend on the face of the plaque said that "he possesses the necessary experience etc. to qualify for this fellowship."[12]

Historically, women were excluded from the legal system. Women could not be judges, jurors, or litigants. The rule was that a jury consisted of "12 good men." Women were also not allowed to attend law school or practice law. In *Bradwell v. Illinois*, the Illinois Supreme Court denied an application for a license to practice law solely because the applicant was female. Law schools also refused to admit women. It was not until 1970 that women were admitted to all law schools.

Admission to the bar for women began in 1869 but developed slowly thereafter. Even in 1948, women were less than 1% of lawyers, and 20 years later, in 1968, women were still only 2.8% of lawyers. Today, in 2019, at least one half of all law students are women. Likewise, the number of law faculty has increased substantially, as have the number of judges and partners in large law firms.[15]

Politicians

Most politicians are lawyers, although many other backgrounds are also found among the 535 members of Congress and the 50 state governors. Although women have made some progress in the political arena since women were first allowed to vote in federal elections in 1920, that progress has been very slow. In part, there may still be some prejudices against women who seek political office. That, however, appears to be a minor obstacle in the effort to promote gender equality in politics. More important reasons for women's failure to gain more success in politics lies in beliefs among women themselves. According to Jennifer Lawless, director of The Women and Politics Institute at American University, women are far more likely to doubt that they are qualified to run for office than men. Only 40% of men but 60% of women surveyed by the Institute doubt their qualifications for office. Therefore, few women choose to run and party officials are less likely to encourage them to do so. This is most unfortunate, because research shows that women are as likely as men to win when they do choose to run.

Some of the results of the 2016 elections show that women candidates failed to win even 25% of the nation's 7383 legislative seats. This means that the percentage of women legislators is approximately 8%, which is about the same it has been for a decade. The total number of women winning in 2016 was 1830, or 22 more than was true in 2010. In 2018, 1,875 women, or 25.1% of legislators, were women.

This failure of American citizens to promote gender equality in politics causes the United States to lag far behind numbers of women in the politics of other countries. In Scandinavia (Latin =dangerous island), that is, in Sweden, Norway, Denmark, Iceland, and Faroe, more than 40% of parliamentary seats are held by women. In other European countries more than 30% of legislative seats are held by women. Even in American state legislatures, women are better represented than in Congress, where women hold only 23% of the House seats and 25% of the Senate seats.[14] In 2018, there were 23 women serving in the Senate and 87 in the House.

The evidence appears to be that female college students, who are a 60% majority, need to be encouraged to seek political office on graduation and /or to gain law degrees, which are the most common qualifications for a seat in county, state, and federal legislatures.

Although there are 50 states in the union, only six women were governors in 2018, and nine in 2019. These include Kay Ivey, Republican Governor of Alabama, who previously held the office of treasurer. In Iowa the governor is Kim Reynolds, a Republican who previously served as Lt. Governor. Susana Martinez is Governor of New Mexico. She had been District Attorney and is a Republican. Mary Falin, Republican of Oklahoma, was Lt. Gov. before she was elected Governor and Kate Brown, Democrat of Oregon, was Secretary of State before assuming the governors position. A sixth woman governor is Gina Ray Mondo, a Democrat from Rhode Island, who was treasurer before being elected Governor. These six were the only women among 50 governors of the United States in 2018.[15]

The 115th U.S. Congress assembled on January 3, 2017. Of the 100 Senators, 22 were women and 84 women were elected to the House of Representatives. Women were 19% of both Houses. Representatives as well as Senators are paid $174,000 a year, although Congress is in session only on a part-time basis.

Undoubtedly the most prominent female member of the House of Representatives is Nancy Pelosi of California. She is 77 years old. Currently she is Speaker of the House representing the Democratic Party. Previously she was House Speaker from 2007- to 2011. Her father was U.S. Congressman and Mayor of Baltimore, as was her brother. She moved to San Francisco in 1960 and participated in politics and by means of various appointments she succeeded in becoming a member of Congress in 1987. Pelosi has a Net Worth of at least $120 million and possibly $202 million.

The oldest United States Senator is Dianne Feinstein of California. She assumed office on November 4, 1992 and has therefore been a senator for 26 years. Feinstein is 84 years old and has been married three times. She has one daughter. Feinstein began her political career in the 1960s when she worked in city government. She was elected to the San Francisco Board of Supervisors in 1970. As President of the Board she succeeded to the position of Mayor of San Francisco after the murder of Mayor George Moscone and city supervisor Harvey Milk. In 1992 she won a special election to the United States Senate and has since then been reelected four times in 1994, 2000, 2006, and 2012. She was elected to a fifth term. She is 85 years of age.[16]

Joni Ernst is the youngest female Senator of the United States. She was born on 1 July, 1970. She was first elected in Iowa in 2014. A Republican, she was a member of the Iowa Senate and previously served as a Lieutenant Colonel in the Iowa Army National Guard. She spent one year in Kuwait during the Iraq war.

Ernst has proposed the elimination of the Internal Revenue Service, the Department of Education and The Environmental Protection Agency as a means of cutting federal spending. She supports allowing citizens to freely carry weapons and cosponsored a resolution to the effect that The Iowa General Assembly shall refuse to recognize any statues or presidential directives or any regulations which conflict with the second amendment of the Constitution of the United States. She has received an "A" rating from The National Rifle Association. She believes that the 10th amendment ensures states' rights and that states have a right to nullify unconstitutional federal laws. In sum, Ernst is a conservative and supporter of the President Trump agenda.

The Income of American Women

It is not possible to record here every occupation listed by the Bureau of Labor Statistics. However, we can reach some conclusions concerning compensation for work by comparing the wages of women to that of men.

It is evident from inspecting the statistical tables exhibited by the Bureau of Labor Statistics that women in 2016 did not earn as much as men. The weekly pay of management positions for men was $1420, and for women it was $1,027.

Professional occupations demonstrate the same discrepancy. While men earned a weekly pay of $1364, women received only $998 per week. The Bureau lists a large number of professional occupations. An example are professors. Male professors earned $1356 per week, women earned $1152 in that occupation for an average by 960,000 professors of both genders of $1247 a week or $64,844. (It is assumed that this salary includes junior colleges).

Predominantly Female Occupations

Social workers, librarians, teacher's assistants, registered nurses, dental hygienists and food servers are predominantly female.[17]

It is significant that those occupations in which women are the distinct majority are also the occupations which are poorly paid. This includes, first of all, social and community service managers or social workers. Of the

421,000 employees in that category, 70.5% are women. Likewise, 74.6% of human resources workers are women, as are the majority of fund raisers.

Social work, undoubtedly the poorest paid occupation among the professions, is staffed by 781,000 employees, of whom 81.5% are women. According to the Bureau of Labor Statistics, the median annual income of social workers in 2016 was $46,890.

McDonald, Postle and Dawson are the authors of a study of the social work profession. Published in May 2008, this study concludes that the social work profession is subject to a bureaucracy which takes little regard of the needs of clients. Social workers, according to that study, display a high level of stress because of the conflict between their professional knowledge and the oppressive bureaucracy which prevents them from applying it for the benefit of the needy. Evidently, a rigid hierarchy discourages the use of practitioner's knowledge. Supervision in social work is interested only on work-flow management rather than professional issues. The practitioners of social work have a good deal of professional knowledge and skills they are afraid to use because supervisors are only interested in procedures and bureaucratic routines. The bureaucracy prevents the clients of social workers from expressing their own views. In addition, a form of paternalism awards clients who show gratitude. In sum, social work practitioners do not rely on social work knowledge but on permission by bureaucrats to act.[18]

Librarians

Women predominate among librarians. 81.8% of the 206,000 American librarians are women, earning a median income of $57,680 annually. Few men who need to support a family could do so on so small an income. It is therefore evident that the reason for the feminization of this profession is low pay.

Librarians need a master's degree in library science which includes the ability to deal with a computerized database, with e-books, and with the Internet. Most librarians work in schools and academic libraries. There are also business libraries as well as law libraries and other specialized libraries serving government. Requirements to enter the profession vary from state to state but include strong communication skills. On a typical day, librarians will help users find the information they need; show users how to find information on the Internet; supervise library assistants; collect and organize books; participate in programs such as storytelling for children and write grants.

Dental Assistants

More than 80% of dental assistants are women earning $36,940 annually. Dental assistants sterilize instruments, pass instruments to the dentist during the procedure, hold suction devices, take impressions, expose dental radiographs, and fabricate provisional crowns.

In some American states, no college education is required to enter this profession, while in other states dental assistants must be licensed and registered. There are over 200 dental assistant school programs in the United States. Certified dental assistants must take the Dental Assisting National Board examinations after completing an accredited dental assisting program.[19]

Pre-school and Kindergarten Teachers

According to the Bureau of Labor Statistics, 97.5% of the 1,565,000 teachers of preschool, kindergarten and elementary children are women. Their average pay is $56,553, although some earn as much as $67,000. This demonstrates the unwillingness of the American public to pay for the education of their children while at the same time demanding that their child receives the best possible education. It is also significant that hardly any men are willing to teach young children.

This means that many young children hardly ever see a man, not only because of our high divorce rate resulting in numerous single mothers, but also because many working men come home shortly before young children go to bed, so that they hardly ever see their fathers.

The National Opinion Research Council has conducted numerous interviews concerning occupational prestige. These interviews show that teaching small children is largely viewed with contempt in this country, although the importance of teaching the young cannot be exaggerated. Obviously all education, and consequently all economic success, depends on elementary learning. Without kindergarten and first grade no one could go to school and no one could eventually succeed. Whatever colleges and universities contribute to American success depends in the first place on those who will teach our youngest children. Here we have one more example of the sociological dictum that "what people believe is real, is real in its consequences."

Medical Assistants

This occupation should not be confused with physician's assistants. Over 90% of medical assistants are women, earning an average of $31,540, according to the Bureau of Labor Statistics. Medical assistants take the patient's temperature, record the patient's pulse and blood pressure, weigh the patient, and insert the results in a medical record. They may also take out stitches or change dressings or explain about a special diet.

Few women are found among the highest earners. Only 25.5% of computer and mathematical workers are women, and women are only 14% of engineering employees.[20]

The Gender Pay Gap

In 2016, the overall gender pay gap in the United States showed that the *median* income of women was $31,781, as compared to the median income of men, which was $45,000. The mean difference between the pay received by men and that received by women is $63,042 for men and $42,640 for women.[21]

It is obvious that although women earn less than men in almost all American occupations, the average American man is not wealthy. Because the American family generally has two children, it is extremely difficult to pay for all expenses incurred by a family of four. That is why the 2018 tax reduction makes considerable difference to working men and women and children who are the poorest Americans.

American demographics exhibit that there is an excess of women over men in the United States, largely due to male risky behavior. Traditionally also, women have been excluded from the economic rewards available to men. This discrepancy has gradually narrowed as a few women have become industrial executives while others have succeeded in becoming physicians, dentists, lawyers, and pharmacists. In politics also, a few women have succeeded in entering Congress or gaining election as governors of states. Nevertheless, women have only gradually achieved a minimum of change in the economic status in this country.

Chapter 2. Women and Men: Status and Role Confusion

The Spanish word "macho" or "machismo" is derived from the Latin meaning masculine. Prior to the end of the 20th century, there was a fairly distinct difference between the status-role of men and women. It was assumed and commonplace that men went to work and women stayed home to care for children and provide their families with all their needs. Even after farming was no longer the principal occupation of American men, the masculine role was defined by the ascendancy of men over women in all phases of life.

At the beginning of the 21st century, this is no longer the case. Men must now adjust their conduct and their expectations to the ever growing power of women in the economic and professional world, which may well lead to a total role reversal between the genders. This frightening scenario provokes American men to exhibit a form of conduct related to beliefs concerning masculinity which have led to a great deal of criticism of male behavior.

A good number of men have been accused of sexual misconduct towards women. In addition, numerous men seek to assert their masculinity by engaging in dangerous behavior. Examples of such conduct is speeding in motorcycles and in cars, committing assault and homicide, killing themselves, and dying from drowning as well as industrial accidents. It would be a gross exaggeration to claim that the higher death rate of men over women is entirely caused by men's voluntary behavior, since industrial accidents are the inevitable outcome of work men must do. Nevertheless, the nearly 5 year excess of the male death rate over the female death rate is largely to be attributed to activities which could be easily avoided.

There is a large amount of literature concerning the possibility that male aggression and so-called macho behavior is the product of natural selection in the sense that men need to be sexually active and impregnate many women in order to guarantee the perpetuation of humanity. This argument has been disputed by numerous scholars who view the differences between male and female behavior as culturally determined. Whatever opinion may eventually prevail, there can be no doubt that at least in American experience, men are a good deal more violent and engage in far more risky behavior than women.[22]

Motor Vehicle Accidents

Among these activities is the riding of motorcycles, which is most dangerous but nevertheless popular among men. The National Center for Health Statistics reports that there were 34,439 fatal motor vehicle accidents in the United States in 2016. This represented 11.6 deaths per 100,000 people, ranging from four in the District of Columbia to 23.1 in Mississippi.

Many more men than women die each year from motor vehicle crashes. Men drive more miles than women, but also engage in risky driving practices this includes not using safety belts, driving while impaired by alcohol, and using motorcycles. Therefore crashes involving men are often more severe than those involving women. For every year from 1975 through 2016, the number of male crash deaths were more than twice the number of female crash deaths. Since 1975, motorcycle deaths have increased, and have more than doubled for both men and women since 1997. In 2016, 4539 men and 434 women were killed in motorcycle crashes. Some 71% of motor vehicle crashes, including cars, involved men in 2016. Even the death rate for passengers in motor vehicle accidents were 2.6 times higher men than for women in 2016.

Age also made a good deal of difference in death rates concerning motor vehicle crashes. For 100 million miles driven, the fatality rate was 50% higher for men than for women, and was particularly high for men aged 16 to 29. This excess of fatalities for men over women also included male passengers.

Another factor which has considerable influence in motor vehicle fatalities is the involvement of alcohol. In 2016, 12,422 male drivers rate were killed with an average blood alcohol concentration of. 32; that same year, 1033 women were killed in motor vehicle accidents while subject to a blood alcohol concentration of 0.20.

Speeding is another factor leading to a greater proportion of male drivers killed in motor vehicle crashes than female drivers killed in crashes. In 2016, 3,466 men were killed because they were speeding. Only 1028 women were killed for the same reason. It is significant that fatalities involving single vehicles outnumber by 55% to 45% fatalities involving several vehicles.[23]

States with the largest populations exhibit more vehicle fatalities than other states, although weather conditions also influence vehicle fatalities.

Fatalities are not the only outcome of motor vehicle accidents. A good number of motorcycle crashes result in permanent injuries, turning the victims into cripples at a young age without hope of recovery.

Single vehicle accidents are mostly caused by excessive speeding or such driver errors as overbraking or running wide on a curve. At last two thirds of multiple vehicle accidents are caused by the other vehicle violating the motorcycle's right-of-way. Men between the ages of 16 and 24 are significantly overrepresented in accidents. This is also true of female passengers, who have no control over the vehicle. The likelihood of injury is extremely high in motorcycle accidents. 98% of multiple vehicle collisions and 96% of single vehicle accidents result in some kind of injury to the motorcycle rider.

Suicide

Suicide is a leading cause of death in the United States. Each year about 45,000 Americans die by suicide. Men commit suicide 3.57 times more often than women. White males account for 70% of all suicides by middle aged men in particular. The highest rate of suicide by age was among adults between 45 and 54. This group was responsible for 20% of all suicides in 2016 while young adults aged 15 to 24 were responsible for 12.5%. Some 51% of all suicides are committed by firearms. There are about 123 suicides each day.

The highest suicide rates in the United States are among whites and the second highest rate is among American natives or Indians. Blacks have a suicide rate of only 6.1%, but exhibit a homicide rate four times higher than that of whites. Although blacks are only 13% of the American population, they accounted for 6115 or 86% of all murders in 2015 out of a total of 7039 murders, according to the Federal Bureau of Investigation's *Uniform Crime Report*.24

The French sociologist Emile Durkheim (1858–1917) published *La Suicide* in 1897. According to Durkheim, suicide is not an individual act nor a personal action. Durkheim rejected the psychological explanation of suicide. He showed that suicide is not psychological but social and that it is the result of social disorganization or lack of social integration or social solidarity. Durkheim therefore classified different types of suicide the basis of different types of relationship between the actor and his society.

According to Durkheim, four kinds of suicide may be distinguished. First is egoistic suicide, which occurs when the victim becomes socially isolated, finds that he has no place in the society, and therefore kills himself. Altruistic suicide occurs when the victim and the group were too close and too intimate. An example is that of the Japanese pilots who, during the Second World War, flew their planes deliberately into American ships in order to die for the Emperor. Anomic suicide occurs when one is suddenly confronted with situations never encountered before and which are both confusing and inexplicable. The stock market crash of 1929 is an excellent example. The fourth form of suicide, according to Durkheim, is fatalistic suicide. An example is suicide by a slave or a woman who cannot have children or a prisoner in a Nazi death camp.[25]

Psychoanalytic theory as first developed by Sigmund Freud (1856–1939) posits to opposing instincts. One is called eros, or the life drive, and the other thanatos, or the death drive. Freud claimed that these two instincts were present in all individuals and acted to reduce tensions in life. Freud believed that all individuals vacillate on a continuum between desiring life and desiring death. Freud argued that depressed individuals do not have the energy to kill themselves unless they identify an object or person whom they wish to kill. These suicidal persons then turn the aggression against themselves, as the psychiatrist Karl Meninger (1893–1990) claimed when he proposed that suicidal persons have three wishes. These, according to Meninger, are the wish to be killed by reason of guilt; the wish to kill for revenge; and the wish to die because of hopelessness. Meninger wrote that individuals who are suicidal wish to be killed in order to relieve their loved ones of a burden. Yet the same people also wish to kill in order to express their anger and aggression at those they feel have wronged them. Finally, these suicidal people wish to die because of the unbearable pain they experience.[26]

These two theories of suicide represent the sociological and psychological views of this bizarre behavior. There is a considerable literature concerning suicide and its possible prevention. Most significant is that persons who have benefited from their status in society are more likely to commit suicide than those who view themselves as losers. Therefore, whites commit more suicide than blacks. Men commit more suicide than women. Army officers commit more suicide than enlisted men and wealthy people commit more suicide than poor people.

Suicide and homicide are affected by the business cycle, in that the level of frustration in the upper and lower status systems influence violence. In times of prosperity, homicide rises as the lower classes feel deprived relative to those above them. In a depression, suicide increases as the middle and upper classes feel their drop in status. These are some of the conclusions reached by Andrew Henry and James Short in their book *Suicide and Homicide*.[27]

There is perhaps nothing more horrendous as murder-suicide, evidently a nearly entirely male behavior. In fact, males account for 93.4% of such crimes. Men who commit such violence are twice as likely to do so when they are over the age of fifty-five. Motives for killing others and oneself have been identified as the need for power, revenge, loyalty, profit, jealousy, and terror.

Expectations of masculine behavior in American society consists of competitiveness, self-reliance, and stoicism. Traditionally men are expected to subordinate women and other men in order to practice what it takes to be a "real man."[28]

American men are expected to be physically strong, powerful, assertive, and in control. American men are also expected to act rather than talk. Schoolboys are influenced to be "cool popular studs," as the media project successful boys and men with great sports ability in football, basketball, and other activities.

Murder

Murder or homicide is almost entirely a male offense. In 2017, the murder rate in the United States rose by 1.5% during the first half of that year. During 2017, the murder rate in Southern and Midwestern states increased while falling noticeably in the Northeast. The increase in Southern states is principally to be attributed to illegal immigrants from Mexico and other Latin American countries, as well as to the black murder rate.[29]

In 2015, there were 13,455 murders known to the police in the United States of these 10,608 committed by men. Hispanics were responsible for 2028 murders and blacks were responsible for 7039 murders. Since the black population of the United States is about 13% it is significant that over one half of murders were committed by blacks.

According to the Centers for Disease Control, blacks have a homicide rate eight times higher than that of whites. [30]

Although murder increased since 2015, violent crime other than murder decreased in most parts of the country outside the South. Thus, rape decreased 2.4% and aggravated assault decreased 1%.[31]

For numerous years, homicide statistics indicated that 73 to 75% of those arrested for murder in the United States were men.[32]

Men at Work

The Bureau Of Labor Statistics lists almost every occupation in which Americans are presently engaged. This indicates that in 2017, there were 153,337,000 persons employed in this country. Men constituted 53.1% of the workforce that year. 1,639 were4 chief executives of large corporations of whom 72% were men. The highest-paid chief executives can earn $130 million a year. Fortune 500 CEO compensation is about 8 ½ million dollars on the average. The average salary for all American chief executives, according to the Bureau of Labor Statistics, is $183,270.[33]

Among computer and information systems managers, 71% are men. Their average salary is $81,928 although some are paid $125,721. Other management positions which are also almost all male are industrial production managers, transportation managers engineering managers and construction managers. Since the vast majority of working men are not managers nor executives of corporations it turns out that in the fourth quarter of 2018 the median salary of American men was $993 per week. Women on the average earned 80% of what men earned, or $794 a week.[34]

Although most American women still earn less than men, since 1980 there has been an ever increasing number of women who are earning more than men. In 1980, 13% of working women earned the same or more than men. This rose to 31% in 2017. Consequently the number of men who earned more than women declined from 87% in 1982 to 69% in 2017.

Still, 71% of the public hold that men are more responsible than women for supporting the family financially. Men themselves place a greater emphasis on their role as financial providers. 81% of Americans whose education is limited to high school or less think that men should be mostly responsible providing the finances of their families. Among college graduates, only 62% believe this.[35]

As the number of women earning more than their husbands grows, the phenomenon of so-called house husbands has grown as well. According to the Census Bureau's Current Population Survey, there has been an increase from about 280,000 house husbands the 1970s to about 550,000 such house fathers staying at home in the first half of the 21st century.[36]

This role reversal between women and men has led to some changes in the attitudes of American fathers towards their families. Younger men who are accustomed to seeing women earning money and graduating from college more often than is true of men have a different view of the identity than is true of older generations. According to Pew Research, fathers are much more involved in child care then they were 50 years ago. In 2015, fathers reported spending on average seven hours a week on child care. That is triple the time spent by fathers on child care in 1965. Because of the fact that it is less common for fathers to be their families' only breadwinner than was true in 1970, it turns out that only 27% of couples are in families where only the father works. In 2016, 66% of families benefited from a dual income.

Although so-called common sense would dictate that a woman earning more than her husband should go to work while he stays home dealing with children and housework, such a role reversal has important emotional consequences.

American culture in 2019 has not adjusted to the proposition that a woman should support the family in which the husband and father of children assumes the role of domestic caretaker. "House husband" is a degrading status in this country, although over half a million American men have assumed that statusrole. There are of course a number of men in this position who have lost their jobs and are looking for work. If successful, they then relinquish "the househusband" status.

The 2010 Census records that then there were often thousand stay at home fathers. Therefore about 16% of preschoolers were being cared for by fathers while mothers worked outside the home. This role reversal has implications for men, which we may call a diminished status. This is true despite the fact that women working outside the home have been generally accepted in this country. The outcome of this arrangement is that men feel threatened because they are no longer the principal providers in the family. In addition to the loss of respect which stay-at-home fathers must accept, many of these men also feel isolated and bored, which are long time complaints of stay-at-home women.[37]

In 2016 a study of 6300 heterosexual couples found that men who were not working full time were 33% more likely to divorce during the following 12 months than husbands who did have full-time jobs. This high divorce rate is principally the result of the failure of these men to fulfill the stereotypical breadwinner role.[38]

Wage Slaves

Every morning during the workweek, long lines of cars travel from the suburbs of America's cities to the downtown area, where their occupants spend eight hours a day in an office or a factory. These are America's wage slaves, people spending their lives, often as working fathers, and performing tasks that others tell them they must do. The proverb "the borrower is the servant of the lender" applies to most of these employees, as a considerable number of young adults owe so much money after getting an education at a college that they begin their working life with a staggering amount of debt. Added to that debt are the usual mortgage, credit card debt, loan debts, and others, so that the average American household is carrying a total of $203,000 of debt. Total American household debt was estimated at $11 trillion in 2017. It is important to consider that the amount of money needed torepay debts will easily be a lot more than what was originally borrowed because of the interest these debts accumulate. These circumstances make a large number of American employees wage slaves.

Most Americans do not own their own homes. The banks own them. Furthermore, homeowners are forced to pay property taxes. Someone who does not pay property taxes will soon find that the politicians would take away the home. Credit card debt approximates about $16,000 in the typical American household, whose members are the target of brutal debt collectors.

Americans also face the national debt, which was $10.6 trillion in 2008 and has now risen to $22 trillion (2019).[39]

One consequence of this situation is that many Americans hate their jobs. It has been estimated that two thirds of the 100 million working Americans are disengaged at work, which means they feel no real connection to their jobs and therefore tend to do the bare minimum.[40]

Sixteen percent of employees resent their jobs so much that they complain incessantly, thereby influencing other workers to do the same. This kind of dissatisfaction has little to do with money but with the behavior of supervisors and bosses, who have no understanding of human relations. Such bosses cause a great deal of absenteeism, employee turnover, low productivity, and even internal theft.[41]

According to Srinivasan S. Pilay, a clinical professor of psychiatry, a random sample 72 senior company executives found that nearly all report signs of "burnout" at work. A Gallup poll shows that only 13% of employees in 142 countries feel engaged at work. Numerous studies have shown that the way people feel at work profoundly influences how they perform. It is also important that employees be allowed to focus on one task at a time. That causes a great deal more success in engagement. The fact is, that an organization which puts its people first, even above customers, is more likely to avoid costly absenteeism coupled with a minimum effort on the part of employees.[42]

A Nation of Employees

Although independence is still highly prized the United States in 2019, few Americans are independent any longer. We have become a nation of employees, so that the livelihood of millions depends on their subordinate positions in large organizations, or even smaller ones, where bosses rule. These millions of employees fear expressing their opinions on any subject for fear of losing their jobs. This is a real threat to American democracy, as freedom of speech has been largely curtailed by economic dependency. Therefore the First Amendment to the Constitution guaranteeing freedom of speech, among other rights, has become irrelevant for most Americans. Instead, silence has become the collective behavior of most employees. At meetings called by bosses, hardly anyone is willing to say anything or make a suggestion or participate in any discussion. This silence among employees betrays a probable fear of confrontation with bosses or others who may have an influence on their job security. Losing one's job is equivalent to an economic death sentence, particularly for men 40 years old or older. Employees will usually keep silent in the face of unethical behavior by superiors for fear of retaliation.

Embarrassment also plays a role in the need to keep silent on the job. Puritan ethics do not allow discussion of sex, money, politics, or one's personal life. Many people keep silent because they feel they don't have the political skills needed to be accepted among bosses and fellow employees. This atmosphere of repression, so common at most places of employment, deprives employers of some of the best ideas that freedom of expression would provide them. Over time, many employees have become so accustomed to keeping silent that they avoid any confrontation on any, even the most minimal, subject.[43]

Protect and Defend

Although there are some women members of American police forces and in the armed services of the United States, the vast majority of law enforcement and the American military are men.

It is assumed that the military is indeed a dangerous occupation. This is largely also true of law enforcement although many citizens still assume that policing should not result in the murder of officers. Unfortunately, police in every state of the union have been shot, wounded or killed in the course of attempting to keep the peace.

In the first two months of 2019, 18 American police were killed. The plurality of these were murdered by firearms, and the second most common cause was traffic related.[44]

An example from the prior year is that on February 10, 2018, several police officers were shot and killed while responding to a domestic abuse complaint. Officers Eric Joering and Anthony Morelli responded at 12:10 PM to a "potential domestic situation." On entering the apartment, they were immediately met with gunfire. Eric Joering died at the scene. Anthony Morelli was transported to the Ohio State University Medical Center where he died. Joering had a wife and four daughters and Morelli had a wife and two children. Their killer is Quentin Lamar Smith, a fairly old man who was wounded when the officers returned fire. He survived.

During the same week, police officer Chase Maddox was shot and killed in Locust Grove, Georgia, and in Richardson, Texas, Officer David Sherard was shot and killed while responding to a domestic disturbance. In Colorado Springs, Colorado, sheriff's deputy Micah Flick was shot and killed as a car theft suspect fired a semi-automatic handgun at him. In 2016, 135 police were killed in the line of duty, and in 2017, 129 police were also murdered in this country.[45]

In addition, 57,180 officers were victims of line of duty assaults. The average age of the officers who were killed was 40. On the average, officers who were murdered had served 13 years at the time they were killed. Two of the officers killed were female and four were African-Americans.

17 of the murdered officers were ambushed and 13 were answering disturbance calls. Nine were investigating suspicious circumstances and six were engaged in tactical situations. Five were performing investigative activities such as searches or interviews and four were conducting traffic pursuits or traffic stops. Three were investigating drug related matters, one was answering a burglary in progress, one was answering a robbery in progress, and four were attempting other arrests. The vast majority of officers killed were murdered by firearms such as handguns, rifles, and shotguns, and a few were killed with vehicles. Many of the assailants had prior criminal arrests.

In 2000, 1652 law enforcement officers were killed in automobile accidents. It is significant that a considerable majority of accidental deaths occurred in the South and fewest in the Northeast.

In addition to all this violence, over 57,000 officers were assaulted in 2016. These assaults were principally related disturbance calls when assailants used hands, fists and feet in 78% of the incidents.[46,25]

Some Case Histories

On October 16, 2016 a 34-year-old sergeant in Fairbanks, Alaska Police Department was shot and fatally wounded while investigating a suspicious person. The officer, with 12 years of law enforcement experience, responded to a call of shots fired at a hotel. As he contacted an individual in the hotel, the man pointed a 9 mm semi-automatic handgun at the officer and fired several rounds at him. The officer returned fire with his service weapon. When the officer fell over a curb and had run out of ammunition, the suspect stomped on the officer victim, took his service weapon, and drove off in the officer's patrol unit. The victim officer was shot in the front of the head, the front of the body, the chest, and in the front below his waist. After two days of investigation, a 20-year-old was arrested and charged with first-degree murder and a number of other violations. The offender was under the influence of alcohol and had a prior criminal record.

The officer was taken to a local hospital, where he died on October 28, 2016.

In San Diego, California, a 32-year-old police officer was shot and wounded and his partner was killed when they stopped a man walking in the middle of the street carrying a weapon. The officers were riding in a patrol car and stopped the car slightly behind the walking man. As the 32-year-old officer left the car and asked the man where he lived, the man turned around and fired at the officer with a. 380 caliber semi-automatic handgun. The officer, having been struck in the throat, fell on his back. The assailant continued to fire and advanced at the officer sitting in the driver's seat of the patrol car. The assailant then shot the 43-year-old officer in the car, hitting the rear of his head, his upper chest, his arms, and his hands, killing him. The younger officer was able to shoot the assailant, who was arrested and charged with murder, attempted murder, and felony possession of a firearm. The assailant had a prior criminal record, including violent crime, drug law violations, and weapons violations.

On November 6, 2016, a 41-year-old police sergeant and a 39-year-old deputy sheriff with the Peach County Sheriff's office were fatally wounded while answering a disturbance in Byron, Georgia.

The two officers first spoke with the residents who called 911, reporting a neighbor threatening them with a firearm. The two officers went to the neighbor's house and told him he was under arrest. The neighbor then pulled a 9mm semi-automatic handgun from under his shirt and shot both officers at close range. One of the officers was shot in the head and the other in the stomach and in the head. The shooting led neighbors to call 911. The Byron

Police Department arrived and fired on the suspect, who was struck and arrested. Both police victims died two days after this incident. The killer had a prior criminal record.

In Iowa, a 24-year-old Urbandale Department member was shot and killed in an ambush at 1 AM on November 2, 2016. On that same day, a 38-year-old police sergeant with the Des Moines Police Department was killed. The 24-year-old officer was found by citizens sitting in his car with fatal gunshot wounds to the side of his head. The Des Moines police sergeant was killed in a similar attack as he sat in his patrol car. He had been wounded in the front of his head, arms, and hands.

These examples can be duplicated in any state of the union, demonstrating that it has become extremely dangerous for the men who risk their lives every day to protect the citizens of this country.

The American Military

In 2017, the United States Armed Forces consisted of 1,429,995 personnel, of whom 210,485 were women. It is therefore evident that men are principally responsible for the defense of the United States against foreign enemies. Over the centuries, military activities have taken the lives of thousands of American men and some women. The Revolutionary War led to the deaths of 4,035 combatants, and the War of 1812 killed 2,260 soldiers. It was the Civil War which led to a minimum of 608,000 deaths, a number greater than American combat deaths in World War I and World War II combined. There were 116,560 war deaths in World War I and 405,399 deaths in World War II. The war in Korea cost the lives of 36,516 Americans, and the Vietnam War led to the deaths of American58,209 Americanmen and women. In Afghanistan, 16 years of fighting killed 2,356 Americans while 4,489 Americans died in Iraq.[47]

The number of Americans who were in the armed services during World War I and World War II, by reason of national mobilization, were very substantial. 16 million served in World War II. 14 times as many Americans served in World War II than did in the first two decades of the 21st century. In more recent years, wars in the Middle East led to one death for every 58 soldiers deployed. In the two world wars about one soldier died for about 40 deployed. Worst was the Civil War, where one out of every five soldiers were lost because so many died of their wounds, for which there was no cure and no help. Innumerable Civil War soldiers suffered horrible agonies lying on the ground and dying slowly from their wounds.[48]

Because the United States has been involved in war in almost every generation, there has never been a time when young men and women have not been buried far from home or brought back in body bags. We have been able to travel to the moon and to explore atomic energy. We have learned to send space capsules into outer space and to conquer some of the most deadly diseases. Yet, like all humans, we have never learned how to keep the peace.

Retirement

Except for the rich and the superrich, retirement from unpleasant work conditions is welcomed by millions of American men and women. However the consequences of retirement, in most cases, are disappointing. This is particularly true for men who spent most of life in a working environment, however disagreeable, and are not accustomed to spending all day at home.

Retirement requires a much greater adjustment from men than women. No doubt there are women who also feel this. It is, of course, even more of a loss for men because the vast majority of men have no second role to assume after leaving work. The most important prestige factor in America is occupation. Therefore, those who are not occupied with productive work are viewed with contempt as burdens and superfluous people. This is not so true of women, because women can assume the role of housewife, which the American public and the media consider legitimate. This is not true for men.

Exclusion from employment has several consequences. One is the reduction in social honor which for men depends on occupation, as shown by The National Opinion Research Council. By means of random telephone calls, the researchers discovered which occupations have the greatest prestige or social honor in the United States. The highest prestige among all American occupations is physician. The least occupational prestige is accorded to shoe shiners, with all other occupations in between.

Many retired men find that their wives are continuing the routines of a housewife, to which the wife has been accustomed for many years. The retired men will then participate in shopping at a grocery store, cleaning the house, washing dishes, and doing other domestic tasks. To some men, this looks like they are being feminized, leading to a sense of uselessness and depression.

American culture dictates that "real men" do not seek help because "real men" are invincible. Men who have retired and find no further purpose in life may become severely depressed and even consider suicide. Yet few men will volunteer to visit a psychologist. It has been estimated that there are 11 million depressed men in America at any one time. This constitutes approximately 9% of the adult male population. The principal reason for such depression is a sense of loss. Many retired men feel that they have lost their identity, which had been related to their work. Unable to transfer such a sense of identity to new interests, they view themselves as useless. It is part of the male culture not to show any vulnerability, for the more vulnerable a man is the less manly he appears.

Some men and women spend their retirement years by traveling by SUV throughout the United States. This allows them to meet numerous other travelers at parking facilities all over the country. At first such constant travel may be of interest. In the long run, however, traveling by SUV here and there separates the retired from their children and grandchildren and finally becomes untenable.

Evidently, therefore, it is vital to those who are retired from their life's work to do something constructive which will not only give them the satisfaction of doing purposeful work but will also avoid the stigma associated with retirement. Someone who has retired from a job or profession can avoid mentioning this to anyone outside the family and now point to his new interest as a means of validating his existence.[49]

A good number of Americans live in poverty after they cease working, having only a Social Security benefit as the only income.

Age segregation is universal in the United States. The American school system is based on age segregation for the young, and retirement communities segregate the old. These retirement communities are usually located in the so-called sunbelt in Arizona, Florida, and California. These communities may be called age ghettos. This means that all who live in these communities will see only other old people. Since there are no children nor middle aged people, these ghettos create an unnatural world, depriving the older generation of all contact with younger people, who become nothing more than voices on the telephone (if that). As longevity increases, more and more Americans disappear into such places.[50,27]

The German poet Goethe wrote: "Nichts ist schwerer zu ertragen als eine Reihe von guten Tagen" (Faust). "Nothing is more difficult to endure than a series of holidays." (This is not a literal translation. Instead it conveys the meaning of that expression.)

Chapter 3. Marriage

Status and Role: Some Statistics

The Traditional Marriage

The most common and universal experience of mankind consists of the relationship between women and men. Two words are used in the English language to describe this connection. A description or reference to the biological differences between women and men is labeled sex. That word is derived from *secare*, a Latin word meaning "to divide," and in this context we use it to mean dividing humanity into males and females. Gender is another English term which refers to the cultural differences between the sexes.

Nature decrees that females and males among the human species and other primates shall associate for the purpose of reproduction. Humans and some animals tend to form permanent relationships between females and males which, because of the enculturation process, leads to marriage.

Marriage is defined according to the culture in which it is practiced. Culture or the man-made environment has three dimensions. Material culture consists of physical objects such as a nail, the atomic bomb, or the chair on which we are sitting. Ideological culture consists of beliefs considered important and behavioral culture consists of what we do. Since culture changes all the time beliefs and behavior as well as physical objects are constantly changing. Therefore, beliefs concerning marriage have changed a great deal over the past 50 years. While it was assumed marriage meant legal association of one heterosexual woman with one heterosexual man, this definition is now limited. In the 21st century, some Americans marry someone of the same sex. Others engage in domestic partnerships, living together with someone of the opposite sex without a marriage ceremony of any kind.

Because this deviant behavior seems to threaten traditional marriage, Congress has passed the Defense of Marriage Act. According to that law, marriage means "only a legal union between one man and one woman as husband and wife."[51] Such a marriage may be called a contract based marriage. This means that both spouses are parties to a contract between them. This 19th and early 20th century view of marriage involved women who had no other source of income. For men and women, contract marriage was the only legal means of participating in sex and procreation. Therefore, in order to have a legal sex life, people had to be married. Non-marital sex was a crime called adultery or fornication.[52]

This earlier family life viewed children as miniature adults who earned their keep by working on the family farm or being an apprentice or servant to supplement the family income, as their pay belonged to their father, while today children are considered an expense. Unmarried women in those days were a burden on the family and divorced or annulled women were viewed as "damaged goods" with little chance of finding a second husband.[53]

In earlier centuries, courts widely recognized common-law marriages when a couple agreed to be married and told the community that they were living in a common-law marriage, because couples who were married without a ceremony or license insured the public that women who were abandoned by their partner or widowed need not rely on public funds for support. Furthermore, recognition of common-law marriage prevented children born to these relationships from suffering the stigma of legal disabilities or illegitimacy.[54]

By the middle of the 20th century, most states had abolished common-law marriages out of a concern that recognizing marriages that had not been formally endorsed led to fraud because there was no written agreement available tying the parties to a marriage contract. Legislators in some states wanted to prevent those who are not really married from claiming to be married for the sake of benefits. As cohabitation became socially and legally acceptable, the existence of common-law marriage could easily deceive the courts by claiming that one intended to get married just because one acted married. There is a distinct difference between common-law marriage and cohabitation. A common-law marriage avoided any ceremony. However a common-law spouse could get a divorce, inherit property, get tax breaks and enjoy all of the other benefits of marriage.[55]

Before 1968, the "man in the house" rule will was part of most states' welfare laws. This rule held that a man's income was available to children of a woman with whom he cohabited even if he was not actually supported by children. In 1968, the Supreme Court struck down these laws.[56]

Marriage Fraud

Polygamy among fundamentalist Mormons has led the Utah legislature to redefine marriage. This new definition seeks to prevent women from seeking welfare because they claim to be single, as their husband is legally married only to his first wife. Women in these polygamous marriages claim to be single and therefore qualify for welfare benefits, although living with an income producing husband.[57]

Marriage fraud by Mormons is minuscule. Immigration marriage fraud is far more extensive. Federal law requires deportation of immigrants who commit immigration marriage fraud and criminal penalties for both the immigrants and citizens who participate in fraudulent marriages. The Department of Homeland Security determines whether a marriage is valid. In 1968, Congress passed the Immigration Marriage Fraud Amendments, which restrict so-called green cards admitting foreigners to the country to immigrants whose marriage is at least two years old. To become a permanent resident, the immigrant and his spouse must petition to remove the conditional immigrant residency status at the end of an additional two-year waiting period. Otherwise, the government will terminate the temporary residency status of the immigrant spouse, who will be deported. Congress enacted this rule to prevent individuals from marrying solely to obtain green cards.

The "New" Marriage

In the middle of the 20th century, a different form of marriage developed. Although these 19th century type marriages have partially survived into the 20th and even the 21st century, around the 1960s, marriages in the United States changed dramatically. From then on, the liberation of women led to marriages which did not only involve the need for private support but were also influenced by support from government programs as well as benefits derived from private agents. Now taxes, immigration laws, pensions, Social Security, military benefits, and insurance played a part in the decision to marry.[58]

According to The Pew Research Center, 88% of Americans marry for love. 83% get married for the sake of a lifelong commitment, and 76% mentioned companionship as the major inducement to marry. 49% of Americans marry in order to have children, 30% are motivated by religion to marry, financial security is mentioned by 28% of the Pew sample, and 23% marry to gain legal rights and benefits. These motivations overlap since evidently the same people can be motivated by some or all of these reasons to marry.[59]

Respondents to the Pew study place considerable emphasis on the ability of male candidates for marriage to be a good financial provider. Better than 70% of respondents said that it is very important for a man to be able to support a family financially, while only 32% said the same for women.[60]

Since 2016, half of Americans age 18 and older were married. In earlier years a much greater number of Americans were married by that age. This indicates that men in particular are staying single longer, as shown by the United States Census Bureau in 2017, when the median age at first marriage reached its highest point on record. At that time, the median age of first marriage for men was 29.5 and for women 27.4 years. Education has a major impact on marriage. Research has shown that marriage declined most among those with a high school diploma or less education. Evidently, only 63% of this group were married in 1990. That marriage rate had dropped to 50% in 2016. In addition, 7% of adults were cohabiting in 2016, which represents about 18 million people. About half of cohabiting people were younger than 35, even as cohabitation is rising among Americans age 50 and older. 65% among those 25 years of age and older with at least a four-year college degree were married in 2015.[61]

As the United States marriage rate has declined, divorce rates have increased among older Americans. In 2015, for every 1000 adults ages 50 and older, 10 had divorced, up from 5 in 1990. Among those ages 65 and older, the divorce rate tripled since 1990. In 2013, 23% of married people had been married before. Most remarried people are men, and 4 in 10 marriages in 2013 had one spouse who had married once before.

Intermarriage is on the rise. There is an increase in the marriage of black newlyweds, who are 18% of newlyweds married to someone of another race or ethnicity.

Interfaith marriage

About four in ten Americans who have married since 2010 are married to someone of a different religious group. The majority of these intermarried couples are between a Christian and a religiously unaffiliated spouse.

According to The American Religious Identity Survey, Jews, Episcopalians, and Buddhists have high rates of intermarriage while Mormons are least likely to marry out.[62]

Interfaith marriage is correlated with higher divorce rates than same faith marriages and is also associated with low rates of religious participation and is therefore a threat to organized, institutionalized religion. In the 21st century, about 22% of Americans marry outside of their own religious tradition. The reason for this development is related to increased individualism and the belief that religious homogeneity is unnecessary. This is also related to the weakening of influence of parents on children. In addition, more and more Americans have become acquainted with religions other than their own. At least 40% of interfaith married who identify with a particular religion say that neither they nor anyone in the household belong to a religious institution. This means that the number unaffiliated with a religion has more than doubled since the 1990s. This loss is most visible among so-called liberal mainline Protestants, while those gaining more adherents are evangelical Christians, who follow high levels doctrinal conformity.[63]

Although Muslims, Buddhists, and Hindus are still a very small percentage of Americans, their numbers have doubled since the 1990s and therefore they have become a potential source of interfaith marriage. Whatever its source, The Institute for American Values has concluded that the weakening of marriage is the single greatest problem facing the United States.[64] The belief in this threat is promoted by a view of the so-called good old days in which father was at work and mother stayed home. This belief is contradicted by historical experiences. In this so-called good old days, many apparently died before their children became adults, and so they produced many orphans as well as blended families of widows and widowers.[65]

In any case, interfaith married couples adopt one or more of four strategies to maintain their families. These include establishing one dominant family faith in friendly dialogue with the other. The second strategy is adopting multi-religious practices, such as attending a synagogue on Jewish holy days and the church on Christian holy days. A third strategy consists of absorbing the practices of both religions at home and a fourth strategy is the adoption of rituals and celebrations such as bar mitzvahs as well as the observance of Christmas.[66]

Because interfaith marriages have become more frequent in the 21st century than ever before, there are now several organizations seeking to facilitate interfaith marriages. The Dovetail Institute for Interfaith Family Relations is a national religiously unaffiliated organization which conducts conferences and helps families work out interfaith arrangements. Other groups with similar interests are the Interfaith Community of New York and the Interfaith Families Project Of Greater Washington DC.

Interfaith marriages do not only concern the married couple. Parents and in-laws and grandparents and families are inevitably involved in the decisions to marry someone outside the faith of the family. The opinions of family members become particularly important when children are born and the religious affinity of the next generation becomes a dominant issue. It is then that women in particular are penalized for acting outside religious affiliations of their family. Many women have been rejected by their own or their partners' families as a consequence of out marrying. This kind of rejection is related to the low rate of religious participation of intermarried couples, as well as the fear on the part of the older generation that their grandchildren will not perpetuate the faith and traditions of their grandparents.[67]

Same-sex marriage has grown considerably since 2000. Public support for same-sex marriage also grew since 2007, when 54% of Americans opposed such marriage. By 2017, 62% of Americans favored same-sex marriage, so that homosexuals could marry legally.[68]

Online dating has become more and more popular since 2013. By 2017, 41% of Americans use online dating, and 29% have entered into a long-term relationship by means of online dating. Online dating is particularly popular among 18- to 24-year-olds.[69]

Age and Marriage

Since 1975, the average age at first marriage in the United States has risen considerably. In addition, the chances of ever marrying have decreased substantially, according to the Census.[70]

Marriage results in significantly better mental health compared to never marrying. This is in part due to social and cultural age norms which cause Americans to wish that their life course resembled the timing which culture imposes on everyone. This means that Americans become uncomfortable when they deviate from the desired age at marriage.

As the average age at marriage is increased, the chances of marrying have decreased. In 1970, approximately 5% of adults age 40 through 44 were never married. By 1996, this had doubled to more than 10% and by 2010, 17% of adults aged 40 to 44 were never married.[71]

The failure to marry can be attributed in part to cohabitation. The increase in women's economic independence as well as economic insecurity and increases in the cost of higher education have all contributed to the rejection of marriage.[72]

Some researchers suggest that people developed the concept of their normal expected lifecycle to the effect that certain lifecycle events will occur at certain times. These lifecycle events, reputedly a major turning point in people's lives, produce changes in self-concept and identity. Therefore, it is argued, failure to attain these changes has a negative outcome for the well-being of those affected.[73]

These negative outcomes include negative social sanctions from one's social network, leading to deprivation of peer support. All this leads to psychological distress and enduring emotional pain over the life course. Not only failure to marry, but also unsatisfactory marriages, leads to mental health problems over time.[74]

It is significant that women's mental health is significantly affected by entering motherhood either earlier or later than expected. This is also true of never married persons who also suffer identity crises and negative social sanctions. Furthermore, those who are dissatisfied with their single status or with their married status can become very much distressed, because they resent the status role that they occupy unwillingly.[75]

Economics of Marriage

Until recently, married couples with children were the norm. In 2019, this is no longer the case, as single parent households and non-married couples became commonplace. In addition, divorce rates have remained at approximately 50% for several years. Moreover, Americans choose to marry late if at all, so that marriage has become more selective than ever before. In addition, work parents have greatly changed, as early earning quality has worsened and the wages of many occupations have failed to increase, although female participation in the labor force has grown considerably. Because of automation, there has been a decided decline in well-paid blue-collar work. Because of the increase in single parenting, income losses have become economic death sentences when there is no second earner in the family.[76]

Marriage tends to raise the levels of income-, employment, and other resources because the families of married people can usually be relied upon to help in finding employment. Two parent married households are generally more stable and well-adjusted and have more resources than single men and women living together.[77]

Several studies have shown that the rise in non-marital births since the 1970s explains a good deal of the poverty associated with this lifestyle. Single parent families were forced into greater maternal employment after the 1996 welfare reforms. This led to a decline in poverty as more single parents worked when welfare was no longer available.

Marriage may have a negative association with poverty, because poorly educated women, the majority, have children earlier than educated women who were delayed in childbirth. Increased work leads to considerable increases in earnings and work hours for both mothers and fathers.[78]

Because there has been a good sized increase in cohabiting couples with children, these cohabiting parents have two earners and therefore fare better economically than single parent households.[79]

In 1996, Congress passed and President Clinton signed the Personal Responsibility and Work Opportunity Act, which was a major welfare reform effort. The bill was promoted by the Contract with America, an aspect of the Republican platform. The purpose of this act was increased labor market participation among public assistance recipients. The message of this act was that full-time mothering was a luxury reserved for people who could afford it. Congress was concerned that welfare receiving people had become too dependent upon public assistance and that those who were on welfare for many years lost any initiative to find work. Therefore, this act increased family earnings as welfare decreased dramatically.[80] It needs to be noted that workers with less than a high school education are earning only slightly more in the 21st century than was true in 1970.[81]

Some Recent Developments

Undoubtedly there are today many couples who found each other by having been introduced by friends or relatives. Others may have met at singles bars or church related events. More recently there are two new means of meeting the opposite sex. One is called speed dating and the other "online dating."

In speed dating events, participants pair off in chairs at tables. A buzzer sounds and the singles move to another chair and a different partner. After the "round robin" is finished, the participants give the organizer a paper listing the names of those they would like to meet again. Those that match are given a phone number of a participant who wants to meet them and are then on their own. Participants in speed dating tend to look for such attributes in others as height, weight, and good looks rather than education or occupation.[82]

Women are a great deal more cautious than men before asking to meet a man a second time. The reason is that women may end up with an unwanted pregnancy and/or years of child raising by making the wrong choice.

A Brief History of Marriage

The earliest marriages were not related to love between the partners but were instead alliances between families. Therefore, families arranged the marriages for the couples. The principal motivation for marriage was economic. The newly married couple had little power to decide their lives together, as the family made these decisions for them. A good example is the arranged marriage depicted in the musical "Fiddler on the Roof." The bible records the marriage of Abraham, the first Jew, who married his half-sister. His son Isaac married his cousin, and Jacob, his grandson, married two cousins. (Genesis 17:15).

American marriages continue to follow some truly ancient traditions. The exchange of rings among the ancient Romans was an indication of eternity in that the ring has no beginning and no end, symbolizing the eternity of marriage, which was expected to last forever. Another interpretation of the ring was that the ring worn at first only by women was to indicate that the woman was the property of the husband, and that the ring was a symbol of the iron chain made of rings which was worn by slaves. [83]

Over the years, several kinds of marriages have evolved. Included are common law marriages, which relied only on the fact that a woman and a man lived together over a long period of time.

First cousin marriage is allowed in 26 states of the Union. Both of these marriages are forms of monogamy, which refers to the marriage of one person to one other person at one time. There is also polyandry, a marriage of a woman to several husbands at the same time. Polyandry is practiced in Nepal, Tibet, and some 50 other societies. Polygyny refers to the marriage of one man to several women. Muslim men are permitted four wives, a practice also known among the ancient Jews in biblical times. Same-sex marriage is known in the United States and is endorsed by some religions. [84]

The earliest marriage contracts ever found by archeologists were Jewish marriages occurring in ancient Egypt. In the sixteenth century, the Roman Catholic Church decreed that marriages were to be celebrated in the presence of a priest and at least two witnesses.

The Pill

In 1960, 18.4% of professional workers were women. In 1998, 36.4% of professional workers in the United States were women. In 2017, nearly one half of professionals were women. For example, 40% of physicians were women and a majority of psychologists were women. In 2017, 36.55% of dentists were women and a majority of pharmacists were women.

These changes began in the 1970s, because young women were able to obtain "the pill" and control pregnancy. The 1970s were years in which feminism emerged forcefully in the United States. Legal changes allowed young married women to gain access to contraceptives and increased the age of first marriage. Thus, after 1970, a sharp change in marriage and childbearing occurred in the United States. Then the age of marriage for those women marrying before age 26 declined from 70% to 54% for those born in the 1950s.[85] After "the Pill" was approved by the Food and Drug Administration in 1960, contraception increased to 40% for married women in one year.

In 1971, the 26th Amendment to the Constitution lowered the voting rights of Americans from 21 to 18. This led to the popular opinion that young people deserved increased rights and therefore the pill was introduced to those 18 years old. This change led more and more married and unmarried women to plan a career unencumbered by pregnancy and fostered by changes in the law. By 1974, most states allowed women less than seventeen years to obtain the pill. This meant that unmarried girls were now on birth control and sexually active. More women than ever before therefore entered colleges and universities, whose family planning clinics provided "the pill" to students. [86]

The pill demonstrates that social movements are often facilitated by technological advances without which the social movement would not succeed. The best example is the feminist movement of the 1920s, which failed because birth control relied on numerous devices which were uncertain and often failed.

CHAPTER 4. PURITAN SEX AND THE WESTERN TRADITION

In the early 16th century, several thousand English immigrants settled in Massachusetts in New England. They called themselves Puritans, as they rejected the Church of England, which they believed was too much like the Roman Catholic Church. The Anglican Church had been founded in 1531 when Henry VIII, and subsequently Parliament, rejected the Pope and made Henry VIII head of a separate church.

Puritanism began in the late 16th century in England. The first Puritans were Protestant reformers, who remained within the Anglican church which they thought they could purify.

Puritans did not observe traditional Christian holy days such as Christmas and Easter, nor did they observe birthdays and weddings. Puritans elected so-called qualified men to govern them in accordance with a covenant with God. They believed that they were chosen by God as long as they were true to that covenant.[87]

The Puritans did not support religious freedom. They believed that the state needed to protect society from heresy, which they suppressed with corporal punishment, banishment, or death. They taught their children that "liberty or freedom is only for that which is just and good" as defined by the clergy. They would not admit people of other religious persuasions.[88]

The Puritans were a repressive society, regarding human sexuality as obnoxious and disgusting, even within marriage. The Massachusetts Bay Colony, founded in 1620 with the arrival of the *Mayflower*, forced its subjects to live a life of autocratic rule by a few clergy, who arrogated to themselves the right to dictate how others should live by using the Hebrew Bible as the authority allowing them to lord it over the entire community in the name of God as they understood it. This popular view was challenged by Edmund S.

Morgan in his essay "The Puritans and Sex," in which Morgan attempted to paint the Puritans as free spirits "Inured to sexual offenses."

Later scholarship proved Morgan wrong, as Morgan himself discovered by reading some of the sermons delivered by Puritan ministers which revealed a "blind zeal and narrow minded bigotry" among the clergy regarding sex.[89]

The Puritan clergy regarded sex, even within marriage, with distaste and even disgust, and as an invitation to damnation. They linked sexuality with atheism, paganism and final judgment. They viewed all sexuality with distrust. To some extent, these attitudes were part of the Protestant Reformation, which reacted against sexual abuses attributed to the celibate Roman Catholic clergy.[90]

Cotton Mather, the most influential clergyman of the Puritans, denounced excessive sexuality among married people, contending that it is a sin to love one's spouse more than God. He wrote that one must not love the creature more than the creator.[91]

The Puritans also worried about uncleanliness, a phrase which referred to "brutish lust," which ended with "fearful desolation," as proved by the story of Sodom in Genesis 19.[92] Not only Genesis but the Five Books of Moses guided the Puritans. This so-called Old Testament was the primary source of Puritan religion. God's deliverance of the Jews from Egypt, the revelation of the 10 commandments to Moses at Mount Sinai, and the journey of the chosen people to the promised land led the Puritans to believe that their own exodus from Europe, their difficult journey to America, and their privileged status in God's eyes and the founding of New England in the colonies were a repetition of all that they read in the Bible.

The Puritans attempted to live by the laws and commandments of the Old Testament and hoped to enforce them. It is significant that the Jews had developed Talmudic Judaism as early as the first century AD. The Talmud interprets the five books of Moses in such a manner as to remove most of the repressive aspects of the 613 laws found therein. This means that the Jews, incessantly accused by Christians of excessive legalism, had in fact liberalized their understanding of the Bible, while the Christian Puritans sought to enforce all that which the Jews had already rejected.

The Puritans were also willing to kill by the use of the so-called death penalty, which they applied extensively.[93]

In 1692, a number of young girls in Salem, Massachusetts, were induced to claim that several women in that community were witches and had caused them to become ill and to see visions and hear voices and be otherwise affected by witchcraft. Since the Bible includes repeated admonitions not to allow a witch to live, the accusations of these hysterical girls were used to kill by hanging 19 women and one man, who was pressed to death. Today, in 2019, there are still a number of states in the United States who kill citizens by means of the so-called death penalty, manifestly pretending that this penalty prevents murder. In fact, hundreds of men and some women have been sent to death row in the United States in the 20th and 21st centuries although they were innocent of any crime. Evidently the latent function of the so-called death penalty is to allow prison guards an opportunity to kill and enjoy sadism while at the same time "keeping the poor in their place," as the victims of these injustices are generally poor men who cannot afford lawyers to defend them. Likewise, the Puritans put to death so-called witches, who were almost always widows who owned property inherited from their deceased husbands. The killers benefited by seizing the property of those they had murdered as witches, so that the latent function of the witchcraft hysteria among Puritans was the seizure of property and the enrichment of the clergy, who were judge and jury in Puritan communities.

Puritan society also suppressed women. Since the oppression of women has continued in the United States until the end of the 20th century, it is not surprising that the Puritans in the 17th century held women in contempt. An outstanding example of this behavior was the condemnation of Anne Hutchinson, who was expelled from the Massachusetts Bay Colony because she discussed the Bible in her home with anyone willing to listen. The Puritans found it obnoxious that a woman had any opinions or even a following. This attitude has persisted in the United States for centuries, so that women could not even vote in a federal election until 1920. Undoubtedly the various disabilities imposed on women for so long owed their persistence to the Puritans.[94]

The Puritans used biblical principles as the basis of their political life. They concluded communal agreements which they claimed were sanctioned by God.

The New Puritans

Until the sexual revolutions of the 1920s and 1960s, it was public policy to claim that women were the victims of male sex needs and were even in marriage forced to endure male sexual aggression. This tool was a remnant of Puritanism, as is the so-called "me too movement," which seeks to extract money from prominent men by accusing those in position to pay large sums to avoid accusations of sexual harassment. There are of course cruel men who harass women by seeking sexual favors. However, the hysteria concerning

sexual harassment which has cost many a prominent man his job and reputation resembles the witchcraft hysteria of the 17th century.

In November 2017 the popular magazine Newsweek published a list
of men who were accused of sexual harassment. Some of these accusations
seem indeed believable. However, the flood of such claims leads a reasonable person to recognize that the so-called female victims provoked many of
these harassments for financial gain and/or an interest in publicity. The film
producer and studio executive Harvey Weinstein was the first to lose his
position amidst widespread publicity, as the New York Times listed over 100
women who accused him of sexual assault.

This opened the floodgates, as the producer Andy Signore and the actor
Ben Affleck were accused, and the prominent filmmaker Oliver Stone was
accused by two actresses of sexual harassment because he made them feel
uncomfortable. The studio executive Roy Price was accused of making lewd
comments and the creator of the Nickelodeon cartoon, Chris Savino, was
accused of inappropriate behavior as well as sexual harassment. Lockhart
Steele, editorial director of Vox Media, was accused of sexual harassment
and inappropriate behavior as was John Besh, the celebrity chef owner of a
restaurant. The screenwriter and film director James Toback was accused
by over 200 women of using vulgar conversation, unwarranted touching,
and masturbating in front of women. Kevin Spacey, an acclaimed actor was
accused of predatory behavior and sexual misconduct toward young men,
and NPR editor Michael Oreskes was accused of unwanted physical contact
and sexual harassment.

This partial list of men accused of sexual harassment is composed
entirely of men working in the movie and entertainment industry. Added to
this group already mentioned is the famous actor Dustin Hoffman, accused
of sexual harassment and lewd comments. Hoffman is known for his acting
in *The Graduate, Tootsie, Kramer versus Kramer*, and *Rainman*.

John Grissom, David Guillod, Brett Ratner, John Singleton, Ed West-
wick, Steven Seagal, Jeffrey Tambor, and numerus other members of the
entertainment industry stand accused of sexual harassment.

Also accused of sexual harassment are Roy Moore, an Alabama politician,
and Al Franken, a former US senator from Minnesota, and Matt Zimmerman,
NBC news executive in charge of booking talent for the *Today Show*. Charlie
Rose, who worked for both PBS and CBS, was accused of appearing naked
in front of female coworkers. James Levine, the longtime conductor of the
Metropolitan Opera was accused in 2017 of sexual abuse of a man in the
1960s. Likewise, Hall of Fame quarterback Warren Moon was accused of
sexual harassment, as were numerous others.[95]

Most egregious was the conviction and imprisonment of Bill Cosby. In April of 2018, Cosby was sentenced to three to ten years in prison for sexually assaulting Andrea Constand. Cosby is 81 years old and nearly blind. By comparison murder carries a usual sentence of 11 years, with three years off for good behavior, so the average murderer serves eight years. Cosby is expected to serve ten years until age 91.

Among those who lost their jobs on the grounds of sexual harassment is Bill O'Reilly, without doubt the top rated cable host in cable news. O'Reilly invited a number of conservative politicians to his show and was evidently himself a defender of Republican politics. It is therefore not unreasonable to suspect that his firing on the grounds of sexual harassment was motivated by political considerations. Obviously it is now possible to rid oneself of colleague or a boss by shouting "sexual harassment."[96]

An excellent example of the use of Puritanism as a means of defeating a political opponent was the effort of Democrats to prevent the accession to the Supreme Court of the United States Judge Brett Kavanaugh. Because Kavanaugh had an outstanding record as a judge of the Court of Appeals, Democrats could not find any means of preventing his approval by the Senate after having been nominated by President Trump. Then, a 51-year-old woman by the name of Christine Ford publicly accused Kavanaugh of drunkenness and sexual harassment which, according to the accuser, had occurred when Kavanaugh was 17 years old and a high school student. It is of course obvious that such accusations can hardly be substantiated 36 years after their reputed occurrence. Furthermore, the complainant granted that she was able to leave the room where this event may have occurred. Kavanaugh claims that he was never at the party the accuser mentioned and that over so many years nobody's memory would be accurate. Moreover it is obvious that if all adults were prevented from earning a livelihood on the grounds of what they did at the age of 17, then hardly anybody would be making a living. The media constantly paint themselves as the judges and juries of all citizens and pretend to be "holier than Thou." We are entitled to ask how many employees of the media would be out of work if their conduct were to become public entertainment.[97]

These constant accusations of sexual harassment have consequences for both women and men. Traditionally senior men have sponsored younger employees and helped them climb the corporate ladder. At one time only men were considered for jobs in America's business community. However, after the sexual revolution of the 1960s and 1970s, women too have become candidates for advancement into leading positions in the business world. The effort of women in this respect was largely promoted by senior men willing to help women achieve. Relationships with senior people in a company led to career advancement for women and men. Now endless sexual harassment complaints have made it dangerous for any man to so much as speak to a woman fellow employee. Even one word or merely being seen in the company of a female employee can lead to the dismissal of a man and the end of his career. Losing one's job in midlife constitutes an economic death sentence. Therefore, women who find it profitable to accuse men will find that their own advancement can be held back, as no senior man will risk his income and the support of his family by so much as talking to them.[98]

An Unholy Alliance

It is remarkable that traditional fundamentalists who have always denounced sex as disgusting, dirty, and immoral are now allied with the so-called liberal establishment who are equally interested in repressing all sex. Fundamentalists even forbid talk about sex and are totally opposed to sex education. This is also true of the anti-sex feminists who dislike men.[99]

Many feminists are stridently opposed to pornography. They seek to control pornography by legislation, although the Supreme Court has ruled that pornography is protected speech under the First Amendment to the Constitution. These decisions include the Roth decision of 1968, Jekyll Bellis versus Ohio of 1964, Ginsburg versus the United States of 1965, Stanley versus Georgia of 1969, Miller versus California, 1973, New York versus Ferber, 1982 and Denver Communications, 1996. There are numerous other decisions with reference to pornography by lower courts. In sum, these decisions uphold freedom of speech despite the objections of those who find pornography disgusting and anti-woman. All courts, including the Supreme Court of the United States, have outlawed child pornography. This prohibition is enforced by police, who watch child pornography in an effort to find the offenders, therefore making the watchers themselves child pornographers.

In 1890, Scottish anthropologist Sir James George Frazer (1854–1941) published a study of mankind's religions since the most ancient days. In his 12 volume book *The Golden Bough*, Frazer wrote these words:

> In Cyprus it appears that before marriage all women were formerly obliged by custom to prostitute themselves to strangers at the sanctuary of the goddess, whether she went by the name of Aphrodite, Astarte, or what not. Similar customs prevailed in many parts of Western Asia. Whatever its motive, the practice was clearly regarded, not as an orgy of lust, but as a solemn religious duty performed in the service of that great Mother Goddess of Western Asia whose name

varied, while her type remained constant, from place to place. Thus at Babylon every woman, whether rich or poor, had once in her life to submit to the embraces of a stranger at the temple of Mylitta, that is, of Ishtar or Astarte, and to dedicate to the goddess the wages earned by this sanctified harlotry. The sacred precinct was crowded with women waiting to observe the custom. Some of them had to wait there for years. At Heliopolis or Baalbec in Syria, famous for the imposing grandeur of its ruined temples, the custom of the country required that every maiden should prostitute herself to a stranger at the temple of Astarte, and matrons as well as maids testified their devotion to the goddess in the same manner. The emperor Constantine abolished the custom, destroyed the temple, and built a church in its stead. In Phoenician temples, women prostituted themselves for hire in the service of religion, believing that by this conduct they propitiated the goddess and won her favor. It was a law of the Amoris, that she who was about to marry should sit in fornication seven days by the gate. At Byblus the people shaved their heads in the annual mourning for Adonis. Women who refused to sacrifice their hair had to give themselves up to strangers on a certain day of the festival, and the money which they thus earned was devoted to the goddess. This custom may have been a mitigation of an older rule which at Byblus as elsewhere formerly compelled every woman without exception to sacrifice her virtue in the service of religion. A Greek inscription found at Tralles in Lydia proves that the practice of religious prostitution survived in that country as late as the second century of our era.

In Armenia the noblest families dedicated their daughters to the service of the goddess Anaitis in her temple of Acilisena, where the damsels acted as prostitutes for a long time before they were given in marriage. Nobody scrupled to take one of these girls to wife when her period of service was over. Here he included the position of temple prostitutes or "sacred women," who used pornography in order to induce male visitors to visit their temples. Temple prostitutes wrote obscene words on walls or displayed obscene symbols to entice men. That was pornography, i.e., the writing of a prostitute.

All around the Mediterranean Sea, in ancient Greece, in Phoenicia and Armenia and numerous other places, people believed that their food supply depended on demonstrating to the gods, whose statues were the object of worship, that the reproduction of the food supply was essential to their survival. Knowing next to nothing of agriculture and having no scientific understanding, primitives used sex to demonstrate in front of the divine statues that reproduction was needed.

Both women and men seek equality for American women and have for years advocated legal regulation of pornography. They wish to treat pornography as an exception to the First Amendment protection concerning freedom of speech and hope to make the production, sale, display and distribution of pornographic materials cause for a civil lawsuit, so that anyone who feels harmed by pornography can collect damages.[100]

Pornography in the American Context

In 21st century America, pornography has lost its religious connotation. Because Americans wish to be Puritans while at the same time seeking to be individualists, pornography is both damned and rejected even as it has been estimated that Americans spend $1 billion a year on this industry. While traditionally objections to pornography were linked to arguments against obscenity, more recently opponents of pornography argue that obscene free speech is not the issue but that pornography causes physical and psychological abuse of women and is a form of a bigotry and contempt for women. The argument seeking to introduce contempt for women as cause for repressing pornography seeks to circumvent the free speech issue, as recorded in the First Amendment of the Constitution.[101]

Over the years the Supreme Court of the United States has struck down almost all anti-pornography laws as unconstitutional by reason of the First Amendment. In 1957, the US Supreme Court rejected the principal that adult matter should be suppressed because it might harm minors. The court struck down a Michigan law prohibiting obscene language that might adversely influence the morals of youth.

In Jacobellis v. Ohio, the court struck down the conviction of Nico Jacobellis on the grounds of having exhibited a film including an explicit three-minute sex scene. This sex scene violated Ohio's obscenity statute. The charge was rejected by the court because the offense did not violate national standards, even if it did violate local standards.[102]

In Redrup v. New York, the Supreme Court overturned three convictions for buying pornographic magazines. The court held that these convictions violated the 1st and 14th Amendments.

In Stanley v. Georgia, the Supreme Court ruled that the state cannot prohibit a citizen from obtaining obscene material for personal use. In this case, sexually explicit films were discovered in the defendant's house by police in the course of an unrelated investigation. Stanley was convicted of violating Georgia's obscenity law. However, the Supreme Court decided: "that mere private possession of obscenity cannot constitutionally be made a crime."[103] Finally, in Miller v. California, the court rejected the conviction of

Marvin Miller for sending a mass mailing of sexually explicit advertisements of films he had for sale.[104] It was only in the case of child pornography that the Supreme Court upheld the right of states to prevent the depiction of children in obscene situations, allowing states the right to prevent possession of child pornography and the viewing of child pornography as well as its distribution.

In May 2011, the then Atty. Gen. of the United States, Eric Holder, spoke to the National Strategy Conference On Combating Child Exploitation. Holder called child pornography a form of child sexual exploitation. According to Holder, the law prohibits child pornography and defines it as any visual depiction of sexual explicit conduct involving a minor, i.e., a person less than 18 years of age. Federal law prohibits the production, distribution, importation, or possession of any image of child pornography. According to Holder, violation of federal child pornography laws is a serious crime.[105]

It needs to be remembered that a film of sexual behavior becomes a permanent record exhibiting those participating in these performances. Therefore, a child engaged in a sex exploitation film is permanently damaged even as an adult. Children are evidently unable to understand the full consequences of being exhibited in such a fashion. Therefore the abuse of the child is not a one-time affair but has long term consequences. Once a child is old enough to understand the outcome of his participation in a pornography film, he/she will have to live with the knowledge that there is a permanent record visible to anyone of his conduct in his younger years.[106]

It is evident from the foregoing Supreme Court decisions that opponents of pornography cannot rely on the law to eliminate it. In addition, supporters of the elimination of pornography have yet another obstacle facing them. That is that the pornography industry will not easily relinquish its huge income, which is supported by millions.[107]

Those who seek to protect free speech may well be sympathetic to the view that pornography is insulting and demeaning of both women and men and that the harm it may do is far less than the harm prohibiting free speech in any fashion, including pornography, because limits on free speech will lead to making the United States a police state. Further it is argued, that some women enjoy viewing pornography and that therefore those who claim to speak for all women are denying other women the right to sexual expression.[108]

Opponents of pornography not only need to deal with First Amendment issues but also confronted by the pornography industry which is unlikely to voluntarily relinquish its huge profits. In addition, the consumers of pornography will equally object to any restrictions concerning their interests.

The Consequences of Pornography

Pornography negates traditional values which favor marriage family and children. It promotes the idea that sexual relations between people who have just met, and who are not committed to each other in any manner, can gain exceptional sexual gratification. The performers in pornographic films are in no way attached to one another, have no commitment, will never see each other again, and have no emotional attachment. Pornography teaches that kindness, caring, and responsibility for one another are meaningless.[109]

Excessive viewing of pornography is generally associated with inability to distinguish fantasy from reality. Such viewing also leads to discontent with one's own sex life in the belief that one is missing great sexual experiences. Excessive viewing of pornography also trivializes rape and criminal offenses against children, leading to insensibility towards the victims of sexual violence. Habitual viewers of pornography are more likely to become sexually callous and violent towards women.[110]

There are some who are addicted to pornography in the same manner as others are addicted to gambling or alcohol or drugs. Such addiction leads to physical, mental, and financial negative consequences also associated with depression and anxiety.[111]

Pornography and crime and financial negative consequences

Over the years that has been an ongoing dispute concerning the relationship of crime to pornography. Some researchers claim that only people already interested in committing sex crimes are induced to do so by viewing pornography. Others say that there is a direct relationship between pornography and sex offenses. Believing that relationship to be dangerous, the Kansas legislature passed a bill in March 2011 requiring police to report any and all pornographic materials during sexual crime investigations.[112] This bill was passed on the grounds that sexual violence is promoted by pornography. According to some psychologists, there are three factors that predict sexual violence. These are hostility toward women, the belief that sex is recreational and non-intimate, and the use of pornography[113]

The relationship of pornography to crime is also important because organized crime earns huge profits from dealing in pornographic films. Because of the huge amount of money earned by supplying viewers of pornographic films, organized criminals usually referred to as the Mafia successfully launched the first commercially popular pornographic movie, called *Deep Throat*, in the 1972. Realistic estimates of the proceeds from this movie are that the producers collected about $100 million, equivalent to about $469 million in 2018. The movie was produced by Louis "Butch" Perino for $47,500, funds which were furnished to Louis Perino by his father, Anthony Perino, a member of the Colombo crime family. *Deep Throat* made the then record $3 million in is first six months of release. In view of the immense income derived from *Deep Throat*, a number of additional Mafia connected movie-makers gained enough money to go into production and distribution of legitimate films. Included among those now producing both porno and legitimate films is James Buckley, one of the founders of the newspaper *Screw*.114

Organized crime is indeed violent, so that it is not surprising that Jack Molinas, a former Columbia basketball star, was shot to death in the backyard of his Hollywood Hills home. Molina had been involved with the Mafia and had previously served five years in prison for fixing basketball games. Likewise, Philip Mainer, having been involved in several Mafia connected distributors of pornographic films, was murdered in Youngstown, after he was suspected of informing on his Mafia associates.115

Because *Deep Throat* was so successful, the Mafia family that Joseph Bonanno headed continued to produce porno films such as *The Devil in Miss Jones*. Included in these films was *Defiance* a film which was stopped by court order because its leading actress, Jean Jennings, was a minor. Since then the Mafia has employed a "front man" to produce pornographic films. A "front man" is somebody associated with the Mafia but not really a member.

The Mafia would not tolerate competition. For example, when in 1973 the brothers Arthur and James Mitchell made a film called Behind the Green Door, the Mitchells were visited by a number of Mafiosi who demanded that they be paid 50% of the profits from Behind the Green Door. When the Mitchells refused the offer, the criminals distributed later printed versions of the film. This drove the Mitchells out of the business.

In 1974, Robert Sommer distributed a pornographic film called *The Life and Times of Xaviera Hollander*. The film was shown in Buffalo, New York, at a theater managed by Don Gaetano. Gaetano suddenly disappeared with the film, which was later shown in New York City in the theater by Ralph Robert DiSalvo, a member of the Mafia.116

For some time throughout the 1970s and later, the production of pornographic films was profitable. But by the middle of the 1990s, the Internet arrived and that put an end to profitable pornographic theater films, even as it also reduced the number of theatergoers watching legitimate movies.

Pornography on the Internet

The Internet and the computer led to the spectacular growth of sexually explicit material. This has created an immense opportunity for individuals to have anonymous and cost free access to a huge number of sexually arousing pictures, movies, and texts. Not only adult men and women but young boys and girls can now view sexuality privately and without cost. Much of the sexual material shown on the Internet is of an antisocial content promoting violence. It is of course true that the vast majority of viewers of pornography do not therefore engage in rape or other atrocities. However, those few already predisposed towards sexually violent behavior will find it far easier to put into action what they have seen on their computer than to do so without inducement provided by the Internet.[117]

Pornography on the Internet has three dimensions. Some pieces may be described simply as erotic. There is also a segment of Internet pornography which is degrading and insulting to women, and thirdly, some Internet pornography is of a violent nature.[118]

In the early 1970s, before the Internet became the prime source of pornographic viewing, such magazines as *Playboy* and *Penthouse* furnished the readers with pornography. These magazines increased material of a sexually violent content from 1% in 1970 to 5% in 1980. This means that sexually violent material was quite rare in print pornography. On the Internet, however, fully 51% of pornographic videos portrayed the rape of a woman. High levels of sexual violence were portrayed on the Internet, in which between 42% and 65% of the performers were women.[119]

According to several researchers, the average user of pornography views Internet sex sites four days per month. Among male college students, research shows that 51% of all men declined to see any sexually explicit videos, while 15% of all college men want to see erotic material which is nonviolent. The remainder view common sexual acts. Since college students are of an age most frequently believed to be interested in pornography, these findings imply that hysterical comments about the saturation of society with Internet pornography is grossly exaggerated.

There are indeed some men engaged in a great deal of sexual promiscuity, who are more likely than others to watch aggressive pornography and who have a history of sexual aggression against women. The majority of men seek out sexually explicit videos without violence, as they have egalitarian and not sexist attitudes towards women.[120]

The Performers

Pornography is a business seeking to make a profit. According to Shira Tarrant, a professor of gender studies at California State Long Beach College and author of *The Pornography Industry*, women earn more than men in the pornography industry. The rates for women appearing alone may be $300-$500 per shoot. A lesbian is paid $800 per shoot and a so-called straight woman acting with a man is paid $1000. An anal scene pays $1200 and so-called double penetration pays $4000.

Male performers' pornographic movies pay $200-$500 in the so-called straight scene and gay men are paid 500 dollars to $1000. Filming costs include makeup artists paid $150 per shoot, lighting specialists paid $350, and photographers, paid $500. A director earns $5000 for each film directed. In addition there are costs for location, camera operators, food, insurance, film permits, and wardrobes.[121]

The actors in porn movies are generally unknown to the public. There are, however, so-called celebrities to a who began their movie career as porn stars. These are very few among the many who come to Los Angeles or Hollywood in the hope of becoming rich and famous. Very few succeed in gaining access to a movie career. Among those who did achieve becoming a so-called star after acting in porn movies are Sylvester Stallone, Arnold Schwarzenegger, Kim Kardashian, Adam West, Marilyn Monroe, Paris Hilton, Jackie Chan, Sibel Kikelli, David Duchovny, Cameron Diaz, and Dustin Diamond.[122]

Although pornography has a vast number of viewers, it is nevertheless stigmatized. Therefore so-called porn stars have a great deal of difficulty telling their families about their occupation. Porn stars face the inescapable fact that they may be seen in a sexual act by their mother or father or other relatives and friends. Once a performer in a porn video is shown on the Internet, he or she cannot ever erase that picture. Therefore some poor performers are rejected by their family and friends and may have great difficulty finding work other than in the movie industry. That industry exploits these performers precisely because almost all of them have no other way of earning a livelihood. The exploitation is not only financial. It is also very difficult to have sex with a random stranger while other strangers, such as directors and a supporting crew making the video, look on. Moreover, porn performers may have three, four, or more scenes in a single day. Performers complain that they are exhausted and sometimes literally incapacitated.[123]

In view of the pain and difficulties porn stars must endure, it is reasonable to wonder why so many women become porn actresses. In 2012, The International Journal of Sexual Health published an article by James Griffith et. al. which describe the reasons that drove 176 porn actresses to this profession. 53% of respondents became porn performers for the money. 27% wanted the sex, and 16% like the attention. 11% considered it fun, and a few others mentioned such motives as acquaintance with someone already in the occupation, a dislike of their prior job, and creative expression.[124]

Working in the pornography industry is degrading and humiliating and painful. Like prostitution, pornography has a huge following among the very same people who hold it in contempt. This illustrates the dichotomy between the Puritan and the individualistic strands in American culture.

The Puritan Catholic Church

For a number of years in the 20th and 21st centuries, an endless series of sex abuse scandals concerning Roman Catholic priests came to light. For example, on August 14, 2018, a Pennsylvania grand jury released a report concerning sexual abuse committed by 300 Roman Catholic priests over seventy years in Pennsylvania. More than 1,000 victims have been identified, and many more are probably victims of sexual abuse by priests. The grand jury also listed a number of ways by which higher ranking clergy covered up these abuses.[125]

This has led to a number of so-called "cover-ups" of such misconduct by priests. Catholic parishioners have accused bishops and even the Pope of doing nothing to prevent parish priests from continuing sexual abuse practices. Instead the church has become even more repressive concerning sex than ever before. Failure of the Catholic clergy to live by their vows represents another example of the failure of Puritanism. Nature has decreed that all men have a sex drive. This cannot be abolished by decree or by vows. Therefore, the embarrassing and painful accusations against Catholic priests can only be resolved by allowing priests to marry women.

The Western Tradition

Americans are clearly at odds with themselves, as individualism is highly valued by the same people who promote the Puritan view. Therefore Henry David Thoreau's dictum "that government is best that governs the least," is widely acclaimed even as government is expected to promote law and order.[126] Most Americans support the Second Amendment to the Constitution allowing citizens to own a firearm. Independence and self-reliance are the subject matter of books and movies concerning the Old West in which culture heroes rely on their guns and their wits and not government to stay alive.

In his Introduction to The Years of Lyndon Johnson, Robert Caro describes the manner in which Johnson's family, who migrated from Tennessee to Texas, survived by having a plow in one hand and a gun in the other, as there was no government to defend them.[127]

An individualist does not follow a particular philosophy but develops his own views based on his personal interests. The individualist is a true liberal, a word derived from the Latin liberalis, "of freedom." Unfortunately, the word liberal has been transformed into the beliefs of so-called "leftists," a phrase derived from the French Revolution of 1789, when those members of the French assembly who wished to abolish the monarchy sat on the left of the speaker's podium while those seeking to maintain the monarchy sat on his right side. Today (2019) so-called liberals are in fact fascists, as they suppress freedom of speech and freedom of assembly, even as American media have become the tool of propaganda for the Democratic Party.

The liberal point of view was originally the so-called Age of Enlightenment, which denied the divine rights of kings and was instrumental in developing French and British democracy. It is of course true that the British parliamentary system as practiced throughout the world does not permit freedom of the press, allows government to censor books, permits government to appeal a not guilty verdict by jury, and limits the rights of citizens, as the head of government is elected by politicians and not by the voters.

In the 21st century, numerous Americans have become self-assertive with respect to their sexual orientation, as women have discarded the ancient prohibition against female sexual expression.

An important aspect of liberalism is the effort to find scientific evidence for any assertion or opinion based on logical principles and objective facts. This view rejects all assertions of supernatural events as well as the existence of any deity. Those who hold these views are generally followers of John Dewey, who taught that the universe is self-created. This is so bizarre a belief that it is in itself a superstition.

Hedonism, a word derived from the Greek hedone or pleasure, was taught by the philosopher Epicurus (341-270 B.C.E.) who thought that pleasure was the principal purpose of life, although he included intellectual pursuits in his definition.

All of these beliefs and philosophical trends have contributed to sexual liberation from the constraints of the Victorian Age, which was briefly interrupted by the failed sexual revolution of the 1920s and continued into the 1950s. The second sexual revolution occurred in the 1960s, primarily supported by successful birth control methods and the decline of such social diseases as syphilis and gonorrhea. In the 21st century, sexual liberation has taken on some unexpected forms, including the celebration of lesbianism, homosexuality, bisexuality, transgender activity, and behavior labeled "queer."[128]

Lesbians

In 630 B.C.E. (Before the Common Era) the poetess Sappho was born on the Greek island of Lesbos. She wrote numerous poems and had a large female following who admired her poetry. There is no evidence that Sappho was sexually connected to any women. Nevertheless, the British writer Aldous Huxley (1894–1963) called homosexual women lesbians. His first wife was a lesbian, leading to his interest in this aberration.[129]

Homosexual behavior was viewed as a crime all over the United States even into the 1970s, when in 1971 a small group of lesbian women founded a commune they called the "The Furies".

In 1973, the American Psychological Association removed homosexuality from the list of mental disorders[130] and in 1993 the armed services adopted the policy "don't ask don't tell" to the effect that the military could not ask service members about their sexual orientation.[131]

All this agitation for lesbian rights led to the legalization of same-sex marriages. San Francisco and the state of Vermont were first to adopt laws permitting same-sex marriage. Then, on June 26, 2015, the Supreme Court of the United States ruled 5-4 in Obergefell v. Hodges that same-sex marriage is legal in the United States. When the Defense of Marriage Act was largely emasculated by the Supreme Court, lesbians and homosexuals seemed to have arrived at total acceptance by the American public. Such a belief is unfounded, because legal decisions do not necessarily reflect public opinion.

Homosexuals or "Gays"

Male homosexuality has been widely recognized since biblical days. The Hebrew Bible refers to homosexuality in Leviticus chapter 18 verse 20 and in chapter 20 verse 13.

In the Bible homosexuality is called an abomination and was punishable by death. Neither Judaism nor Christianity today seeks to apply the death penalty to this activity. However, both religions view homosexuality from the point of view of their denominational attitudes and beliefs. Orthodox Jews and Fundamentalist Christians reject homosexual behavior on the grounds of its Biblical prohibition. They view homosexuality as a sin and claim that they can teach a homosexual to convert to heterosexual behavior. [132]

Homosexuals are approximately 7.3%% of Americans and 7.3% identify as lesbian, gay, bisexual and transgender.[133]

The belief that homosexuals are free to be heterosexuals if they so choose is not confined to fundamentalist Christians. People who are interested in religion and exhibit a high association with religious institutions are also more likely than non-participants in religion to hold homosexuals responsible for a choice they made. Catholics and mainline Protestants such as Episcopalians, Presbyterians and Methodists are a good deal less likely to believe that homosexuals chose that lifestyle than is true of fundamentalists.

Finally, Jews and Christians who view the Bible literally and who think God is active in human affairs view homosexuality as a deliberate sin which the sinner can abandon if he so chooses.

Men, more than women, are generally more likely to believe that homosexuality is a matter of choice. This is also true of people who view themselves as politically conservative.

As education increases, the belief that homosexuality is a matter of choice decreases.[134]

Same Sex Marriage

These beliefs are related to opinions concerning same sex marriage. Evidently, older Americans are less likely to support same sex marriage than is true of young people. However, as income increases, support of same sex marriage also increases. Those who attend religious services regularly are less likely to support same sex marriages than those who seldom or never attend religious events. Despite religious objections, there has been a marked liberalization in attitudes by the American public concerning same-sex marriage. Between 1988 and 2006, same-sex marriage was accepted by far more people than was true at the beginning of those years. This considerable increase in acceptance of same-sex marriages may be attributed to secularization and education, both of which lead to more liberal attitudes.[135]

Political affiliation influences attitudes towards same-sex marriage. Republicans are less likely to approve of same sex marriage than is true of Democrats. Evangelical Protestants are likely to disapprove of same-sex marriage, as demonstrated by Kim Davis, the county clerk of Rowan County, Morehead, Kentucky. Davis refused to issue marriage licenses to David Etmold and David More. Davis based her refusal to issue such a license on the Bible, which labels homosexual conduct a sin. Davis was briefly jailed until she agreed to let someone else issue such licenses.[136]

The Children of Same-Sex Marriages

Because the number of same-sex marriages is small, it is difficult to gain much information concerning childhood in a same-sex marriage. Only 1% of all couples in the 2000 census were same-sex couples. Despite the dearth of information concerning children's welfare in same-sex marriages, all investigators agree the children raised by their married biological parents have several advantages over those raised in same-sex marriages. This is true for number of reasons, including that married couples tend to be more prosperous then same-sex married couples.[137]

Nevertheless, several studies of children in same-sex marriages have found no statistically significant disadvantages for children raised by gay and lesbian parents compared to other children. Same-sex couples may adopt children. Some lesbian women use artificial insemination, and other lesbians and/or homosexuals have children they acquired by natural means that they bring with them into a same-sex marriage.

Since all children six years of age and not yet 16 must go to school, grade retention, which refers to being held back from promotion to the next higher grade is one measure of school failure. Apparently, there is a minor disadvantage to being the child of a same-sex couple, as such children are more often held back from promotion than is true for children of permanently married biological parents. In short, long term married couples have the best outcomes for their children, as is visible by the evidence that the children of heterosexual married couples have the lowest rate of grade retention as compared to children of lesbian mothers and gay fathers.[138]

Those who have become well acquainted with children of same-sex parents report that such children are often embarrassed when they discover that almost everybody else has two parents of different sexes. While such children may not understand the reasons for their peculiar family life, they fail to recognize the differences in gender roles between males and females. This would be particularly true of children of lesbian couples, because almost all grade school teachers are female, so that such children may never experience the presence of a man.

Transgender Men/Women

Bruce Jenner is a woman who calls himself Caitlyn after having his sex changed. Although there are others change their sex, Jenner's move from male to female has attracted worldwide attention because Jenner won a gold medal in the decathlon competition at the 1976 Olympic games in Montréal, Canada. He broke every decathlon record and was labeled the world's greatest athlete by the media. The Greek word decathlon means "ten contests." These are:

the 100 m sprint, long jump, shot put, high jump, 400 meter run, 110 meter hurdles, discus, pole vault, javelin throw, and 1,500 meter run.

It was therefore a source of true amazement when in 2015 Bruce Jenner reputedly began to make a transition from male to female. Jenner had been displayed on the Wheaties box. He had been a Playgirl cover boy, authored sports books, and was generally regarded as America's "Superman." No one was considered more of a male role model the Jenner. Yet, his prominence as an athlete has led to a good deal of public discussion concerning transgender conversions. And so the former Mr. Jenner has now become Caitlyn Jenner, wearing makeup and a female hairdo. In an interview on ABC's 2020, Jenner said that he identifies as a woman. He said that he had been given hormone treatments. Bruce Jenner was married and divorced three times and has six children.

There have been other prominent Americans who have undergone a sex change. Included are the former Chastity Bono, who became a man, the screenwriter Larry Wachowski, who became a woman, Bradley Manning, a soldier convicted of leaking classified documents, became a woman, and Richard Raskind, who became René Richards and played tennis on the women's circuit.[139]

The number of people who have changed their sex is quite small. Those who believe that they should belong to the opposite sex say that they felt this compulsion at a young age. The reason for this is not known.

Bisexuals

A bisexual is someone who engages in sexual conduct with women and men.[140]

In September 2016, Okay Magazine reported that the access Angelina Jolie Voight announced that she is bisexual and that she deals with women as well as men. Divorced three times, Angelina Jolie, as she prefers to be called, is one of a list of other celebrities who are bisexual.[141] Because movie actors, sports figures and elected officials are role models in American society, their deviant sexual conduct influences others to do the same. An outstanding example is former President Bill Clinton.

Bisexuality is by no means confined to celebrities. Bisexuality has been seen in various societies and even in the animal kingdom. Because sexual orientation occurs along a continuum, there are people who are not exclusively homosexual or heterosexual but engage in both. A number of different terms have been applied to this conduct, including the term pansexuality.[142]

In the 1940s, the zoologist Alfred Kinsey created a scale to measure the continuum of sexual orientation from heterosexuality to homosexuality. This scale ranged from 0 for those exclusively heterosexual to 6, meaning exclusively homosexual. Those ranking between two and four were considered bisexual.[143]

There is no agreement amongst students of sexuality as to the cause of bisexual or homosexual orientation. The American Psychological Association published that there are many reasons for a person's sexual orientation, which will be different in different people. Magnus Hirschfeld, one of the earliest students of sexology, thought that in every embryo there is one rudimentary neutral center for attraction to males and another for attraction to females.[144]

The National Center for Health Statistics found in 2002 that 1.8% of American men aged 18–41 consider themselves bisexual. The study also showed that 2.8% of women aged 18-44 consider themselves bisexual. In 2007, *The New York Times* reported that 1.5% of American women and 1.7% of American men identified themselves as bisexual.[145]

Because there is no agreement among investigators as to the cause of bisexuality, various forms of speculation concerning this phenomenon must suffice. Some claim that genetic factors are responsible for bisexuality. [146] There are also studies which attribute bi-sexuality to environmental conditions such as birth order. This argument rests on the theory that a boy with a number of older brothers is more likely to become homosexual than a boy with no older brothers. Another theory rests on the view that prenatal hormone exposure is responsible for bisexuality and/or prenatal stress on the mother.[147]

Sigmund Freud believed that every human being is bisexual in the sense of incorporating general attributes of both sexes. Freud did not claim that everyone is bisexual in the sense of feeling the same level of sexual attraction to both sexes. Nevertheless, the psychoanalyst Sandor Rado argued that there is no biological bisexuality in humans,[148] and Edmund Bergler claimed that bisexuality does not exist and that all supposed bisexuals are homosexuals.[149]

The sociologists Bell, Weinberg, and Hammersmith wrote that bisexuality is more influenced by social and sexual learning then exclusive homosexuality.[150]

Finally it is the observation of psychotherapists that bisexuality is related to abusive parents. This means that a parent, be it a mother or father, who beats or otherwise abuses a child may cause the victim to become bisexual as an avoidance mechanism concerning the abusive gender.

Compulsive Sexual Behavior

In July of 1977 the Chicago Tribune published a story concerning, in part, one Jodi Stutz, who had been a secretary at a farm machinery manufacturing company in Moline, Ill. While so employed, she repeatedly made Xerox copies of her face by placing her face against the glass of the Xerox copier. Subsequently she decided to copy her buttocks by sitting on the Xerox machine with her bare posterior. Claiming that "it looked great," she distributed the resulting picture throughout the offices of her company. Consequently she was fired.[151]

Since then there have been other women who did the same thing with the same consequences. This type of behavior is labeled exhibitionism or voyeurism, or sexual compulsion. It is estimated that 3.5% to 6.5% of Americans suffer from this condition. Included is excessive use of pornography, sex with multiple anonymous partners, excessive use of the Internet for sexual purposes, and a disproportionate amount of thinking about sex.[152]

Psychological symptoms associated with sexual compulsion are low self-esteem, loneliness, anxiety, guilt, poor social skills, and impulse control problems. Sexual compulsivity also leads to psychological distress, interpersonal problems, financial difficulties associated with paying for sex or pornography, and difficulties by reason of failure to meet one's responsibilities.

Women with same gender sexual experiences are more likely to report dysfunctional drug use compared to other women. The use of drugs is related to homosexuals who frequent bars and dance clubs. These homosexual and bisexual people generally absorb drugs before sex. This includes those who are HIV-positive but nevertheless engage in sexually risky behavior.[153]

Male exhibitionism begins around ages 11 to 15 and sometimes as late as age 25. Ages of female victims begin around age 19. Exhibitionism is widespread in America as well as in Europe. Some exhibitionists exposed themselves to females several hundred times without ever being apprehended by police or being treated by psychotherapy. Exhibitionism is often viewed as a victimless nuisance or a harmless abnormality. Nevertheless there are women who view this as a severely disturbing experience. This is true of about 11% of women, which therefore involves millions of women.

The true incidence of exhibitionism is underestimated because it is not adequately reported to police or other agencies because the victim does not know the perpetrator.[154]

In addition, sexual compulsion is also related to so-called fetish oriented sexual exhibitionism. Both men and women who suffer from sexual compulsion may associate with sexual exhibitionism. The reason for this kind of conduct by compulsive sexual practitioners is the need for attention. Among women who exhibit their proclivities are those who seek to counteract the popular view that women are sexually uninterested and sexually passive.[155]

This discussion of deviant sexual behavior demonstrates that Americans are torn between two philosophical orientations. One is Puritanism, derived from 16th century doctrines which have been carried over in the course of 500 years and now appear in the form of accusations of sexual harassment, sexual abstinence, sexual imitation in the form of pornography, and religious denunciation of sexual activity.

The American Western tradition contradicts Puritanism and emphasizes individualism. Therefore there are Americans who engage in deviant sexual activity in which they are supported by role models such as President Clinton and many a movie star and other entertainers, as well as sports heroes.

Essentially the conflict between the Puritan and the Western tradition leads to role confusion between the genders. It leads to a great deal of pain for those who spoil their gender relations with lifelong efforts to find satisfaction chasing after the mirage of great sexual experiences which could never be satisfied by those bringing their erotic conduct with them.

CHAPTER 5. THE ASSAULT ON AMERICAN MARRIAGE.

Sociologists who study marriage and the family have discovered some major differences between couples were married for life those deviate from this norm in several ways. The evidence is that in married families both adults and children suffer less psychological distress that is true among divorced or cohabiting families. Married men have lower levels of stress hormones and married women experience less psychological distress married mothers experience less conflict husbands then either cohabiting single women with their partners.[156] Biological parents and adoptive parents who are married experience this parenting stress than single mothers or those living in any other type of family arrangement.[157]Furthermore depression and suicide as well as drug and alcohol use are considerably less, among permanently married than those deviate from that standard

Co-Habitation

Demographers use the term cohabitation concerning single adult heterosexual couples who live together. According to Pew Research, the number of American cohabiting adults ages 50 and older has, in 2017, risen 75% since 2007. It is estimated that in 2017 there were 17.5 million adults living in cohabitation. Among those age 18 t0 34 that increase from 7.2 million in 2007 to 8.9 million in 2017 constitutes an increase of 24%. In 2007 3.9 million Americans age 3549 cohabited. In 2017 this age group was represented by 4.7 million constituting an increase of 20%.[158]

Approximately one half of cohabiters are younger than 35. Yet, an increasing number all Americans age 50 and older are in a cohabiting relationship representing about a quarter of all cohabiting adults. These collaborators represent only 4% of adults 50 and older. 14% of Americans age 25 to 34 are collaborating and one in 10 adults age 18-24 are co-habiting.

Among the older cohabitants increasing divorce rates are responsible for partnering without the benefit of marriage. Most collaborators age 50 or older have previously been married. In 2017, 61% of adults ages 50 and older were married compared with 64% in 1999. Only about 10% of cohabitants 50 and older are widowed. About 3 in 10 of cohabitants are in their 60s and 1 in 10 are in their 70s.[159]

In the 21st century two thirds of newlyweds have cohabited prior to their first marriage.[160] The announced purpose of cohabitation is to allow young adults to test their relationship in order to determine whether they are compatible before they are married. Because a number of researchers have found a positive association between cohabitation and marital dissolution it is possible that cohabitation itself provokes marital failure. Although there is some evidence that as cohabitation becomes more popular, its effect on marital instability may weaken somewhat.[161]

More popular means that between 1985 and 1999 44% of women cohabited prior to their first marriage and that 67% of women have done so since 2000. About one half of these marriages have ended in divorce. Therefore, the hope that cohabitation makes subsequent marriage divorce proof has not materialized

In recent years 70% of high school seniors reported that living together before marriage is a good way to test compatibility. Evidently a majority of those who cohabit failed that test as empirical studies find that couples who cohabited prior to marriage experience significant higher odds of marital dissolution than those who did not cohabit before marriage.[162]

In recent years two fifth of cohabitors were engaged or had definite plans to marry their partner when they started cohabiting. Those cohabitors who had marriage plans experienced as much stress as those who were married and had not cohabited. Cohabitors who did not have marriage plans experienced lower marital quality and higher marital distress.[163]

Some cohabiting women face greater risks of marital dissolution than is true of the majority. Included in this subgroup are women who are black, had less education than a college degree, were raised in a single or step-parent family or had more than the median number of sex partners.[164]

Black and Hispanic cohabiting women are more likely to conceive a child that is true of white women. And a small proportion of women with who conceived a child during cohabitation came from families with two biological parents. Women who had a child during cohabitation had lower education levels than those without a child. Women who bore children during cohabitation have less than 12 years education and were less likely than those without children to be employed full-time.[165]

Divorce

In 1980 there were 23 divorces per 1000 women in the United States. This was the highest rate of divorce ever attained in this country. But 2014 the divorce rate it declined to 17.6 per 1000 women. Marriages have also declined. In 1970 there were nearly 77 marriages for every 1000 unmarried women aged 15 and older. In 2015 there were 32 marriages for every 1000 unmarried in the United States. The so-called millennial generation has experienced both a marriage decline and a divorce decline. The average age at first marriage for women is 26 and 29 for men in 2018. The so-called baby boomer generation experienced a doubling of divorce for married adults 50 and older since 1990 for those over 65 the divorce rate is triple what it had been in 1990 this is in part due to the longer lifespan has a number of older people don't want to be stuck with the same partner to the end of their lives.

It is significant that married couples with a college education have a 40% lower divorce rate than high school graduates. Divorce rates also differ according to regions of the country. The District of Columbia has the highest divorce rate in the US, followed closely by Wyoming, Nevada and Alaska and Arkansas. The lowest divorce rate in the United States is in Hawaii.[166]

The United States has experienced a divorce culture for many years. A divorce culture considers the marriage is conditional, with divorce an option if the marriage does not work. For that reason one in two American marriages ends in divorce. This high divorce rate is related to gender equality in marriage. The high divorce rate is also related to low fertility rates, late age at marriage, as well as less spousal violence.[167]

Since the last part of the 20th century there has been an ever increasing labor force participation by women which is the outcome of high divorce rates. 21st-century women are far less willing be financially dependent on men than was true at any time in the past. This financial independence has led to far greater gender equality in marriage than ever before.[168]

There is in any marriage a divorce threat point. This means that in marriages which are insecure and troubled, both partners consider whether the relationship should end because the alternative, divorce, seems better than their current condition of married cohabitation. The divorce threat point is related to such conditions as the level of public assistance divorce single mothers as well as divorce roars regarding the division of property. In the past women usually stayed in unsatisfactory relationships because they had no alternatives as their lack of education and experience seldom allowed them to earn a livelihood for themselves and their children. Conversely, now there is a high correlation between equality in marriage and the divorce culture. [169]

A list of tasks common to all but the wealthiest families will consist of shopping for groceries, deciding what is for dinner, doing the laundry and caring for the sick. Traditionally all of these tasks are done by women often resent the failure of the husband to participate in any of these efforts.

The divorce culture is also highly subject to beliefs within the society in which the marriage has taken place. In 21st-century America divorce is accepted as a legitimate option available to both genders in the form of no-fault divorce. The fact is that marriage does not occur in a vacuum but is a segment of social life and subject to cultural expectations. Family relationships ae shaped not only by the members of the family but also by the culture in which it exists. Culture, or the man-made environment, has three aspects: material culture consisting of physical objects; ideological culture consisting of beliefs; and behavioral culture consisting of conduct. All three influenced marriage and therefore divorce.

Parental Divorce and Childhood

Children who experience the divorce of their parents tend to exhibit a number of problems as adults. These children of divorce are likely to have less education, earn less income, have more troubled marriages, have weak ties to parents, and suffer more psychological distress than people whose parents stayed together. Anyone who has ever studied this phenomenon agrees that while most children of divorced parents become well-adjusted adults a good-sized minority of such children are damaged by parental divorce.[170]

The offspring of divorced parents are more likely to drop out of high school and less likely to attend college, and more likely to be unemployed, than people whose parents remained together. These outcomes develop because divorce usually of children and their custodial parent who is usually the mother.[171]

This occurs because women generally earn less than men and a considerable number of fathers failed to pay child support. The result of this financial decline for schoolchildren may well be that they cannot have books, computers travel, private or help with college expenses. Disputes between parents frequently do not end with divorce. Divorced mothers must off a new and cheaper neighborhood leaving to changing schools. Children will also be faced with the next marriage of their parent, forcing them to adjust a stepfather or stepmother. All these stresses can make it difficult for children to do well in school. Research has shown that divorced single mothers are less affectionate to their children than married mothers and engage in harsher punishments than married mothers[172]

The noncustodial parent after most divorces is the father. These divorced fathers have a great deal of difficulty maintaining close relationships with their children. As a result many divorced fathers visit their children less and less and finally distance themselves from their children altogether[173]

It is obvious that children acquire their interpersonal skills by observing their parents and other adults. Therefore, the children of divorced parents are more negative themselves as adults more critical of their partners, resent criticism of themselves withdraw from problem solving discussions and are more jealous and have difficulty controlling anger.[174]

Divorce is emotionally charged and is preceded by a good deal of anger and hostility. Children of such parents often feel emotionally insecure, find it hard to trust other people and do not like to depend on others. Divorces disrupt parent-child relationships so that children of divorce may develop into emotionally insecure adults.[175]

The consequences of divorce are therefore not confined to one generation. This would deal of evidence that the emotional distress on children by divorced parents leads to further difficulties on the part of the grandchildren of the divorced grandparents. It has been found that marital aggression on the part of one generation frequently leads to marital aggression in the second-generation which in turn brings on aggression in the third-generation.[176]

It is therefore reasonable to predict that people grew up amidst the divorce of their parents will influence the next generation and numerous generations thereafter unless some time during the mating effort of a descendent of divorce a person or event intervenes leading to more positive interpersonal relationships and more stable marriages. I

In an average year about 2.4 million marriages and 1.2 million divorces occur in the United States.[177]

Divorce became a public issue in the United States in the middle of the 19th century. This was the result of the women's movement which first raised the issue the right of women to sue for divorce. Thus, in the 19th century women were slowly challenging men's absolute power in both the family and society. At that time and for so many earlier years a wives identity was subsumed under that of her husband. These legal disabilities for women reduced problems when a number of states past Married Women's Property

Actsd to bring about as divorce was becoming more prevalent and women were the primary initiators of these divorces.[178]

The reason for this thread was that women were becoming more confident of surviving outside of marriage as an organized women's movement was fighting for the cause of women's rights including the right to divorce for low-priced women. The women's movement managed to bring about uniformity divorce laws because at that time every state decided for itself who could divorce and for what reasons. These old divorce laws sought to find fault on the part of one party while the other party had to be the innocent victim of the other party's behavior. This means that divorce was fault driven until California became the first state in the union to pass a no fault divorce law when in 1969 that state's legislature passed the first no-fault divorce law. By the end of the 20th century all 50 states and the District of Columbia followed California's example until all states of the union permit no fault divorce [179]

In the 19th century the custody of children of divorce began to shift from fathers to mothers particularly because women are generally the innocent victims of mistreatment by the husband. Also at this time payment of child support became a legal issue. By the end of the Second World War public pressure about no-fault divorce increased considerably as judges, lawyers and others sought an end to fault based divorce. No-fault divorce makes divorce victimless. This interpretation of divorce was the product of the social constructionist view of social problems. According to that view a social problem is constructed by interest groups who succeed in making their claims a matter of public concern once a social condition has been defined as disagreeable. In 21st-century America divorce seems to be no social problem any longer as it is so common that is accepted as a matter of course has no stigma attaches to it any longer. In fact, divorce can now be obtained "on line" by filling out a form available on the computer. Although every state has somewhat different procedures in different forms the New York "divorce writer" is a good example of how one can obtain a divorce by filing my bail. The New York divorce form as such questions as: "Do you qualify for and online divorce? "Is this a same-sex marriage?" "Has at least one of lived in New York for the past year?" "Do you have debts to split between you and your spouse?" "Do you have children under 18 from this marriage?" "Is your spouse willing sign the divorce papers?" "Is your divorce uncontested??"

These examples of questions on divorce by mail forms are only a few examples but not unlike of what is asked all the other states. The purpose of all this is to make divorce easy as one files by mail, there is no divorce hearing no mandatory waiting period. All this is dependent on mutual consent between the two parties. In the event of a dispute concerning property or any other dispute the divorce was still heard Family Court judge.[180]

Divorce has a religious dimension although American Protestantism has accepted secular divorce. This means Protestant churchesin discourage divorce not prohibit it.

Although most American Jews participate in secular divorce, Jewish law requires that divorce involves a divorce ceremony which the husband gives the wife a document of divorce in the presence of witnesses. This is called a get in Hebrew.

Get is described in the Bible. Jewish theology teaches that God joins the souls of husband and wife at marriage and that therefore divorce can only be attained by following God's command as written in Deuteronomy 24:1-2. Jewish law requires a secular divorce in addition to a Jewish divorce. Nevertheless, without a get a couple remains married in the eyes of Jewish law and cannot marry anyone else. Jewish law also requires that husband and wife seeking a divorce must appear before a rabbinical court may or may not grant the divorce.[181]

Roman Catholicism does not allow divorce. The Church views marriage as a sacred union. According to the catechism (instruction) of the Catholic Church marriage is indissoluble because God holds that a marriage cannot be dissolved by any human power. Therefore, the Catholic catechism lists a number of offenses against the dignity of marriage. These are adultery, incest, sexual abuse of children, so-called free unions in which women and men live together without marriage, so-called trial marriages and divorce.[182]

Abandonment

About 5000 American children live in foster care. Children are placed in foster care because they have been physically, emotionally abused, sexually or because no family member willing to care the child. It has been reported that about 600 children are abused or neglected in the United States. In addition it has been estimated that about 900 children are the victims of violence each year. Furthermore, 40,000 new infants are placed in foster care each year. 25% of those who end up in prison spent time foster care. 30% of all people who are homeless spent time in foster care. The average number of home placement per child is three. Girls in foster care are six times more likely to give birth before the age of 21, 50% of foster youth are unemployed four years after leaving foster care. 37% to 48% of foster children don't finish high school. Only 7% of foster children attend a four-year college. Only 1% of foster children graduate from a four-year college. Foster care programs cost the American taxpayer $25.7 billion a year and another $100 billion is annually spent all the consequences of child abuse.[183]

The consequences of foster care are by no means the only outcome of parental neglect and abandonment. The facts are that abandoned children of four times more likely to live in poverty than children whose parents are present. Abandoned girls are seven times more likely to be pregnant. Abandoned children are more likely to be a behavioral problem and are more likely to themselves abuse and neglect their children. The infant mortality rate is half times greater among abandoned children than those who remain with the parents. Abandoned children are more likely to use drugs and alcohol and are also more likely to go to prison than is expected in the general population. Obesity is small, among abandoned children and they commit more crimes than is normally expected and that 2 ½ times more likely to drop out of high school that is usual. All this comes about because 19.7 billion American children, one in four, live without a father in the home.[184]

Annulment

A secular marriage can be annulled for a number of reasons. This is also true of Catholic marriages. Popular opinion refers to Catholic annulment as "Catholic Divorce." This opinion is mistake because in annulment is concerned with the religious and spiritual element or the sacrament of marriage while the divorce is concerned with only the legal issues concerning marriage. And annulment relates to the church doctrine not to secular law. It is commonly believed that annulment means the marriage never took place. That is a myth. The Catholic catechism teaches that annulment cannot erase the past. Indeed the marriage did exist but then annulment holds that the sacrament was never present in the marriage although the marriage did indeed exist.

Before 1970 the American Catholic Church granted approximately 400 annulments annually. Since 1980 the American Catholic Church has granted more than 50,000 annulments each year. This considerable change came about because of the reforms instituted during the second Vatican Council.[185]

Catholic annulments are granted or refused by a tribunal of judges. The work of the tribunals is done in writing although it is possible to appear in person. In that event the testimony is given in a private interview. [186]

Incest

Every American state prohibits incest, which is defined as sexual activity between family members and/or close relatives. These are defined as a lineal ancestor and a lineal descendent such as parent or grandparent with a child or grandchild or brothers and sisters or aunt-nephew or uncle-niece marriages. States differ widely concerning the criminality of such sexual relationships. In Rhode Island criminal incest statutes have been repealed although incestuous marriages remain prohibited. In Ohio only incest between parents and children is prohibited and New Jersey applies no penalties if both partners are 18 years old or more. By contrast, Massachusetts, Virginia, Oregon and Texas punish incest with up to two decades in prison. In Georgia the penalty for incest is up to 30 years in prison and in Wisconsin the penalty for incest is up to 40 years in prison.

And some state, such as Nevada, Montana, Idaho sex between brothers and sisters involves a life sentence. Marriages involving incest can be annulled.[187]

A bizarre example of incest was discovered in September 2016 in North Carolina. A 44-year-old mother was arrested for having married her twenty five-year-old son. Melissa Kitchens and her son, Shaun T. Pfeiffer were charged with incest. According to the charges the mother and son had sex although the son was married and was living with both mother and his wife.[188]

Fraud

Fraud is another cause for the annulment of a marriage. And outstanding example of this kind of fraud is immigration fraud. In 2011 twenty individuals were arrested by US Immigration and Customs Enforcement of the Department of Homeland Security. The defendants were members of an organization that arranged the illegal entry of Russian women into the United States to work as exotic dancers in clubs controlled by the Gambino and Bonanno crime families. The women were induced to enter into sham marriages with American citizens. The defendants were charged with visa fraud and harboring and inducing the entry of illegal aliens. [189]

In 2002 and alien named Vy Dinh came to the United States as an F-1 student but dropped out of school and therefore lost his legal status. Because she had lost her legal status she paid $12,000 to a middleman named Hao who arranged for Dinh to marry a citizen named Prince. They married at once and Dinh directly thereafter married another American citizen named Duran. That marriage took place in 2004. Dinh filed papers so that his new bride could become a legal resident. Yet Dinh had no intention of moving in with Duran. Instead they were divorced.

Meanwhile Hao was indicted for taking money to arrange marriages between American men and Vietnamese women in which she allegedly received a kickback as the women were allegedly unaware of this scam. Durand pled guilty in Utah federal court to a misdemeanor aiding and abetting the attempted illegal entry of an alien.[190]

Failure to "consummate" a marriage is also grounds for annulment. "Consummate" is a legal term meaning sexual intercourse. American law assumes that married couples engage in sexual intercourse. Failure to do so is cause for an annulment.

A brother and sister were charged with setting up a sham marriage scheme to prevent immigration officials from removing the brother from the United States.

Selmir Sakanovic a 27 year old citizen of Bosnia had overstayed his tourist visa in 2017. His sister, Salena Dedic, paid a US citizen to marry her brother in order to defeat American immigration law. Both brother and sister were indicted on conspiracy to commit marriage fraud. Dedic paid a woman money and gave her a Ford Taurus as part of the $5000 deal to marry Salkanovic. Since Dedic and his "wife" never consummated the marriage and never lived together the marriage was void and violated American immigration law. Because Sakanovic had not returned to Bosnia when his travel visa expired he was arrested by the Cedar Rapids Immigration and Customs Enforcement Office. On agreeing to leave the United States on June 18, 2017 he was released. When June arrived the siblings asked the woman to marry Salkanovic. This fraud led to the deportation of Salkanovic.[191]

Bigamy is the condition of having two wives or two husbands at the same time.

The second marriage someone who is already legally married is void and will be annulled. A person knowingly commits bigamy is guilty of a crime. It is possible that bigamy occurs accidentally when a previous divorce was not finalized due to technicality or one of the spouses is presumed dead because he or she has not been heard from for 7 years.[192]

In 1828 the United States Supreme Court in Reynolds versus the United States ruled that a plurality of wives as at one time permitted by the Mormon religion violates criminal law. (95 U.S145) the court also held that religious duty was not a defense to a criminal indictment.

George Reynolds was a member of the Church of Jesus Christ of latter-day Saints. He was charged with bigamy under the Morrill Anti-Bigamy Act after marrying Amelia Jane Schofield while still married to Mary Ann Tuddenham. Reynolds was secretary to Brigham Young and wanted to test the federal government's attempt to outlaw polygamy.[193]

The Latter-Day Saints believed that the law was unconstitutional to provide its members of their First Amendment right to freely practice their religion. Nevertheless Reynolds was convicted of bigamy and sentenced to two years hard labor in prison and a fine of $500. [194]

After Reynolds, the United States government threatened to seize all assets of the Church of Jesus Christ of Latter-Day Saints unless they renounced polygamy. Fearing destruction, the Latter-Day Saints officially ended polygamy in 1890. Some so-called fundamentalist Mormons nevertheless continue the practice; fundamentalist Mormon men intentionally marry two or more women. Although polygamy is extremely unpopular in the United States, the conviction of Reynolds and forced renunciation of polygamy indicate that the First Amendment of the Constitution guaranteeing freedom of religion is applied only as long as a religious practice is popular.

Under-Age Marriages

In the course of six years, over two hundred thousand minors are married in the United States. Almost all of these marriages were between a child and an adult. The considerable majority of married children were girls.[195]

In 2018, 48 states have laws allowing children to marry. However two states, Delaware and New Jersey have completely prohibited child marriage. Of the 48 states allow child marriage 18 have no minimum age for minors to marry/. 32 states have a minimum age at marriage ranging 14 to seventeen.

Since 2016 several states have raised the minimum age for minors to marry. It is remarkable that in many cases minors married when they were under the age of sexual consent. In some states minors cannot legally divorce, leave their spouse or enter a shelter to escape abuse.[196]

In Alabama a 74 year old man married a 14 year old girl and in Tennessee three ten year old girls were married to men aged 24-31. The famous singer Elvis Presley married Priscilla when she was fourteen. More recently both states have raised the minimum age of marriage to seventeen (in Tennessee) and sixteen (in Alabama). In most states the minimum age at marriage is eighteen. Although very young, married children are considered adults by the law so that they can get a divorce and benefit from social services. About 80% of teenage marriages end in divorce. In some states, including Massachusetts, married minors cannot get a divorce.[197]

Statistics concerning Child Marriages.

Nearly five in every la thousand 15–17-year-old Americans are married — a ratio of one in two hundred. Between 2000 and 2010, there were 248,000 children married in the United States. [198]

In Florida, 16,000 children some as young as 13 were married which is the second highest incidence of child marriage after Texas.[199] in Texas, 2000 to about 40,000 children were married and in New York more than 3800 children were married between 2000 and 2010. In Virginia between 2004 and 2013 nearly 45,000 children were married. In Alabama there were over 8600 child marriages from 2000 to 2015.[200]

The marriage of children, which usually means girls marrying adult men is principally a rural phenomenon related to poverty. Black girls are about 1 ½ times more likely to marry under the age than is true of US-born white. girls.

In 2013 The Violence against Women Reauthorization Act mandated that The US Secretary of State establish and implement a strategy ending child marriage.

Forced Marriages

In addition to childhood marriages among the American Christian population the entrance all numerous Muslims into the United States during the past two decades (1998-2018) has led to a number of forced marriages of American children in Muslim families.

In December 2017 a New York girl, Amina Ajmal Chaudhry, testified in a Brooklyn courtroom that her father, Mohammed, had arranged the killing of a young man's relatives because the man had helped Amina escape forced marriage. Several years earlier her father had tricked her into leaving their home in Brooklyn in order to return to Pakistan where he forced her to marry her cousin. This forced marriage resembles so many other forced marriages in which a girl is married against her will or is so young that she cannot give informed consent.[201]

Forced marriages are illegal in the United States and in England. These marriages are vastly underreported but are accepted as part of family tradition in most Muslim communities.

Yamine Koenig was born in Chicago of Palestinian parents. Her father was killed during a robbery at a gas station where he worked. Yamine, raised as a Muslim by her mother, wore a headscarf and went to mosque on holidays. Yasmine had two sisters who were sent to Palestine by their mother. Yasmine did not go to school because her mother did not want her to go.

With the help of her cousin she dated a young Christian man who came to her house and asked if she was home. This led her mother to scream at the young man, who told her "I'm Yasmine's boyfriend." Her mother told him to leave and threatened to call the police. She slammed the door and screamed at Yasmine, "Go to your room, you are grounded." The next day her mother left the house but locked the glass storm door from the outside so that Yasmine could not leave. This continued for two weeks. Then her mother told her: "Pack your bags; we're going to Palestine to visit your sisters."

Once in Palestine, her mother contacted her two sisters. One of them introduced her to a Muslim man who met her in the company of his mother and his uncle and spoke to her in Arabic. A second meeting with a marriage-able man was arranged by her sister. The man repulsed Yasmine because of his looks, his missing teeth and his extremely short stature; nevertheless her mother and grandmother said that they thought she should marry as he had a job at a house.

Jasmine was forced to meet this man three times. At the third meeting her mother sisters and grandmother as well as the men in his family read the engagement from the Muslim marriage manual and told her that that she would have to marry this man whom she disliked intensely.

Without money and without her passport which her mother held, she was contemplating suicide. When Yasmine confronted her mother and refused to marry this man, her grandmother slapped her in the face shouting: "don't disrespect your mother." It turned out that her grandmother had made all arrangements for her to marry this man because he owned a restaurant. The grandmother arranged to have a wedding 1 ½ weeks later. The wedding actually took place, although Yamine would not come near the new husband with his family. She used their computer and sent a friend and message and told her where she was and how she had been entrapped. The friend told her to call the American Embassy. An American embassy employee met her in a car in a parking lot and took her to the US Embassy in Jerusalem where she was entered into the foster care system back in the United States. That night an American diplomat took her to the airport with two bodyguards and she was put on the plane to Chicago. By email she was told by her mother and sisters that she was ruining their reputation. They had not one good word to say to her. Since she was only 15 at the time she was introduced the Illinois Child Protective Services were arranged for her to live in a foster home. Child Protective Services arranged court date to decide from the custody of her mother whether or not she should be removed the custody of her mother. Her mother was present but would not speak to her nor even look at her. After the hearing she became a ward of the state, living with her foster mother. She went to school, graduated and was accepted at a state university with a full scholarship.[202]

Sarah Tasneem was born in Colorado. She had just finished her freshman year of high school in Colorado when she was told it this time get married. She was 15 years old and had hoped to join The Reserve Officers Training Corps (ROTC) and apply the US Air Force Academy. Eventually she hoped to become a lawyer. All this was voided when her mother discovered that a boy from her school interested in Tasneem. Her mother discussed her dating. Her father demanded that Tasneem go to California with him. She was no longer allowed to speak to her mother. Her father then told her that their religious leader had chosen a man for her to marry. The father took her to Los Angeles where his religious group was holding a conference, it was there that she met her future husband — a man 13 years her senior. She was married to this man by religious officials although this was not a legal union under California law. After the marriage ceremony this strange man took custody of her as she was underage and took her out of the United States. At 15 she became pregnant almost immediately. Her husband therefore decided to return to the United States so the baby would be an American citizen. They settled in the San Francisco Bay area but shortly thereafter moved to Reno, Nevada. In Reno at age 16 she was married again under Nevada law.

Whenever her husband was out of the house Tasmeen entered an adult school earned a general education degree or GED. Shortly thereafter, she was pregnant again. She wanted to leave her marriage but had no money. As soon as her husband went on a vacation to his home country, she filed divorce papers. Her husband followed her when she went to Colorado and physically attacked her. Nevertheless the court finalized her divorce and ordered her husband to pay $500 a month in child support.[203]

In view of these atrocities committed against American children it is good news that on May 10, 2018, Delaware became the first state in the union to bad child marriage and that on June 22, 2018 ,New Jersey became the second state in the US and child marriage. Delaware raised the minimum age of marriage to 18 without exceptions thereby banning child marriage and New Jersey did the same. It is nevertheless disheartening that there are still 48 states who have not commended their legislation so that many children continue to face pressure to give up that childhood long before they are ready.

CHAPTER 6. ABORTION

Some Abortion Statistics

According to the *Guttmacher Policy Review*, 45% of pregnancies in the United States are unintended, and about four in ten of those are terminated by abortion. In sum, 19% end in abortion or miscarriage. Approximately 926,200 abortions performed in the year 2014 constituted a decline of 12% from 1.06 million in 2011. Approximately 1.5% of American women aged 15–44 have an abortion and 45% have had a previous abortion. In the course of the year there are in the United States about 15 abortions per thousand women aged 15 to 44. It is projected that 20 years from now, one in 20 women in the United States will have had an abortion by age 20, one in five by age 30 and one in four by age 45. More than one half of American abortion patients are in their 20s and 34% are attributed to women aged 20 to 24. Ages age 25 to 29 obtained 27% of abortions.

About 12% of abortion patients are adolescents. Those age 18 to 19 account for 8% of all abortions and those younger than 15 for 0.2%. Those who are 15- to 17-year-olds account for 3% of abortions.[204]

In 2015, the abortion rate was 11.8 abortions per 1000 women aged 15 to 44. Among teenage women 15 to 19, the abortion rate decreased 54% from 2006 to 2015. This sharp decline came about because a number of states restricted women's access to the procedure. In 2015, the total number of abortions was 638,169, or 188 abortions per 1000 live births.[205]

Religion influences abortion. Thus Catholics, who were 23% of the American population, had 24% of the abortions in the United States in that year. They therefore have an abortion rate that represents their proportion in the population of the United States. Protestants annually represent 17% of all abortions, evangelicals 13%, and 38% report no religious affiliation. 8% of abortions identified as "something else."[206]

White abortion patients account for 39% of abortion procedures although whites are 74% of the American population. Blacks, who are 13% of the American population, account for 28% of abortion patients. Hispanics, who are 14% of the American population, are 25% of abortion patients. Other ethnic groups account for the rest of abortion patients.[207]

At least 75% of all abortion patients in the United States are poor. Only 26% have an income one or two times the federal poverty level, and 49% have incomes that put them below the federal poverty level, which is $15,730 for a family of two.[208]

A Brief History of Abortion

Abortion was commonly practiced in the United States until the American Medical Association criminalized this practice in 1857 by inducing state legislatures to prohibit it. By the end of the 19th century, every state in the union had passed legislation against it. This resulted in the passage of the Comstock Act, which Congress passed in 1873. The act prohibited abortion as well as "obscene literature and articles for immoral use."[209] In 1938, Judge August Hand lifted the federal ban on birth control, thereby ending the use of the Comstock laws. The AMA was motivated to bring about prohibition of abortion in order to rid themselves of such competitors as midwives, homeopaths, and others.

These laws made the state the regulator of sexual and reproductive behavior. To obtain evidence against abortionists, physicians were obliged to report abortions and collect dying declarations from patients who generally died from the infections associated with the operation and for which the was no cure.[210]

The criminalization of abortion not only prohibited abortion but also forced conformity to gender norms. A norm is expected behavior. Thus norms throughout the 19th century and into the first half of the 20th century required men and women to marry, and for women to bear children and for men to alone carry the financial burden of supporting a family. Unmarried men who were implicated in abortion deaths were publicly questioned about their sexual behavior and could be arrested and jailed.[211]

During the many years when these rules were in force, women, mainly immigrants, often used inexpensive and dangerous self-induced measures. The poor usually delayed calling doctors if they suffered complications. As a result they had a high death rate and their case came to the attention of state officials. Wealthy women were usually acquainted with doctors who offer falsified death certificates of those who died from abortion.[212]

Until 1930, the state usually prosecuted abortionists after a woman died. However, juries usually nullified the law and would not convict abortionists.[213]

State investigators also questioned women who had an abortion. They sought dying declarations from these women in which the women admitted their abortion and named their abortionists.[214]

When abortions were illegal, those who cared for such patients were in danger of prosecution. Physicians repaired uterine tracts and wounds stopped hemorrhaging. Most important was that fetal infections could hardly be defeated because there were no antibiotics. Women who had widespread septic infections usually died. This then led to making doctors suspects in criminal abortion cases. Police often arrested doctors because they were the last person attending a patient. Doctors who were associated with abortions risked losing their medical licenses. In some states a doctor had to be convicted before losing his license, but in other states doctors' licenses were revoked without any trial.[215] Doctors were compelled to regard all miscarriages as possible attempts at abortion. Women's health care suffered. Physicians treated their female patients badly. Doctors often refused to provide needed medical care.[216]

After a woman died of complications resulting from abortion, an investigation into the death was a shameful event for her relatives and friends because state officials demanded they speak publicly about sexual matters. For example, a police officer testified that the sister of a dead woman had translated the policeman's questions so that relatives could understand them. Yet, when the questioning dealt with using instruments on her privates, the sister would not interpret anymore. Another immigrant woman said that during questioning by the coroner about her friends abortion, "I am ashamed to tell."[217]

State officials generally prosecuted single men who were responsible for the pregnancy leading to criminal abortion deaths. Young men who had engaged in premarital intercourse and then failed to marry the woman were incarcerated as accomplices in the crime of abortion.[218]

Two scientific developments gradually ended the suppression and persecution women and men associated with abortion. The first of these was the birth control plan parent movement and the second the discovery of antibiotics.

In the 19th century and the first half of the 20th century, birth control was opposed until considerable changes in law, public opinion and medical advances led to nearly universal acceptance of birth control. These changes came about as social activists religious groups and physicians participated in the American birth control movement. The most effective leader in the early birth control movement was Margaret Sanger (1879–1966) who founded the American Birth Control League which was later known as Planned Parenthood Federation of America. By the 1920s Sanger had gained a good deal of support not only from women but also from physicians.[219]

As a result, these efforts by Sanger birth control became increasingly popular so that by 1978 a survey light ever married women found that 71% that used contraceptive techniques at some time in their married life. 20% had diaphragms or IUDs (intra-uterine devices) obtained from physicians.[220] Wealthy couples in the 1930s who had access to physicians were far more likely to receive these devices than was true of the poor who could not afford physicians. at a time when the protection of maternal health was the only legal justification for the use of countries. In 1936 a Fortune magazine survey found that 63% of the American population favored the teaching and practice of birth control and a Gallup poll in 1938 found that 76% of women polled supported birth control in consideration of the family income[221].

In 1937 the American Medical Association which had at one time been responsible for criminalizing abortion, endorsed birth control. Then in the 1940s mostly under the control birth control became ever more popular so that by the 1950s the issue of the morality of birth control no longer received any consideration. In 1960, 93% the American population favored birth control as more and more Americans sought to have smaller families. This led to family planning mostly under control of the medical profession.[222]

Because abortion was at one time as dangerous a procedure as well all operations a good number of women died from the infections which these procedures promoted. It was only after the discovery of a number of antibiotics that it became possible for physicians to fight bacterial infections. It wasn't until 1907 that Paul Ehrlich discovered an antibiotic called Salversan[223]. In 1932 Gerhard: Domagk developed Sulfonamide the first systematically active antibacterial drug.[224] Then, in 1928 Alexander Fleming discovered penicillin, which had a major effect on the prevention and cure of infections resulting from operation including abortion. Innumerable additional discoveries by medical of the scientists made abortion far less dangerous than it had ever been before. Therefore, as public opinion and medical science together led to more and more support for both birth control and abortion law also changed. The Comstock act had already been repealed when in 1973 the Supreme Court of the United States in *Roe v. Wade* decided that abortion is legal United States. This case concerned Norma Nelson who for the sake of anonymity, use the name Roe. In in this this 1973 decision the Supreme Court ruled that women have a constitutional right to abortion, and that this right on an implied righto privacy as reported by the ninth and 14th amendments of the Constitution. The court held that a fetus is not a person but potential life and that this does not have constitutional rights of its own. The court then proceeded to limit abortion. Accordingly, during the first trimester of pregnancy this statement may not regulate abortion for any reason. During the second trimester the state may regulate abortion only to protect the health of the woman. During the third trimester the state may regulate or prohibit abortion the interests in the potential life of the fetus- except where abortion is necessary to premature the woman's life or health.[225] After Roe versus Wade had been decided a number of states attempted to defeat that decision by all kinds of legislation designed to create numerous obstacles for those seeking to gain an abortion which was their right. This anti-abortion effort can be recognized by the several additional Supreme Court decisions such as *Doe v. Bolton* (1973) in which the US Supreme Court modified *Roe v. Wade* and decided that a woman's right to an abortion could not be limited by the state if abortion was sought to maintain a woman's health. In *Planned Parenthood v. Danforth*, the court invalidated a large portion of Missouri's abortion law. That law prohibited abortions by saline injection, required and married woman to obtain the consent of her husband before an abortion, and required consent of parents before and abortion could be performed on their minor daughter. Several other Supreme Court decisions also defeated these efforts to get around Roe versus Wade. Therefore some antiabortionists resorted to violence and murder in a fanatical effort to and abortion United States.

Anti-abortion violence

The United States is an achievement driven competitive society. School-children are taught to excel in sports and to do well in high school in order to go to college. Adults compete with each other for money and social honor, Whether achieving the highest bowling score or making more money than one's friend's relatives and associates. It is therefore evident that those who have achieved very little or nothing at all may view themselves as losers in our competitive world. Of course a loser is somebody who views himself as a loser. Some people earn very little and have never been the sports hero in school or anywhere else, yet they may nevertheless feel good about themselves because they have a high bowling score. There are however also those who resent being on the bottom of the prestige ladder, in particular compared to friends and relatives.

This kind of competition for honor and prestige is centered on occupation which is the most important measure of success in the United States. Therefore resentment against achievement is very common in the America of 2018. Exceptional achievers in any area may find that the ostracized rejected and resented. Even the great Albert Einstein was denounced as a charlatan when he overthrew the physics of his day and proved that the universe was not what Newton had proclaimed. History is full of advanced thinkers who were denounced for their achievements. It is therefore not surprising that those who have not done well in school, did not participate in sports, adults who do not have high incomes, who are in jobs with not much of a future, may resort to getting even with that world by using violence as a last resort to gain attention and a sense of power — even if it costs them their lives. Politicians are frequently people who run for office in order to be known and to gain attention. In particular, prosecutors love to send people to prison or even the death row, thereby making themselves masters of other people's lives and enjoying a sense of power. An example was Henry Wade, known particularly for the *Roe vs Wade* case. Wade prided himself on being so good a lawyer that he could send innocent people to prison and death row. He enjoyed convicting the innocent and repeatedly said that anyone could convict a guilty person but he was able to persuade juries to convict innocent people.[226]

This kind of thinking is part of the reason why there were 11 murders of abortion doctors and others working in abortion clinics between 1977 and 2017. In the same period of time there were 26 attempted murders, 41 bombings of abortion clinics, 187 arson attacks on abortion facilities, 99 attempted bombings, and 1755 cases of vandalism. 3745 instances of trespassing at abortion clinics and innumerable threats of violence were also reported. There were four kidnapping and hundreds of other cases of verbal and physical attacks of those associated with abortion.[227]

There is a good possibility that many an angry person will resort to violence because of the disappoint he suffered in his life. Seeking to justify his aggression such an angry individual will then attach this violent behavior some cause such as antiabortion. The cause which such violent people are attached means little to them as it is only a vehicle for the expression dictated by the inner demons Such a person is Scott Roeder who murdered Dr. George Tiller an abortion doctor on March 31,.2009. Was shot in the head while standing in the lobby of the Reformation Lutheran Church in Wichita

Kansas where he was serving as an usher and handing out church bulletins. Scott Roeder fled in his car but was arrested three hours after the shooting about 570 miles in a suburban of Kansas City. On June 2, 2009 Roeder was charged with first-degree murder and was convicted in January 2010 and sent to life imprisonment without parole for 50 years.[228]

In October 1998 Dr. Barnett Slepian, an obstetrician in the Buffalo suburb of Amherst returned home with his wife Lynn on Friday night from the Sabbath services at his synagogue (Greek for assembly). A few minutes later he stepped into his kitchen when a sniper's bullet crashed through a back window striking him in the chest. He fell to the floor and called for help but died within two hours. Dr. Slepian, 51, was the third abortion doctor killed in the United States after years of picketing and harassment.[229] The killer who murdered a doctor was James Kopp.

Kopp had stood for a while in the dark of the backyard of Slepian's home. He could see the occupants of the lit up kitchen without being seen in the dark backyard. Kopp was a Catholic convert became an antiabortionist after his girlfriend underwent an abortion. He was known by the nickname Atomic Dog and had designed locks that protesters fastened to abortion clinic doors. After the attack Kopp disappeared for 2 ½ years. He used multiple passports and alliases as he traveled in Ireland and finally in France. There he was arrested in 2001. At his court appearances Kopp claimed he had a right to kill abortion doctors on moral grounds.[230]

Paul Jennings Hill killed Dr. John Britton and Britton's bodyguard James Barrett in 1994. He justified his actions with his antiabortion beliefs. Hill was murdered by lethal injection on September 3, 2003 at the Florida State prison at age 49. Those who killed Hill, including the judge, were of course performing the same actions for which Hill died, except that Hill was not paid to do it, whereas the professional killers in the Florida State prison were paid to commit murder.

Hill was a Presbyterian minister. Hill told reporters at his final interview that he felt honored that he would be killed for what he did. His supporters is somebody outside the prison holding up such signs as "Doctors can kill, therefore killing baby killers is justifiable homicide," and "extremism in defense of life is not extreme." Hill had advocated violence against abortion doctors sometime. He appeared on television shows such as "Nightline" and "Donahue" where you said that killing abortion doctors was the same as killing Hitler. On July 29, 1990 Dr. Britton had just arrived at the Pensacola Ladies Center when Hill shot him with a 12 gauge gun. Then he killed James H Barrett who had driven Dr. Britton[231]

In 1993 Dr. David Gunn was murdered outside of his Pensacola, Florida clinic. At age 47 Dr. Gunn was the first abortion provider to be killed by an ant-abortionist. He was murdered by Michael Frederick Griffin who put three bullets into Gunn's back. Griffin called the police. His friends who came to protest abortion stood calmly by while Gunn bled to death. Griffin was convicted of first-degree murder and sentenced to life in a Florida State prison. At a television interview while in prison, Griffin claimed that he was protecting the innocent children that he had accepted that responsibility. Griffin has become a cult hero who inspires his followers who were the same people who had put Dr. Gunn's face and phone number on a "wanted" poster including even his daughter's school. It was shortly after Gunn's murder that Paul Hill collected signatures for his defense action statement which was signed by 34 antiabortion individuals.[232]

Rachelle Shannon attempted to murder Dr. George Tiller in 1995. She was sentenced to 11 years behind bars for shooting and wounding Dr. Tiller in both arms. She was also found guilty of six fire bombings and two acid attacks at abortion clinics in California, Oregon and Nevada. After her release she supported the same opinions held before going to prison. She did not view her shooting of Dr. Tiller is wrong but on the contrary she called the shooting of the doctor most holy and most righteous, and reported that she had no regrets. On her computer she detailed clinic arsons and acid attacks that she had committed.[233]

In January 1995 John C. Salvi 3rd murdered two employees and wounded five others at an abortion clinic in Norfolk, Massachusetts. He used his 22 caliber Ruger rifle to shoot into an open door at the Hillcrest clinic. Which had been the site of an attempt at bobbing 1984. Salvi had participated in protests outside the Planned Parenthood offices in Brookline, Massachusetts.

Salvi was known as a friendless recluse who lived alone in a largely deserted street of Hampton Beach. He was training a hairdresser and was isolated from his full five years family. His victims were two women, one of whom was 25 years old and the other 38 years old. Salvi's victims were is typical of other mass murderers who take out their anger and frustration on anonymous victims.[234]

Eric Rudolph was on the FBI's 10 most wanted fugitives list for five years until he was captured in 2003. On January 29, 19 98 Eric Rudolph bombed a n abortion clinic in Birmingham Alabama killing Robert Sanderson an off-duty police officer who worked as a security guard at the clinic. Eric Rudolph was also responsible for three Atlanta bombings including the 1977 bombing of ab abortion center and the 1996 Centennial Olympic Park bombing during the 1996 Summer Olympics and the bombing of a lesbian nightclub.[235]

According to Rudolph the bombing was motivated by a wish on his part to embarrass United States government eyes of the world for the sanctioning of abortion on demand.[236] Immediately after the bombing the media including television attributed this crime to Richard Jewell a security guard who was the first one to spot Rudolph's explosive device. Caring nothing about the cruelty of accusing an innocent man be repeated the second patients so that you'll was fired from his job and denounced nationwide. Later Rudolph confessed to the Olympic Park bombing. Nevertheless it was too late for Jewell who died shortly after this humiliation. Rudolph also confess of bombing an abortion clinic in Sandy Spring Georgia and killing and police officer Alabama and a part-time security guard Robert Sanderson and critically injuring nurse Emily Lyons. Bombs they acted as charrette notes of the victims. Rudolph was identified Department of Justice February 1998 was two witnesses had seen running from the scene of his bombings and remembered his appearance. The FBI offered $1 million for his capture or for information leading to his arrest. Nevertheless spent more than five years in the Appalachian wilderness during which time neither law enforcement nor volunteers found him. Rudolph was able to remain at large for so long because his closest family and friends supported him while camping in the Pisgah National Forest. After his arrest in May 2003, Rudolph pled guilty to all charges and was sentenced to life in prison. In prison he wrote a number of essays justifying his actions on the grounds that his victims were murdering little children.[237].

Robert Lewis Dear entered the Planned Parenthood clinic in Colorado Springs one November day in 2015. He brought with him a high-powered rifle and fired a police and civilians outside the building. He killed three people including a police officer and wounded five others. Questioned after his arrest, he shouted, "no more baby parts." Although there is no evidence that Planned Parenthood sells baby parts, antiabortionists continue to make that claim.

Robert Lewis Dear was found incompetent and delusional by psychologists who interviewed him after his arrest. Therefore judge Martinez ruled that Dear lacked rational understanding of the court proceedings and was therefore incarcerated in a mental institution.[238]

On December 18, 1998 Dr. Calvin Jackson of New Orleans was stab 15 times, losing four pints of blood. Donald Cooper was charged with second-degree attempted murder and sentenced to 20 years in prison.[239] On October 28, 1997, Dr. David Gandell of Rochester New York was seriously injured after an unidentified sniper fired through a window at the doctor's home. And on the same day Emily Lyons, a nurse, lost an eye in a bombing that killed off-duty police officer Robert Sanderson.[240]

Not all antiabortion activities are violent. In an effort to damage the reputation of Planned Parenthood —which promotes abortion — David Daleiden and Sandra Merritt were charged with illegally recording employees of Planned Parenthood selling tissue from aborted children. Evidently Daleiden and Merritt wanted to make money and have Planned Parenthood shut down. However the activities were discovered and both were charged with fraud and entering a federal office in order to discredit plan parent. In some states recording the circumstances related to such behavior' is a crime. Therefore Daleiden and Merritt were charged with 14 counts of illegal recording and conspiracy concerning Planned Parenthood who,, they claimed, were selling tissue from aborted fetuses for profit Such sales are illegal. Daleiden and Merritt claim was made because the profit from aborted fetuses are unlawful. State investigators found no evidence for this claim.[241]

Although David Leach did not use violence he nevertheless has endangered the lives of abortionists and those who promote their views. The owner of a music store in Des Moines, Leach commented on You Tube that, "it will be a blessing to the babies" if someone shoots the people who opened a Kansas abortion clinic. Leach posted a recorded phone compensation he had with Scott Roeder who was sentenced to life imprisonment for the murder of Dr. George Tiller. Leach, in earlier rants claimed that it was justified that abortion providers be killed.

Kidnapping is another method used by some antiabortionists against abortion doctors. In August 1980 23 when identifying as the Army of God kidnapped Dr. Hector Zevallos and his wife Rosalie Jean and held them for eight days.[242]

On June 15, 1984, Father Edward Markley, a Benedictine priest, entered a Birmingham clinic and destroyed equipment. He then assaulted tree clinic workers. One of these women received back injuries and a broken neck vertebra trying to prevent Markley from splashing red paint on the clinics equipment. Markley was convicted of first-degree criminal mischief, one count of third-degree assault and one count of harassment.[243]

In more recent years attacks on abortion clinics continued.

Religion and Abortion

Judaism

Modern Judaism is based primarily on the Bible (called the Torah, in Hebrew) and on the Talmud or scholarship which is the root of post-Biblical Judaism. According to Jewish teaching the rights of the mother is a crucial concept concerning abortion in Judaism. Over the years numerous rabbinical authorities have commented on abortion not all agree. However, in the case of rape abortion is allowed in Judaism. The Jewish attitude towards the termination fetal life holds that the fetus is an organic part of the mother but that the fetus is less than a person. Jewish law defines abortion as a form of depravation but not murder. Nevertheless, abortion is considered immoral unless it can be justified for medical or other serious reasons. Abortion to save the mother's life is definitely allowed. Even non-life-threatening reasons affecting the mother may lead to abortion. If the fetus endangers the mother's life it should be destroyed for to let the mother die would be a violation of the sanctity of human life.[244]

Orthodox Jews reject abortion entirely. The birthrate is 4.1 for women age 15 to 30 while the general Jewish birthrate is only 1.4 for women age 15 to 30.[245]

Islam allows abortion before the pregnancy is four months old. Thereafter abortion can only be permitted in instances in which the mother's life is in danger or in case of rape.

The Catholic View of Abortion

The Catholic Church opposes all forms of abortion procedures whose direct purpose is the destruction of zygotes, embryos or fetuses on the grounds that human life must be respected and protected absolutely from the moment of conception.[246]

In 21st century United States, a majority of Catholics disagree with the official position of the Church concerning abortion. Although frequent mass attendees tend to agree with the Church, those who attend infrequently are more likely to be pro-choice than pro-life. The documentary released by the United States conference of Catholic Bishops Committee on Pro-Life Activities the Catholic Church condemned procured abortion as immoral. There are however some exceptions to this teaching which reflect the concern of the Church for the life of the mother. Accordingly, a doctor who believes abortion is always morally wrong may nevertheless remove the uterus or fallopian tubes of pregnant women, knowing the procedure will cause the death of the embryo or fetus in cases in which the woman is certain to die without the procedure. In cases in which the intended effect is to save the woman's life and the death of the embryo or fetus is a side effect, the death of the fetus is an undesirable but unavoidable consequence.[247] Over the year a number of polls of American Catholics concerning abortion have been conducted. These polls reveal that 36% of American Catholics in some circumstances or support unqualified acceptance of abortion in all cases.[248]

A survey by Pew Research Center showed that 47% of American Catholics believe that abortion should be legal in all or most cases while 42% of American Catholics believe that abortion should be illegal in all or most cases.[249]

These public opinion polls demonstrate that American Catholics are individualists and do not march in goosestep to the Popes declarations or the bishops opinions.

The American Protestant Opinion Concerning Abortion

America is a Protestant country. This has been true since Colonial days and continues to be true today, (2019). 23% of Americans are Roman Catholic and less than 2% are Jewish. Islam, Hinduism and Buddhism are also represented among Americans as are a number of other denominations in small numbers. Protestants are therefore at least 70% of the American population including atheists and agnostics of Protestant descent. Therefore it is legitimate to regard the United States as a Protestant country.

Protestants celebrated the 45th anniversary of the *Roe vs Wade* decision making abortion a Constitutionally guaranteed right. The Southern Baptists, one of the largest Protestant denominations in this country, back *Roe vs Wade*. A Christian life commission Baptists and MethodistsC and others organize a correlation abortion-rights. The United Methodists first helped with abortion in 1971 when in fact abortion-rights as Jews and others in 1970. In sum it can be said that most American Protestants support abortion.[250]

The American Baptist churches in the USA do not condemn abortion. However, The General Board asks couples spiritual counsel before deciding on abortion. The board opposes abortion as a means of birth control. The Church of Jesus Christ of Latter-Day Saints teaches that elective abortion personal or social convenience is contrary to the will and commandments of God. The church nevertheless allows abortion in the event that the pregnancy threatens the life of the mother or that pregnancy came about as a result of rape or incest. The Episcopal Church recognizes a new right to terminate a pregnancy, only in cases of rape or incest, and in all cases in which the mother's physical or mental health is at risk, or in cases of fetal formalities. The Church forbids abortion as a means of birth control, family planning, or any reason for mere convenience. The Evangelical Lutheran Church in America holds that abortion prior to viability of a fetus shall not be prohibited but that abortion after the point of viability should be prohibited except where the life of a mother is threatened or when fetal abnormalities pose a fatal threat to a newborn. The Lutheran Church Missouri Synod allows no abortion except when \ a mother's life is at risk. Likewise the National Association of Evangelicals rejects all abortion except in order to protect the life of the mother or in cases of rape or incest; the Presbyterian Church USA affirms that termination of the pregnancy is a personal decision; the Church disapproves of abortion as a means of birth control or for convenience but recognizes that different Christians may come to diverse conclusions and actions concerning abortion. The United Church of Christ supports reproductive rights including the right to a safe abortion. The United Methodist Church opposes some abortions; while this Church sanctions the legal option of abortion under the proper medical procedures the Church rejects abortion as a method of birth control or gender selection[251]

The Casey decision and the decline of abortion in the United States

In 1992 the Supreme Court of the United States decided in Planned Parenthood of Southern Pennsylvania v. Casey. This case dealt with a Pennsylvania law that required spousal awareness prior to obtaining an abortion. This law was rejected because of n the 14th Amendment on the grounds that it created an undue burden on married women seeking an abortion. The court also ruled that parental consent, informed consent and a 24-hour waiting period were constitutionally valid.[252]

Since *Casey*, the number of abortions has declined. In the states reporting to The Centers for Disease Control and Prevention, the number of abortions fell from 1,054,719 in 1990 to 926,200 in 2014 down 12% 1 06 million in 2011. In 2014 ½% of women aged 15 to 44 had an abortion[253] More than half of all US abortion patients in 2014 were in the age range 20 to 24 as they obtain 34% of all abortions; 20% of abortion patients in 2014 were adolescents accounting for 8% of all abortions. Those aged 15 to 17 years of age were 3% of all abortions. The abortion rate in 2014 was 14.6 abortions per 1000 women aged 15 to 44. This is the lowest rate ever observed in the United States. In 1973 when abortion became legal, the rate was 16.3. It is estimated that one in 20 women will have an abortion by age 20 and one in five by age 30 and one in four by age 45.[254]

White patients amount to 39% of abortion procedures. Blacks have 28% of abortion procedures although they are only 13% of the American population.

17% abortion patients identified as mainline Protestants, 13% as evangelical Protestant and 24% as Catholics. 23% of Americans are Catholics.

38% of abortion patients report no religion and 8% belong to a small religious community. 94% of abortion patients are heterosexuals, 4% consider themselves bisexuals, 0.3 of 1% are identified as homosexuals and the others identified as something else.[255]

RU 486

Abortion is an issue about which Americans disagree vehemently. Millions of Americans believe that a woman has a right to abortion if she chooses it, because it is her body which is involved. Then there are other Americans who believe that abortion is murder and therefore wish for abortion to be illegal. Because the Supreme Court has ruled that abortion is in fact legal in the United States some antiabortionists have resorted to violence while many others sought to circumvent the ruling of the Supreme Court in *Roe v. Wade*.

The dispute concerning abortion has not abated despite court rulings and religious opposition. American chemical companies failed to seek chemical means to bring about abortion for fear of losing the business for all their products, at least on the part of abortion opponents. It was therefore the French chemical industry which invented abortion pill labeled RU-486 after the French pharmaceutical company Roussett-Uclaf which succeeded in producing a drug in 1988 called Mifepristone.

This drug was not available to American women until 2000 when it was approved by the FDA. During the 12 years prior to its approval the drug was smuggled into the United States for the benefit of those who were able to afford it. The drug is approved only until the seventh week of pregnancy.[256]

The research which led to the development of this drug was not intended to provide abortions. The chemist Etienne Emile Baulieu recognized its use as an abortion drug. It therefore became available to French women as early as RU48j6 is also useful in the treatment of some types of breast cancer, glaucoma and Cushing's syndrome. For some time Roussett-Uclaf would not export the drug because they did not want to entangled in the abortion, controversy in the United States. In 1994 the company decided the US rights to the New York City population Council who in turn license RU486 to Danco laboratories. RU-486 has given women the option of taking a few pills to end a pregnancy. This means that abortion has become more accessible as women will no longer have to travel to clinics to gain a surgical abortion.[257]

It is obvious from the foregoing that abortion is here to stay and that American women will continue its use despite all obstacles. The fact is that innumerable disputes were in the end settled by science which is nonpartisan and hardly influenced by religion. The middle of the 19th century when scientific developments first began to be a revolutionary influence on American life, disputes which seemed insurmountable were in the end settled by the discovery of scientific fact. For example, the invention of the steam engine James Watt in 1776 lend some clergy to argue that the steam engine was an immoral development because if God had wanted us to move as fast as steam engines allowed, He would've given us legs with which to do so. Likewise slavery was defended by Christian clergy on the grounds that slavery existed in biblical days, in ancient Israel. Yet, in the end science led industrial production without slavery making that issue moot. The liberation of women in the 20th and 21st centuries came about because chemistry invented efficient birth control methods, making it possible for women to reduce their domestic obligations, gain education and income, and thus were liberated from the dictates of men. It was not feminist organizers but science which liberated women.

CHAPTER 7. PROSTITUTION: STIGMA, DEGRADATION, AND HUMILIATION

"Sordidness and ugliness are the concomitants of prostitutes' commonplace, everyday routines of living. Here are people narcotized to accept hurts, humiliations, and abasements as their daily portions. Here are people who know nothing of hope or joy or uplift." So say Judge John Murtagh and social worker Sara Harris in their classic book on prostitution, *Cast the First Stone*. For surely, if there is any occupation that is stigmatized, it is that of prostitution.[258]

It was not always so. According to Sir James G. Frazer, the great British student of religion, no doubt the foremost authority on ancient rituals, magic, and religion, the practice of prostitution was clearly regarded not as an orgy of lust but as a solemn religious duty performed in the service of that great Mother Goddess of Western Asia, as discussed above.[259]

The Greco-Roman goddess Aphrodite was the goddess of love and the ancient Greek city of Corinth was dedicated to her. Here a great temple was erected in honor of the goddess whose devotees established there a "paradise of sacred sex." The sacred prostitutes who serviced men in the confines of that temple prayed there for the salvation of the Greeks from the invading Persians in the early fifth century B.C.E. "so that all of Greece took seriously the temple-prostitutes of Corinth."[260]

Likewise in India some "servants of the gods" were in fact prostitutes who were also called "sacred women" and whose duties included entertaining Brahmans, or the priestly class. This behavior was by no means viewed as immoral, as respectable women now and then dedicated a daughter to the role of temple prostitute in a manner resembling the dedication of a son to the priesthood today.[261]

Because the very word "prostitution" is stigmatized and arouses contempt and rejection, a great deal of dispute has arisen over the years concerning the ancient practice of sacred prostitution as practiced in most parts of western Asia, in India, and elsewhere. The dispute arose chiefly in the nineteenth century when British and other students of ancient civilizations first discovered descriptions of sacred or temple prostitution. A good number of those who made these discoveries were clergy who had an interest in classical scholarship and were unwilling to admit or recognize that prostitution was not always and everywhere the target of stigma and rejection. These "Victorian divines" kept silent about this subject or denied the evidence for fear of offending those who delighted in upholding everything Greek and ancient.[262]

In ancient Greek society, those whom others would later refer to contemptuously as whores achieved a level of autonomy leading to education and high status. With the rise of Christianity, however, whores lost that standing and were contrasted with the ideal of the good wife and mother. That contrast led to the stigmatization of whores as bad girls and sinners, particularly in Protestantism. In the Victorian era in England and America, ideals of social purity and morality contrasted even more strongly with these ancient ways, so that the clergy in particular found prostitution despicable.[263] That is still true in current American thinking despite the evidence that prostitution is widespread and by no means abating at the end of the twentieth century. In fact, sociologists estimate that despite the threat of AIDS there are about 336,000 prostitutes in the United States today. The number of prostitutes appears to be increasing in America. In New York City, also called the Prostitution Capital of the United States, escort services increased their supplies of prostitutes to hotel guests by 400% during the 1990s, and there has been no abatement since then.[264]

There are several explanations for the continuing existence of prostitution. First among these is the functionalist argument that prostitution serves the strengthening of "morality." According to proponents of that view, prostitution serves an important function for society because it helps to "protect the family and keeps the wives and daughters of the respectable citizenry morally pure." This belief is based on the assumption that men who visit prostitutes will therefore avoid driving "respectable" girls into premarital sex, extramarital sex, or "immoral" sex as defined in the law or in the broader social mores.[265]

The functional view of prostitution was undoubtedly supported by nineteenth-century and early twentieth-century sexual conduct in America. However, ever since the "sexual revolution" of the 1960s and 1970s, functionalism is very much in doubt. This is so because sex among single women and men has become commonplace, extramarital sex is practiced by a large minority of both sexes, homosexuality is much more accepted than ever before in American experience, and "cybersex" has taken the opprobrium out of pornography because it is hidden and private despite its appearance on the Internet.[266]

Nevertheless, the functional point of view is frequently supported by the customers of prostitutes generally called "johns." Men who visit prostitutes have rarely been studied by sociologists although they are the vast majority in the economic exchange that prostitution implies.

Normally, sexual relations between women and men occur in a close relationship which may be called a "gift exchange." Therefore, both participants in the exchange give of themselves freely with a view of establishing and reaffirming a reciprocal connection. Therefore, relational sex carries no stigma because the actors are "in a state of reciprocal independence." Such exchanges occur between actors in an established social relationship such as marriage or friendship and therefore support a community's social fabric. Social life is more secure and a community is more stable as reciprocal sexual relationships increase, because each party to such a relationship affirms willingness to be held accountable and responsible for the welfare of the "other."[267]

This view can of course be criticized as hypocritical because there are undoubtedly those who withdraw any emotional support from casual sex partners. Nevertheless, even the most casual sexual interchange, not based on money payments, retains a sentimental function and lacks the economic contract conditions pertaining to prostitution. Prostitution does not pretend to have any sentimental content. Unlike sex between committed partners and unlike even casual sex partners, prostitution is free of even the appearance of love, honor, or generosity. This lack of sentiment is a necessity for the prostitute. This excerpt from an interview with a "john" reveals the business of prostitution as it was experienced by a first-time customer: "She kept talking me out of more money, and I didn't understand what was going on. It was like she was offering me more stuff if I would pay her more money before we did anything. So I kept pulling out more money... and then it was over real quick and she hustled me out of there. Until the point when the act was completed she seemed interested in me... and then it was like get this guy out on the street and do the next one."[268]

In part, then, the stigma of prostitution arises from the fear that prostitution might compete successfully with marriage and/or other stable social relations and that it could therefore threaten that stability. To put it bluntly, we might ask: "Could a society survive for long if all marriage and all sentimental alliances between the sexes were replaced by prostitution?" No matter how that question is answered, it transforms prostitution into a threat and a danger and drives its practitioners into the role of outsiders.

Prostitution is a commodity exchange. In a capitalist economy, such an exchange resembles the purchase of other services such as medical care, legal advice, and the payment of psychologists, accountants, and other providers. There is, however, a limit to what may be provided even in a capitalist economy that tends to affirm the right of citizens to turn any service into a profit-making venture. For example, selling babies, body organs, or political favors are all prohibited, as is prostitution, even in capitalist economies. There are some things that, although done, are stigmatized because they violate the moral order and reach the limits of what money can buy. Plainly then, the opponents of prostitution who stigmatize this kind of work are also opponents of extreme capitalism. The customers of prostitutes and the prostitutes themselves, however, are supporters of pure capitalism and say that they have every right to buy and sell whatever they please, including sex.[269]

This belief, that sex may be sold for money, is embodied in the "freedom of contract" doctrine that drives the capitalist world. Therefore, prostitution, like any other commodity, depends on the ready availability of the goods or objects to be sold and the willingness of buyers to pay. This is evidently true of prostitution since willing women and even men are available at all levels of the market for anyone who can afford one. The contract between a prostitute and the client is regarded as a private transaction, as are all capitalist contracts not involving government. Approximately 1.5 million Americans, almost all of them men, avail themselves of the services of a prostitute every week.[270]

There was a time, prior to the effort of women to liberate themselves from economic dependence on men, when some writers argued that marriage and prostitution were at bottom the same thing. Emma Goldman, Simone de Beauvoir, and Cicely Hamilton, all writers active in women's causes, agreed with the sentiment that "it is merely a question of degree whether a woman sells herself to one man, in or out of marriage, or to many men." De Beauvoir wrote that a wife is "hired for life by one man; the prostitute has several clients who pay her by the piece. The one is protected by one male against all the others; the other is defended by all against the exclusive tyranny of each."[271]

In 1909, Cicely Hamilton wrote that women were prevented from bargaining freely in the only trade open to them, marriage, but that they could exercise this freedom in their illegitimate trade, prostitution. Since those words were written, a radical change has occurred in the status of American women, so that Hamilton's view of marriage is utterly antiquated in contemporary society.[272]

Now, when almost all adult women work and have access to any occupation of their choosing, prostitution is seen by some feminists as just another form of work. This argument holds that prostitutes, like all workers, are paid for their efforts and ability. That effort and ability is called labor power and is therefore to be rewarded with money like all work. The erstwhile view was that a prostitute sells herself or her sexual parts. The present argument is that a prostitute sells her services, just like the doctor or the dentist or the lawyer. Just as these servers of man's needs sell not themselves but their services, so the prostitute sells her services. She is therefore to be called a "sex worker," argue these feminists who view prostitution as an industry which includes a trade fit for the entrance of anyone wishing to do so. The defenders of these views call prostitutes "therapists" and liken them to psychologists, social workers, and nurses.[273]

It needs to be noted here that some prostitutes are men and that therefore the view of prostitutes as "sex workers" must be extended to men as well. Most male prostitutes service other men, although male prostitutes who service women are increasing as the needs of unattached, working, and traveling females also increase. Nevertheless, as always, women are the major suppliers of prostitution and men almost the exclusive buyers. However, because prostitution is traditionally criticized as a woman's problem, or as a problem caused by women, the male participants, either as providers or as consumers, are generally ignored.

Because the male role in the transaction between prostitute and "john" is usually ignored, the principal question that arises in this connection is seldom answered. That question is: "Why do so many men believe that satisfaction of a natural drive must take the form of public access to women's bodies in exchange for money?" Evidently, the day when "decent" women did not deal sexually with men outside of marriage is over in the United States and Europe. Therefore, sex outside of marriage is readily available, and it is reasonable to assume that prostitution flourishes even now because the men who rent the services of a prostitute do so to gain power and ascendancy over a woman or several women by means of the sex act. We argue here that prostitution from the male point of view resembles rape, which is also an effort to gain ascendancy and power over women. Both prostitution and rape are indeed sexual in nature. Yet, the motive for both actions is power and the male need to dominate. The evidence for this view is found in the observation that "nearly all men... complain[ed] about the emotional coldness and mercenary approach of many prostitutes they had contact with," so that the wish to dominate is defeated by the attitudes of prostitutes generally.[274]

The complaint by male patrons concerning prostitutes is voiced by many men who want to pay not only for the sexual service rendered by prostitutes but also for some sentimental attachment. That, however, is impossible since the very nature of prostitution negates any sentiment on the part of the prostitute in favor of the money paid for her services. Furthermore, men who employ prostitutes in a society that allows considerable access to sexual expression in and out of marriage are announcing their wish to divorce sex from emotional attachments of any kind. Almost every study of the male customers of prostitutes concludes that men who buy the services of a prostitute do want to engage in sex without having to express any commitment to their sex partners. This means that men can buy and use women as objects.[275]

Therefore, proponents of conflict theory hold that prostitution is the very epitome of exploitation and that prostitution reinforces the old patriarchal system of male dominance over women. The patriarchal system of social organization from which the United States is only now emerging encourages prostitution by socializing boys to be dominant over girls and men to dominate women. Simultaneously, girls are socialized in any patriarchal society to be submissive to boys and men at play, at work, and in sex. In fact, women are relegated to many low-status jobs in any patriarchal society, so that as late as 1999 the average income of American women was only 75% of the average income of American men. Prostitution therefore fits into this arrangement since it is a low-status job. In traditional male-dominated societies, prostitution reflects the entire gender arrangement prevailing there. This assumes of course that in a traditional patriarchal society, marked by great gender inequality, there is no free choice for women who become prostitutes.[276]

While this analysis of prostitution in a traditional patriarchal society may fit many areas of the world today, it does not reflect the current reality of gender relations in the United States. In 2019, American women who enter prostitution do have a choice to refrain from that occupation. There are, however, some women who see prostitution as the best job they can get. Viewing sexual relations with strange men as a commercial transaction and not an emotional experience, these women enter prostitution in interaction with friends already associated with prostitution or because of the offer of money from men or because of the protection offered by pimps. Because a majority of prostitutes have been abused by their fathers, that majority has learned to detach themselves emotionally from sex with strange men. Parental abuse teaches children not to feel affectionate toward the abusive parent and to be emotionally detached in almost any relationship. It is that emotional detachment that makes prostitution possible for many engaged in that occupation.[277]

Sexologists Vern L. Bullough and Bonnie Bullough, following Stein, report that a study involving 1,230 men who had encountered "call girls" found that all wanted their sex needs met conveniently, professionally, and "without obligation but the momentary one...."[278] Emotional detachment has always been a mark of occupational relationships. Millions of Americans work every day in numerous occupations without becoming emotionally attached to those with whom they work. In fact, it is an underlying assumption of work in capitalist societies. Work is a means of satisfying needs. Many kinds of employment are also tedious and lead to alienation. Author Studs Terkel in his well-known book *Working* illustrates by means of workers' words how dull and alienating work is for millions of Americans. Terkel shows that because the product of work belongs to the capitalist and not the worker, workers do not invest themselves in their work. Human companionship and positive relations with other workers are therefore limited or nonexistent. Factory work in particular is a dehumanizing experience, although many professions, particularly the academic profession, are equally alienating and devoid of emotional attachments.[279]

Prostitution may therefore be seen as just another form of work in a capitalist market. In light of that insight, prostitutes have recently organized and formed a number of unions devoted to insuring their rights as workers. Most prominent among these organizations is COYOTE, which uses an acronym for "Call Off Your Old Tired Ethics." There is also PONY or "Prostitutes of New York," HUM or "Hookers Union of Maryland," NTFP or "National Task Force on Prostitution," PUMA or "Prostitutes Union of Massachusetts Association," and many others around the country. Those who organize prostitutes in this manner seek to remove the stigma of prostitution by legitimizing the sex trade and even "celebrating it." Demanding the rights enjoyed by workers in other industries, organized prostitutes engage in public debates on television programs. There they have demanded the end of discriminatory law enforcement such as entrapment and quarantining. Entrapment refers to the instigation of a crime by law-enforcement officers in order to find grounds for criminal prosecution. Quarantining refers to the isolation of prostitutes in jails for the purpose of a physical examination to detect sexually transmitted diseases. Further, they demand the passage of the Equal Rights Amendment to the United States Constitution, the suppression of pornography, the end to the unjustified belief that they are the cause of the AIDS epidemic, and an end to violence against women.[280]

COYOTE leaders have also insisted that most prostitutes chose their occupation and were not coerced into that line of work as is popularly believed. Sociologists estimate that only 15% of American prostitutes are coerced into their work either by force or by the need to survive. Hence, prostitute organizations have made that occupation into a civil rights issue. These organizations argue that prostitutes have the right to work as freelance workers just as nurses, typists, doctors, lawyers, or anyone else. Those who defend this position also hold that "sex is a commodity just like anything else and, like any other commodity, operates on the law of supply and demand."[281] In addition, organized prostitutes demand that they be given paid vacations, health insurance, workers' compensation, and Social Security. Above all other demands is the demand that prostitution be legalized.[282]

Legalization has had many defenders who think that when sex work is clean, safe, and less publicly visible it is preferable to street prostitution that has none of these characteristics. Many sex workers, however, and in particular the International Committee for Prostitutes' Rights, do not support legalization of prostitution. To them, legalization represents a yet more blatant male method of control of female sexuality than is true under existing laws. Moreover, they point out that in countries such as Germany where prostitution is legal it has not proved successful. There, and elsewhere, many women refuse to provide sex for taxed pay in a state brothel and work illegally and privately instead. In addition, women who are barred from the legal brothels in Germany because of diseases or other sickness continue to work outside the law. Therefore, the International Committee for Prostitutes' Rights includes in their "World Charter" the total abolition of all laws limiting or prohibiting prostitution in favor of the granting of a benefits system to sex workers. These benefits are to include support for women seeking to leave that occupation, enforcement of existing legislation concerning coercion of sex workers, rape, fraud, and child abuse.[283]

Child abuse is also the principal focus of the United Nations Children's Fund Convention of the Rights of the Child. According to Article 34 of that convention: States Parties undertake to protect the child from all forms of sexual abuse. For these purposes, States Parties shall in particular take all appropriate national, bilateral, and multilateral measures to prevent (a) the inducement or coercion of a child to engage in any unlawful sexual activity; (b) the exploitative use of children in prostitution or other unlawful sexual practice; (c) the exploitative use of children in pornographic performances and materials. That convention also includes the findings of the Congress Against the Commercial Sexual Exploitation of Children. This congress represents 133 nations, each of which has declared that there is a child-prostitution problem in their country. Despite the considerable participation of so many nations in the congress, unanimity concerning child prostitution has not developed among them. This is true because there are different interpretations of the word "child." In the United States a child is generally someone not yet eighteen years old or, at the most, someone under the age of sixteen. In primarily rural societies, however, the word "child" refers to those much younger than eighteen and sexual maturity is often attributed to children as young as thirteen. Hence the definition of "child" is a combination of emotional, physical, mental, and sexual attributes in which the family and the social environment also play a role. Therefore, the ages at which various nations confer the status of adulthood range from ten to twenty-four, including the assumption that a young person can consent to sex at such an age.[284]

Therefore, in order to accommodate these differing views and also avoid making government-supervised brothels legal employers of prostitutes, there are those who suggest that the prostitutes themselves be licensed. The advantage of such a move would be that the prostitute would not depend for her livelihood on a madam or a pimp but only on herself. Such licensing would also serve to decriminalize prostitutes. Feminists have long argued that criminalizing prostitutes intensifies female inequality and discriminates against women. In addition to all the other difficulties associated with prostitution, the policy of criminalization forces prostitutes to bear the additional burden of being identified as criminals. This is particularly true for the street prostitutes who are victimized daily by police, judges, prosecutors, and pimps. Feminists therefore argue that sexual behavior should be the choice of each adult woman or man and that prostitutes should have the right to protection without such demands as mandatory physical examinations, which are seen by feminists as efforts to "increase male control over women's bodies."[285]

We have already seen that there are those who seek the decriminalizing of prostitution and the issuing of a state license to all prostitutes. Such a licensed prostitute could then work for herself almost anywhere. Those who favor licensing prostitutes want to establish state boards of prostitution similar to the boards that now regulate medicine, law, and social work. Those prostitutes who feel vulnerable vis-a-vis men could be encouraged to form a cooperative that could help in defending them from violence by providing security. Such a license would also give prostitutes near-professional status, thereby giving them the right to protest the lack of sex workers' rights. A license would make sex workers less dependent on large, commercial interests and would render prostitutes less vulnerable to pimps, customers, and the police. Finally, a license would give customers reassurance that some standards concerning the health of the prostitute have been observed.[286]

There are those feminists who argue that prostitution should not be legal. They defend their position on the grounds that prostitution is mainly caused by poverty and that poverty deprives those who enter prostitution of free choice. Opponents of legalizing prostitution also argue that women's bodies should not be for sale any more than there should be an open market for babies or human organs. It is further argued by opponents of legalizing prostitution that such legalization would reduce the number of work opportunities for women in other occupations and that legalizing prostitution would insure the subordination of women by law.[287]

Social Stratification In The "Oldest Profession"

All occupations are stratified subcultures. This means that every occupation has practitioners who have high prestige within the occupation and some whose prestige is ranked lower. A subculture is a variation on a mainstream culture and consists of a group whose values and norms or expectations set them apart from the broader culture. In addition, all subcultures use language not in general use by those who do not belong to the subculture. That is true of lawyers, accountants, physicians, and prostitutes.[288]

Examples of such language are these: A "john" or a "mark" is a customer of a prostitute, a "trick" is a sexual performance, a "pimp" is an agent for prostitutes, a "madam" owns a brothel, a "hooker" is a female prostitute, a "jane" is a lesbian customer of a prostitute, a "stable" is a group of prostitutes controlled by one pimp, to "get burned" is to give service without getting paid, and a "quota" is the number of johns a prostitute must see each day.[289]

Among those who practice this occupation are prostitutes who manage to collect a large fee for their services because they wear expensive clothes and have a veneer of education permitting them to converse with or listen to the customer. Such prostitutes generally make a glamorous appearance and can serve as escorts for men with large wallets and expensive tastes.

In 1984 the police closed a house of prostitution run by Sydney Biddle Barrows, whom the media labeled "The Mayflower Madam." Her "escort service" in New York City earned $1 million per year renting twenty women to her clients at rents from $125 per hour to $400 an hour. Barrows kept 60% of their take. Because Barrows was the descendant of a socially prominent family who did indeed arrive with the ship *Mayflower*, her conduct became a media sensation. Not only was Barrows from an establishment family but, according to police, her appointment book read like a social register.

As is true with so many prostitutes, Barrows learned about the opportunity to earn a good deal of money from a coworker. Since Barrows earned no more than a department store salesclerk's wage, the large fee collected by a prostitute for one night's work attracted her. She says that she had no moral problem in entering the prostitution business because she believed that prostitution "filled a human and age-old need." She believes that her male clients were gentlemen who were paying for an "elegant escort." Therefore she opened an escort service that employed only women who looked good and knew how to dress well. Barrows and her employees were of course only interested in the money to be earned. Unlike lower-ranking prostitutes, Barrows taught her girls to be most polite and to use a variety of speech patterns that would make the "client" feel important and that would produce a maximum of income.

Prostitutes at all levels of occupational prestige learn their trade from those already involved. This is not surprising, since all occupational skills and the values associated with such skills must be learned in association with those already holding these skills. First, prostitution novices learn "The Hustling Rap." This "rap" concerns the initial conversation between the client and the prostitute and deals with the wishes of the client and the money demanded by the prostitute for rendering a service. The hustler must maintain a steady patter of verbal coaxing, during which her tone of voice may be more important than her actual words."

Madams and other teachers of prostitutes also instruct the needed physical skills and the values associated with the profession. Lectures and discussions are used to teach these skills. The lessons often include guest speakers who have a good deal of experience. Evidently, then, escort services are good businesses.[290]

Many of the women who worked for the escort service also held daytime jobs in business and industry or were college students. Yet others were actresses; Barrows says that she liked to hire actresses because they were more capable of pretending an interest in the client. These actresses also faked enjoyment where there was only money and were also capable of portraying a whole scene demanded by the client. The prostitutes hired by Barrows sold not only sex but also companionship and intimacy. This means that many male customers of the prostitutes spent a good deal of time discussing their professional and family problems with the paid prostitutes they were now engaging. Many of the men who used prostitutes to discuss their life situation claimed that they had no one else willing to listen to them, not even their wives. Others, however, were indeed close to their wives but used prostitutes to talk to them and be intimate with them whenever they were out of town and had no opportunity to see their wives. Barrows claims that a good number of such men were getting along fine at home but were lonely when in New York on business and in need of companionship.

For centuries prostitutes have been used to initiate young men into sexual experiences. This was also true of the Mayflower Madam and her employees, who were sometimes paid by the father of a young boy in order to teach him all about sex.

In sum, Biddle described the so-called high-class whore who costs more because she appears closer to the American ideal of womanhood than those with lesser prestige. Nevertheless there can be no doubt that even the Mayflower Madam and those associated with her were and are held in contempt by large numbers of Americans and that all of these women were and are stigmatized for who they are and what they do.[291]

"Call girls" have been labeled the "aristocrats of prostitution." They charge customers $1,500 per night and can earn over $100,000 a year. Some gain clients through employment in escort services or by other means that permit them to develop independent customer lists. Many call girls come from middle-class families and service upper-class customers. To dispel the notion that they merely provide sex for money, they give the clients the impression that they are fascinated by the clients' importance, intelligence, and competence. "Call girls," as the term implies, make dates on the telephone with men whose names they obtain from bellhops, cab drivers, waiters, and other employees working in various service industries. These girls either entertain clients in their own apartments or visit the client at his home or hotel. Evidently, this occupation is very risky, since the call girl is not protected against violence and other forms of abuse.[292]

Although violence occurs only on occasion and is by no means the rule, all prostitutes have at some time been the subject of violence and are always aware that violence may occur at any time. The reason for much of the violence experienced by call girls and other prostitutes is that for some johns prostitution is not about sex but about power. In present-day American society a good deal of power and authority is still vested in men. Despite "women's liberation," which has affected mostly the educated segment of the American population during the past fifty years, large numbers of Americans, even now, expect that the relationships between men and women continue to be structured along the lines of male superiority and male dominance.

Although rapists are hardly an example of the average American man, it is nonetheless instructive to note that one justification rapists use for their action has traditionally been that their female victims are at fault. Such justification for so brutal an act includes the belief that women who were raped brought it on themselves by dressing in a provocative fashion, or by ingesting too much drugs or alcohol. Rapists and their apologists believe that a woman who engages in such behavior has waived her right to be treated with respect. Men who rape evidently seek to assert their dominance over women, and in particular women who are "forward." Because prostitutes are sexually available, it is believed by many Americans that rape is less of a crime when a prostitute is victimized than when so-called good women are so treated. In fact, sexual solicitation is viewed by some to invite violence so that there are even those who argue that prostitutes cannot be raped because of the work they do. The belief that prostitutes are subject to violence because of their work is supported by the evidence that violence against prostitutes is hardly ever reported to the police and is generally ignored by the police when it is reported. Even judges have been heard to say that a prostitute who has been raped is less damaged emotionally by such an experience than other women because of their line of work. All of this indicates more forcefully than anything else that prostitution is severely stigmatized, so that the stigma alone removes normal protection against violence from prostitutes.

Because protection against violence is so hard for call girls and street prostitutes to achieve, another method of delivering the services of prostitutes to men willing to pay is the so-called brothel, bordello, house of ill repute, sporting house, or cat house. Such establishments were most common in the nineteenth century but are still available today. Generally, these houses are run by "madams" who employ the prostitutes, supervise their behavior, protect them from violence, and receive the fees for the "working girls" in their establishments. Out of these fees the madam usually pays the prostitutes between 40% and 60% of their earnings. Usually the madam in such an establishment is a retired prostitute who makes arrangements for bringing in customers, hiring prostitutes, bribing the police, and dealing with neighbors.[293]

Ranking a good deal lower in the hierarchy of prostitution are "circuit travelers." These are women who move around in groups of two or three to lumber camps, labor camps, and agricultural camps. With permission of the foreman, these "circuit travelers" will service all the men in a camp on one night and then travel on. Some "circuit travelers" seek clients at truck stops and rest areas. There are "circuit travelers" who have been forced into prostitution by brutal pimps who lure young Mexican women into Florida and other southern states with promises of employment in restaurants, nursing homes, and with other healthcare providers. Raped, beaten, and forced to have abortions, these foreign women, unable to speak English, are helpless victims of so-called ticketeros who charge the customer $20 for each sex act and give the prostitute $3.

On the bottom of the prostitution hierarchy are "skeezers." These are women who barter sex for drugs. An investigation in Chicago and New York revealed that more than half of all prostitutes are drug users who support their habit with prostitution. Psychologist Paul Goldstein and his associates have studied this behavior in some detail and found that contrary to popular opinion, skeezers are not exploited but view themselves as engaged in an economic transaction in which they come out ahead. The skeezers believe that gaining drugs for a few minutes of sex is a transaction that favors them.[294] These skeezers and other streetwalkers are of course the most visible of the prostitutes working in American cities. The street prostitutes, more than any others, are subject to a whole spectrum of behavior by the communities they enter. Street prostitutes are exposed to name-calling, physical assault, and occasionally rape and murder. There are people who "cruise" in areas where street prostitutes wait and shout insults and obscenities at them. An example of such violence is recorded by Neil McKeganey, professor at the University of Glasgow:

> Marina and I were approached by a woman whom we have chatted to on many nights. She had a black eye and a heavily swollen cheek-bone. She explained that she had been set upon by a punter earlier that week. [A "punter" is the British term for a prostitute's client.] He had stopped and had asked her for business. Although she had been a bit weary he had used her name. Once in the car she had given him her usual directions to the place she normally used but he had turned onto the motorway. She had protested but he turned off near the fruit market, pulled the car up near some darkened factories, ordered her to strip and then tied her hands with bin liners. He then punched her in the face and pushed her out of the car. She thought for sure he intended running her over but she managed to scramble over a fence and into a nearby field.[295]

This and numerous other examples, including the use of guns and knives, are the constant companions of prostitutes' lives.

Assault from customers is not the only source of violence suffered by prostitutes. Pimps, men who control prostitutes and furnish them with some protection, are notorious for beating and even knifing these women. Many pimps have violent tempers and make it a practice to savagely beat the girls working for them. Yet, few prostitutes ever complain about such beatings because they have incorporated into their own self-evaluation the belief that they deserve nothing better. It is very common for all who are rejected and stigmatized to finally accept the view of others as their own and to reject themselves and to view themselves in the same ugly light that their persecutors have imposed on them. That is certainly as true of prostitutes as it is of racial and ethnic minorities, homeless people, and obese people.

Male Prostitutes And Johns

The participation of men in prostitution is generally overlooked as male prostitutes call themselves "hustlers" rather than prostitutes. These "hustlers" frequent gay bars and homosexual baths or walk the streets looking for business. Some "hustlers" are "kept boys" by one wealthy man while yet others are "call boys" or work in a "massage parlor" which is in fact a homosexual brothel. There are also "gigolos," a word derived from the French giguer meaning "to dance." "Gigolos" are male prostitutes who service women. They operate out of escort agencies or dance studios and offer companionship and sex for money. Some are "kept" by wealthy women.[296]

Male prostitution is practiced unevenly in the United States. While there are undoubtedly some male prostitutes in all parts of the country, San Francisco has been the capital of male homosexual activity for some time and therefore houses a larger contingent of male prostitutes than any other American city. Unlike female prostitutes who chiefly service men, most male prostitutes service homosexuals and not women. Hence the customers of male prostitutes are ordinarily men, so that both sexes service men more than women.

It is claimed that San Francisco's involvement with male prostitution began during the "gold rush" when boy brothels operated there from 1840 until 1910. It was not only the entrance of so many men into California in search of gold which led San Francisco to become the American headquarters of homosexual prostitution. A second reason for this development was the diversity of the California population, which led to a far greater tolerance in that state for deviant lifestyles than is true in other parts of the country.

During the 1960s "hippie" era, male prostitution received more attention than ever before. At that time a good number of drug-addicted young men moved into San Francisco. These young men were usually heterosexual but permitted homosexuals to use them for the money they needed to feed their drug habits. Such heterosexual youths may be called "situational hustlers" as they prostituted only on some occasions. These "situational hustlers" are distinguished from "habitual hustlers" consisting of homosexual males who prostituted regularly. There are also "vocational" male prostitutes who consider themselves professionals.[297]

While there is a massive amount of research describing the background of female prostitutes, there are very few studies of male prostitutes. D. Kelly Weisberg, professor of law at Hastings College in San Francisco, did make such a study including research in the metropolitan areas of Boston, Houston, Los Angeles, Minneapolis, New York, San Francisco, and Seattle. Because Weisberg's study is national in scope it is reliable as a source of knowledge concerning American male prostitution generally.

It is surely not unexpected that the Weisberg study found family background to have a major influence on prostitution. Evidently, many prostitutes, both male and female, come from homes involving parental alcoholism and frequent fighting among parents. Long absences of the father or his permanent desertion of the family are common experiences of such boys (and girls). Many prostitutes, both male and female, come from homes dissolved by death or divorce. In fact, the Weisberg study showed that only one-third of all the boys Weisberg studied came from intact families. A large number of prostitutes are raised by a single parent, usually the mother.

Another study of male prostitutes shows that only eighteen of ninety-eight youths in that study had an intact family, but even in these families poor relationships were the rule. Physical and emotional abuse were also common in the families of prostitutes, both male and female. Such abuse often included severe beatings and constant humiliation. Neglect and abandonment are also common experiences of prostitutes. There are children who are kicked out of the house at very young ages, so that they have no choice but to become street people. "I lived on the streets since I was nine," says one boy interviewed by psychologist Robert W. Deischer in his study of male prostitutes in San Francisco, while another boy told an interviewer: "My mom moved. She told me I am on my own."[298]

Although the sexual exploitation of children is known in the United States, it is far more common in Asian countries such as the Philippines, which for years hosted a number of American naval and military bases. There "thousands of children were under the control of pimps and performed any service for anyone who could pay." Australian news commentator Cameron Forbes claimed that "thousands of boys and girls were for sale (in the Philippines). The youngest was five years old." Forbes then describes prostitution in the Philippine town of Pagsanjan. "Pedophiles flocked to the lodges along the river and took their pick of the boys in the swimming pools. And they all fed on the poverty of Pagsanjan."[299]

Sexual abuse is a common characteristic of the family background of male and female prostitutes. The abusers include fathers, mothers, siblings, and other relatives. Others report that they were sexually abused by nonfamily members at very young ages. Even those who do not report sexual abuse generally recount sexual experiences at ages as young as five or six. Most male prostitutes were paid for sexual acts before they were eleven years old. Weisberg concluded that 74% of her respondents began prostitution on a regular basis within the year in which they were paid for their first encounter. Regular prostitution was defined by Weisberg as participating in prostitution several times a month. The interest in engaging in "regular prostitution" is of course aroused by the realization that prostitution is a source of money or other rewards. While money is the principal reason for engaging in male prostitution, drugs, sex, and adventure are also mentioned as motivations. Whatever the motivation, prostitution, like all occupations, involves certain norms or expectations that must be learned if one is to be successful. Generally, these norms are learned from a friend already engaged in the occupation and involve instructions as to how to "pick up" a customer, how to charge for the service, and how to perform.[300]

Male prostitutes have paid and unpaid sex with multiple partners. Many engage in risky sexual behavior involving illicit drugs. Their partners may be homosexuals, heterosexuals, or bisexual men and women. Sociologists Jacqueline Boles and Kirk W. Elifson report that their study of male prostitutes revealed that one-half of the men in their sample consider themselves heterosexuals.

"Sex Work": Organized Prostitution

As I have already stated, prostitution has most recently been relabeled "sex work." The reason for this change is of course to escape the stigma associated with that kind of barter. The phrase "sex work" also serves to ally prostitutes with other working people so that prostitution may appear as "normal" work. The effort to normalize prostitution has been challenged by those who agree with the stigmatization of prostitution and whose objections may be summarized in the following seven propositions. First, that "sex work" or prostitution is inherently immoral. Those who disagree with that view claim that the very designation "immoral" precludes any rational discussion and that therefore such a designation is ipso facto useless. The second objection against prostitution is that sex between a "sex worker" and her client is cold, unemotional, and impersonal. The counterclaim here is that even in marriage sex can have those characteristics. It is further argued that sex without love is not necessarily "bad" sex. Third, those opposed to prostitution argue that sex workers are defenseless against physical violence and that many sex workers are themselves prone to physical and mental illness. The counterclaim is that there are many hazardous occupations and that the difficulties sex workers encounter are the outcome of the stigma that attaches to their work. Absent the stigma, sex work would no longer be dangerous. Therefore, those who are opposed to sex work and want to rehabilitate the prostitutes are confronted with the argument that we need to minimize the risk of doing sex work rather than creating difficulties for these workers. Yet another argument against prostitution is a reflection of the old Marxist idea that prostitution represents exploitation of all workers. Marx had argued that prostitution exists only in capitalist societies and is an example of how all labor is exploited. Yet today prostitution exists in all countries, many of which are not capitalist. Then there is the feminist argument contending that the prostitute has the status/role of an object while the customer is the subject. This is best expressed by the claim that the prostitute is "merchandise." The counterclaim here is that prostitutes do not sell themselves but only their services. It is argued that if the prostitute is only "merchandise" then that would also have to be true of all professionals who render a service. Furthermore, those who find the "merchandise" argument spurious say that sex is as important as food and drink and that nourishment as well as sex can be bought. The sixth objection against prostitution is commercialization. Those who counter this objection claim that the sex industry is a symptom and not a cause of capitalist commercialization of everything. Finally, it is argued that prostitutes are subject to a disturbed emotional life caused by the exploitation they suffer. That argument is countered with the insistence that it is not "sex work" per se, but the stigma associated with that kind of work which leads to emotional problems on the part of the worker.[301]

Whatever the arguments for or against prostitution, it is evident in the twenty-first century that prostitution in the United States is faced with competition from a number of sources. First and foremost among these sources is the ever-increasing willingness of young unmarried women to engage in sexual activity. Today the rate of premarital sex relations for women is approaching that of men, so that prostitutes are by no means the only sexual outlets available to unmarried men. Furthermore, women no longer believe that they are not sexual beings and must merely endure male sexual advances. The "sexual revolution" of the 1960s led to the assumption that women are equally interested in sex and hence more accessible than before. In addition, effective contraception such as "the pill" and the cervical cap have allowed men greater and more frequent access to their spouses without fear of unwanted pregnancy, thereby making visits to prostitutes less necessary. Divorce is more frequent than ever before, so that couples who are sexually incompatible need not stay together, which might have steered the husband toward the services of a prostitute. There are also singles bars, swing parties, and a good deal of premarital cohabitation, all of which compete effectively with prostitution.[302]

In view of these developments, there are those who believe that prostitution will soon come to an end as the "market" arrangement between customers and "workers" will have too much competition. This view overlooks the fact that many of the customers of prostitutes are men who do not want to enter into any close relationship with any woman and even shy away from the temporary obligations which a sexual liaison implies. These men want to pay and "get it over with."

There is yet another reason for the perpetuation of prostitution despite the "amateur" competition to which it is subject. That is the recent introduction of the drug culture into the sphere of the American prostitute. Drug addiction has led girls as young as eleven to be used by gang members to make money. These gangs were at one time engaged in robbery and assault but later found that they can use girls, including children, as a means to attract customers to their drug business. According to the Federal Office of Juvenile Justice and Delinquency Prevention, women and girls constitute 11% of the gang members in the United States. In some cities female gang members account for 20% of all members. As long ago as October of 1998, more than one hundred members of seven gangs operating in Manhattan were arrested on charges of using prostitutes to sell drugs. Richard J. Estes, professor of social work at the University of Pennsylvania, claims that "all across the United States young women [are] joining gangs where their major contribution is sex."[303]

There are some areas of large cities where gangs have high social standing and where girls join such gangs in order to share in that status arrangement. The need to belong, the need for the money and the protection such gangs afford these girls leads them to independence from parental supervision and consequently to prostitution and drug addiction.

Although Western civilization generally stigmatizes prostitution today, this sex activity was at one time considered a sacred occupation, since it was believed that demonstration of human sexuality would induce the gods to permit agricultural growth. Until the rise of Christianity, prostitutes were held in high esteem in ancient Greece and Rome. Later, prostitution was seen as functional and a method of preserving the chastity of "good" women. Yet, prostitution resembles a capitalist commodity exchange because it lacks all sentiment.

We have seen that "sacred" prostitution was acceptable and in fact commendable in the ancient Near East. This was true because the idea that women were more than male appendages never occurred to these ancient people. It is unlikely that the concept of social disease was known to the ancients, as the germ theory did not exist. Therefore, prostitution served the purpose of illustrating the wishes of the population for the reproduction of food. This had to be conveyed to gods that were in fact dumb statues.

Once Judaism and its daughter, Christianity, became influential in the Greco-Roman world, these customs changed. Foremost, Judeo-Christian scriptures denounce prostitution vigorously. That was possible because it came to be believed that an invisible god could be approached through sacrifice and prayer so that demonstrations of what was wanted were no longer needed. Furthermore, Judaism and thereafter Christianity viewed sexual intercourse as a sacred institution to be practiced inside marriage only. The reason for this was the need to insure that offspring could be identified as being certainly from only one father. The ancient peoples did not understand the relationship between coitus and birth because these events do not necessarily follow one another. However, later developments led to that recognition and to the patrilineal requirements just outlined.

With the rise of Christianity women were given a somewhat better status than was true in the ancient world. Married women could object to the practice of husbands visiting prostitutes. As Christianity progressed, prostitutes came to be seen as rivals of married women. Since Judaism and Christianity did not include prostitutes in religious rites, their function changed. Prostitutes now serviced men in a manner that "moral" married women would not. As centuries of prudery taught that women did not really like sex but were mere passive objects of men's lust, some men sought the company of prostitutes who were not included in these female prohibitions and who did all those things the in-group married woman was enjoined not to do. This served the function of securing marriages which would otherwise have been dissolved or held together miserably because of the sexual frustration of husbands. In short, prostitution served the function of maintaining the group, as out-groups always do. The married woman was told that if she did not behave as she should, then she would be as despised and as miserable as the prostitute. This meant that prostitutes were needed to keep women "in line." In this sense, prostitutes served the same function as Jews. Christians were told that they would be as miserable as the Jews if they did not believe what the clergy taught them.

All this continued into the first half of the twenty-first century in Western civilization and is still true in much of the world. However, the advance of science and education has liberated women and given them greater economic opportunities than were available before the 1960s. Prostitution then became even more stigmatized than before, because many people now believe that those who prostitute themselves could do something else to earn a livelihood. That may not be true, because almost all prostitutes are involved in the use of drugs and are therefore dependent on not only these illegal substances but also on male "pimps." In American society, occupation is the most important criterion of social prestige. Not only money but also the means by which money is earned are decisive in determining prestige or social standing in the twenty-first century. Those occupations which require the most education, have the greatest autonomy, supply the public with important services, and allow practitioners a great deal of "conspicuous consumption" have the highest rank among the occupations. Therefore it is not surprising that physicians have consistently outranked all occupations in all public opinion surveys concerning occupational prestige.

Evidently, then, prostitution ranks the lowest among occupations because it is believed that it requires no skill or education, it appears to be socially harmful, and its practitioners are viewed as utter dependents. This is not entirely true, but it is the perception of an occupation, and not its actual condition, that creates prestige.

In addition to all these negative evaluations, prostitution is also seen as a health hazard even for those who never visit a prostitute. AIDS and the fear of AIDS have led to a real concern for those who may become infected by men or women who have had contacts with prostitutes and then seek out other sex partners. The threat to marriage is obvious.

In view of all of these negative evaluations, the prostitution business continues to exist. This is true despite the "sexual revolution" of the 1960s and beyond which has made sexual intercourse available to unmarried women and men to a greater degree than ever before. It is therefore not the lack of sexual opportunity that leads "johns" to visit prostitutes but the belief that prostitutes will somehow satisfy men more than "decent" women. That belief is fostered by the entertainment industry and therefore contributes to the stigma associated with prostitution.

Prior to the "sexual revolution" of the 1960s there were some who equated marriage with prostitution, an argument that can no longer be supported in the twenty-first century. Instead, there are those who now seek to label prostitution "sex work" and hope to unionize "sex workers" with a view of giving them the same benefits other unionized workers already have. Likewise, sex workers seek the decriminalization of prostitution.

Prostitution is learned by association with those already in the "profession." There is a hierarchy of prostitutes ranging from "call girls" to drug-dependent street prostitutes. There are also male prostitutes who service both homosexuals and heterosexuals of both sexes.

In the main, prostitutes, both male and female, are the children of dysfunctional families. Abandoned and "thrown away," many become involved in drug and alcohol dependency, creating a close link between addiction and prostitution.

CHAPTER 8. ROLE MODELS, AND CULTURE HEROES

All mankind lives in two environments. One is nature, which determines much of human experience including the lifecycle. The over 7 billion people living on earth are also dependent on culture, which is the man-made environment. Culture has three dimensions. One is material culture consisting of all human inventions and discoveries from the stone age to the present. Material culture includes the chair we are sitting on as well as the atomic bomb. Birth control is also an aspect of material culture. A second form of culture is ideological and consists of beliefs and opinions. Evidently, these beliefs are in part dictated by the material culture. For example, no one had anything to say about automobiles before they were invented. Yet today, in the 21st century, beliefs concerning the automobile are widespread. Ideological culture also includes religion which, unlike science, is considered absolutely true by the believers despite the fact that religion too changes over the centuries according to the developments in material culture. For example, the belief that women must conform to the housewife role and may not earn a livelihood outside the home has been abandoned in the United States with the advent of effective birth control. Thirdly, there is behavioral culture. Behavioral culture consists of that which we do by reason of what we believe and by reason of the material objects available to us. [304]

Sexual behavior, like all human behavior, is therefore determined by the culture in which it is conducted. This means that sexual behavior is subject to the principle of legitimacy. Every culture determines how this sex drive shall be expressed. During the 19th century, also known as the Victorian age, Americans seldom mentioned the word sex. The years of Queen Victoria's reign in England from 1819 to 1901 were named after her as she suppressed all mention of sex after her husband Albert died in 1861. The puritanical Victorian age was undoubtedly the product of the inability of the population to limit the number of children born to each family and to protect oneself from social diseases. The only means available to defend against these two conditions was abstinence. In fact, it was not until 1920, after the First World War, that an effort was made by American women to liberate themselves from household slavery. This failed, because birth control failed. Therefore, the liberation of women was postponed for another 40 years and did not become effective until the end of the 1960s.

From then on into the 21st century, sexual expression by both women and men became more and more acceptable. Finally the view of many Americans became that sexuality is purely a private matter to be decided as each individual pleased. The outcome of this major change which we may call the sexual revolution has been an attack on the erstwhile Puritan attitudes concerning sex as well as an assault on the traditional family. All of this was accompanied by the conduct of those we may call American role models and culture heroes who receive wide publicity not only for their achievements in politics, sports, and entertainment, but also for their sexual exploits. Many Americans imitate the sexual behavior of these culture heroes who include politicians such as presidents of the United States, major movie stars, and highly visible sports personalities.

Politicians

An excellent example of a politician whose sexual behavior became a public scandal was the conduct of President William Jefferson Clinton, who was impeached and connected with his this sexual encounter in the Oval Office with a 20-year-old intern woman. The scandal surrounding President Clinton's conduct was of course produced by the media who benefit financially from reporting stories with sexual contents. The behavior of President Clinton would probably not be tolerated on the part of the chief executive officer of a corporation, a professor, a military commander or anyone else in the position of power and responsibility. Yet President Clinton continued to maintain a high level of public approval of his presidency despite the fact that he was viewed as an errant family member. Many identified with him because his sins were also their sins, the public generally felt that is excessive behavior was appealing, and his public support represented the feelings of the majority of Americans. [305]

Although criticized by some, President Clinton became a role model, as millions of American television viewers and newspaper readers were sympathetic to the president's conduct. [306] A public opinion poll revealed that 64%

of those responding said the public did not need to know the details of the president's relationship with the female intern.[307] A December 1998 ABC poll found that 86% of the American public believed the president had lied under oath, and 63% believed that he had obstructed justice. Yet 60% did not support his removal from office.

President Clinton was not the first president to commit adultery while in office. President Harding as well as Presidents Kennedy, Lyndon Johnson, and Franklin Roosevelt did the same. Kennedy dealt with Judith Campbell Exner even though she was also connected to organized crime figures. Lyndon Johnson prided himself and bragged, "I had more women by accident then he Kennedy had on purpose."[308]

Infidelity and adultery are common occurrences among the congressional delegations in Washington DC. No doubt one reason for this behavior is that the representatives and senators are separated from their wives and families for extended periods of time. An example of this kind of relationship among legislators was reported by the Detroit Free Press in 2015. According to their assistants or staffers, Cynthia Gamrat, (R., Michigan) and Todd Courser (R., Michigan) were sexually involved with each other, although both were married and had children at home. Both eventually resigned from the House.

U.S. Representative Chris Collins of Western New York was arrested in August 2018 in connection with his role on the board of a biotech firm, "Innate Immunotherapeutics." According to federal prosecutors, Collins let his son know about a failed test for drug. This allowed his son and his father-in-law to avoid $750,000 in losses by selling the company stock before it dropped, because the drug, which was expected to successfully treat secondary multiple sclerosis, failed. Collins is charged with securities fraud, conspiracy, wire fraud, and making false statements. Collins also had sponsored several bills in the House that would have directly affected his company. Nevertheless Collins won reelection to the House of Representatives in November 2018. His opponent, Nate McMurray, repeatedly reminded the voters that Collins had defrauded the owners of stock in the drug company. It made no difference to the voters. Collins was re-elected to another term in Congress.[309] It is by no means uncommon that legislators on the federal and state level are elected without regard to their moral character or their support of fidelity and monogamy. There can be little doubt that American voters are influenced by politicians who have become role models and culture heroes in the American society of the 21st century.

In November 2017, Wes Goodman, a representative to the Ohio House of representatives, was asked to resign because he was discovered to have sex with a man in his office.[310] He was the second lawmaker in Ohio whose inappropriate sexual behavior became public knowledge in the same year. It may well be that the voting public does not always know about the sex life of candidates. This is so because it is not held important by the voters. One major consequence of this attitude is that politicians influence the public, so that the politicians thereby create a disregard for family life within the confines of "moral" conduct.

During the eight years including 2010 through 2017, four hundred and fifty six

American politicians were convicted of a variety of crimes. The vast majority of these are of a financial nature or dealt with violations of the election laws. 18 of these convictions involved sexual misconduct and others consistent with violating their oath of office. For example, the mayor of San Diego, Bob Filer, were convicted of sexual misconduct.

In 2011, a state senator of Arizona, Scott Bundgaard, was convicted of assaulting his girlfriend. He resigned before he was expelled from the Arizona legislature. A heavy drinker, he was involved in other altercations.[311]

In 2013, the mayor of San Diego, Robert Filner, was forced to resign and pled guilty to charges of sexual harassment. These charges involve false imprisonment and battery of three women. He was accused by 18 women of sexual harassment. He was accused of using a headlock on a woman during a fundraising event. He was also accused of kissing a woman on the lips without her consent. A woman who asked him to photograph her said that he touched her buttocks. Filner had represented San Diego in Congress 20 years.[312]

John McGee, a member of the Idaho Senate, was arrested on June 19, 2011, for taking a stranger's sports utility vehicle and crashing into the front lawn of a residence. His blood alcohol level measured nearly double the legal driving limit.

In 2012, McGee was accused by a woman staffer of propositioning her in his fourth floor office and again the following week, suggesting she perform oral sex. The lady also said that McGee grabbed her buttocks on another occasion and that he masturbated in front of her.[313]

It is significant that McGee was installed in a responsible public position even after his drinking and sexual behavior were widely known from newspaper and public media reports.

In May 2015, former state representative Keith Farnham began an eight year prison term for distributing child pornography over the Internet. At age 69, Farnham was suffering from bladder cancer, pulmonary fibrosis, and hepatitis C.

Nevertheless he was incarcerated after investigators seized computers at his home in Elgin, Illinois, and his Springfield office. The investigators found 2750 sexually explicit images and videos of children, some as young as six months old.

The average prison term served for murder is eight years. It appears that the Illinois judiciary views distributing pornography as a crime equal to muder.[314]

Senator Virgil Smith of Michigan was jailed in March 2016 for shooting at his ex-wife's Mercedes-Benz car. He continued to receive his $71,785 salary while in prison for 10 months. Smith continue to receive the money because he did not resign from the Senate. According to the Michigan Constitution, a legislator cannot be forced to resign, although he could be expelled. Smith was also accused of attacking a woman by punching her and ramming her head into the floor.[315]

Stuart Dunning, a prosecutor in Lansing, Michigan, was charged with 15 prostitution related offenses in March 2016. Dunning was accused of using his power as prosecutor to coerce women into prostitution. Although his conduct could have led to a 20 year felony conviction, the charges were dropped in exchange for a five year felony conviction, leading him to plead guilty to misconduct in office. Dunning was evidently a steady customer of a woman who ran an escort service. Dunning's attorney arranged a plea deal for him that involved only one year in jail.[316]

In March 2016, New Hampshire representative Kyle Tasker was arrested for drug possession and intent to sexually assault a minor. Since only a mind reader can know what someone else intends, the New Hampshire police must have supernatural powers.

Tasker was charged with using Facebook messages to arrange a meeting with a 14-year-old girl with the intent to commit aggravated felonious sexual assault. Ta was also charged with offering the girl drops for sex and providing the 14-year-old with pornographic videos. Tasker was also accused of harassing a young female. Thereupon the police pretended that a 14-year-old girl meant to meet with Tasker. The 14-year-old girl was in fact a police officer. When Tasker arrived at the agreed-upon meeting place, he was armed with a loaded gun. A search of his house revealed that he was in possession of marijuana and the drug Suboxone, which the police assumed he meant to sell. Tasker was jailed and told by House Speaker of New Hampshire Sean Jasper to resign.

The facts of this case are that Tasker assaulted no one and sold no drugs. His crime was that he might have done these things at the provocation of the police.[317]

New York State Senator Marc Panepinto was imprisoned for two months in December 2018 on the grounds of having made unwanted advances toward a female staff member. Panepinto was jailed two years after he left the New York State Senate. The victim of Panepinto's sexual advances complained that these advances were unwanted. In an effort to keep the woman from complaining, Panepinto offered her a job and money. Panepinto's conduct was referred to the Joint Commission of Public Ethics. The FBI investigated in Panepinto's efforts in gaining the attentions of the complaining female. Gary Loeffert, in charge of the FBI Buffalo office, referred to Panepinto's sexual interests as public corruption and criminal misconduct.[318]

Lance Mason, a Cleveland, Ohio judge, was arrested for stabbing his wife to death on November 19, 2018. In 2015, Mason served nine months in prison for punching his wife 20 times in front of the children. Mason held the position of minority business administrator in the Cleveland government. He was arrested after the police found his former wife dead in her driveway. Mason attempted to kill himself after the death of his wife.

Ralph Shortey, a former Oklahoma state senator, was arrested for child sex trafficking in November 2017. He was charged with soliciting sex from a 17-year-old boy. He was also charged with participating in child pornography. By pleading guilty, Shortey of avoided the possibility of being sent to prison for 30 years. Shortey was also charged with engaging in child prostitution, transporting a minor for prostitution, and engaging in prostitution within 1000 feet of a church. Shortley used Facebook and Craigslist to gain access to these children. Shortey attended Heartland Baptist Bible College in Oklahoma City.[319]

Joseph F. Brennan, a state representative from Bethlehem, Pennsylvania, was sentenced in April 2018 for a third offense of drunk driving. In 2012, Brendan was charged with beating his then wife and driving away drunk, for which he served a 23 month sentence. Brendan's blood alcohol level while driving was above 0.3% at the time, which is four times the legal limit for driving.[320]

The number of elected officials who have been charged with a variety of sex offenses indicates that the American public in general resembles the behavior of the elected representatives. The sex offenses with which these elected officials are charged are a product of the Puritan spirit, which is still with us 400 years after the Massachusetts Bay colony was founded. The Puritans and such like-minded members of other denominations who have denounced sex as a crime or as sin are largely responsible for the sexual deviations leading to criminal convictions in this country. The hatred for sex leads to an effort to defeat nature. That effort must fail, as all humanity is born with a sex drive, which cannot be abolished by denunciations, criminal convictions, and imprisonment. The fact is that prostitution, pornography, sexual assault, sexual harassment, and all kinds of deviant sexual conduct come out when normal sexual expression is suppressed and criminalized. Nature cannot be defeated by religious fanaticism or the financial interests of the media.

Sports "Heroes"

Americans are very much impressed by achievements in sports. The faces of Olympic winners, and professional football, baseball, and hockey players, are exhibited on food cans and packages, and television advertisers pay well known sports "heroes" for endorsing their products. It is therefore evident that American sexual conduct is influenced by sports personalities, many of whom have been convicted of sexual assault and other forms of violence.

For example, Hector Olivera, a former Atlanta Braves outfielder, was found guilty of domestic assault and ordered to serve 10 days in jail. Olivera assaulted his girlfriend so that she needed to be treated in the hospital. There- fore major league baseball put Olivera on paid leave and suspended him 82 games under major league baseball's Domestic Violence, Sexual Assault, and Child Abuse Policy.[321]

On August 18, 2016, Darren Sharper, New Orleans Saints football player, was sentenced to 18 years in prison for drugging women in order to rape them. He committed these crimes in Louisiana, Arizona, California, and Nevada. It is noteworthy that he kept drugging and raping women even after state and federal investigators had been contacted by one of his victims. Sharper will also be supervised for three years after he gets out of prison. Sharper had been named all pro six times. He had played with the Green Bay Packers and then the Minnesota Vikings before joining the Saints. He ended a 14 year career in 2011.

On August 6, 2016, former NFL linebacker Aldon Smith was sentenced to three years' probation for drunken driving and possession of three assault rifles, as just one of multiple offenses with which Smith was charged at various times.[322]

The Entertainment Industry

Actors and actresses who appear in the movies are without doubt major role models for the American people. This is demonstrated by the numerous tabloids sold at the checkout counters of grocery stores. These tabloids incessantly recite the romantic activities of movie and television actors.

Therefore those who are most prominent also have considerable influence, per the principle of legitimacy in American culture.

It is therefore not surprising that when Hedwig Kiesler died in Orlando, Florida, in 2000, she was remembered not only in the entertainment industry among whom she was known as Hedy Lamarr, but also as an inventor of traffic stoplights, carbonated drinks, and wireless communication.

Hedy Lamarr was married six times and was elevated by the media to the most beautiful woman on earth. That was not an exaggeration, as an old photograph of her will show, which made her one of the most admired women ever in the movie industry. Lamarr had three children. James Markey was the child of Gene Markey, her second husband. She had two children with John Loder, her third husband.

However, after her movie career was over, she lived alone in Orlando, Florida. In her old age she was arrested for shoplifting and exhibited other peculiar behaviors. When she died at the age of 86 in 2000, she left $3.5 million dollars in her estate.[23]

Elizabeth Taylor was born in 1932 to a wealthy American family then living in London, England. She was raised in Los Angeles. She died in 2011 at age 79 of heart failure. She had become an alcoholic and a heavy smoker. Elizabeth Taylor had a phenomenal career as an actress, starring in many movies produced by Metro-Goldwyn-Mayer. Taylor had seven husbands and was married eight times because she married Richard Burton twice. Her first husband was Conrad Hilton, heir of Hilton hotel chain. She divorced Hilton after eight months, after meeting British actor Michael Wilding during the filming of *Ivanhoe*. Wilding became her second husband. With him she had two sons, Christopher Edward and Michael Howard. She divorced Wilding in 1957 when she met Mike Todd, her third husband, with whom she had one daughter, Elizabeth Francis. Todd died in a plane crash in 1958. Taylor began an affair with singer Eddie Fisher in 1958 and married him in a Jewish ceremony in 1959. Three years later, in 1962, Taylor starred in *Cleopatra* and met her costar Richard Burton. She and Burton entered into an "affair," leading her to divorce Fisher and marry Burton, her 5th husband. She divorced him in 1974 and remarried him in 1975, only to divorce again. Her 6th husband was Senator John Warner, whom she married in 1976 and divorced in 1989. Taylor then married Larry Forrtensky, a construction worker whom she met at the Betty Ford Center in 1988. The Betty Ford Center is a residence for alcoholics. She divorced Forrtensky in 1996 when she was 64 years old. In 1959 she had converted from Christianity to Judaism and was therefore buried in a Jewish cemetery.[24]

Frances Gumm was born in 1922. In her professional life, she was known as Judy Garland, undoubtedly one of the most talented entertainers of all time. Yet, she died at age 47 from an overdose of barbiturates. Judy Garland had five husbands, including David Rose, with whom she became pregnant but aborted the child. After divorcing Rose, she married and divorced Vincent Minelli, Sydney Luft, and Mark Harron, whom she divorced after six months. She died while married to Mickey Deans. Garland had three children, including the actress Liza Minelli, and two children with Sydney Luft. She also had "affairs" with Johnny Mercer and Orson Wells. Garland is best known for acting Dorothy in "The Wizard of Oz," which can be seen on television repeatedly. Despite her success, Garland attempted suicide for the first time in 1947. In that year also she developed a serious problem with alcohol. In 1950, she attempted suicide a second time by slashing her throat. Although she earned a great deal of money, she owed the tax collectors at the Internal Revenue Service $50,000. As a result, IRS agents seized the majority of her earnings.

Norma Jeane Mortenson was born in Los Angeles, California, in 1926 and died as Marilyn Monroe in 1962 at the age of 36 from an overdose of drugs.[325] Because she was widely advertised as a sex symbol, numerous unfounded rumors accompanied her life. There can be little doubt that she was the victim of aggressive journalists who flew helicopters over her house and implied all kinds of escapades to her.

Marilyn Monroe was married three times. Her first husband was Jimmy Dougherty, followed by baseball player Joe DiMaggio and the playwright Arthur Miller. Monroe appeared in over forty movies, including "Gentlemen Prefer Blondes," "The Misfits," "Niagara," and others.

Monroe never met her father. Her mother was incarcerated in a mental institution. She therefore spent her youth in foster homes, where she was sexually assaulted. Her life was permanently influenced by her painful childhood, which no success could eradicate. Like so many other actors, she died alone and unloved. Her life is a gross example of how fame and good fortune can be a road to misery.

Elvis Presley died on April 16, 1977. He was 6 feet tall and weighed 350 pounds. While there was some dispute as to the cause of death, there can be no doubt that drugs, particularly codeine, were present in his body at 10 times the prescribed dose. At the time of his death, Elvis Presley was undoubtedly the most well-known popular singer in America. He had developed a style of singing which made him unique, not only among the performers of his day but for all the years since he died. His former home is visited by thousands each year and he is labeled The King in popular culture. Presley not only sang rock 'n roll songs but also performed in several movies. He had a very high income and a large following and yet he died of drugs, which he believed he needed. From January 1977 to the day of his death, August 16, 1977, Presley took 8805 pills and numerous injections. Back in January 1975 he had absorbed 19,012 pills.

It is significant that Presley appeared to be very successful but yet was miserable and needed pills to live in reality. Presley was and is a role model for many Americans, to their detriment.

Presley was born on January 8, 1935, to a poor family in Tupelo, Mississippi. His success was the result of his exceptional talent and determination. In 1950, Elvis Presley met 14 year old Priscilla Beaulieu, whom he married in 1967 and divorced in 1973. They had one child, Lisa Marie. After Elvis Presley's death, his ex-wife transformed his former home, Graceland, into a tourist attraction. Since his death, Elvis Presley has been named one of the most popular entertainers ever. In 2018, a two-part documentary was released which explores his life, his rise to fame, and his musical influence.[326]

The Drug Epidemic

The Center for Disease Control has published the ever-increasing number of drug overdose deaths occurring in the United States in this century. According to the CDC, from 1999 to 2017, 700,000 people have died from a drug overdose. In 2017, the overdose deaths involving opioids like heroin were six times higher than in 1999. About 130 Americans die every day from opioid overdose. In 2013, significant numbers of synthetic opioids were manufactured.[327]

The Entertainment Industry and the "Me Too" movement

In the early 21st century, the role of American women had changed dramatically if compared to their condition in the 20th century. By 2000, American women had become emancipated enough to gain considerable economic successes, to become the majority of college students, and to enter into the major professions, which were at one time the province of men alone.[328]

The entertainment industry also changed in the 21st century, so that women began to assert themselves and began to resist the casting couch tradition, which for generations allowed men in control of casting women in theater and movie roles to exploit women sexually.

Among those men who had for years use their power to give women an opportunity to act in the movie industry was Harvey Weinstein, founder and president of Miramax Pictures, one of the most productive and successful movie studios in Hollywood. Weinstein became one of the richest Americans because of his success in producing movies which employed many of the most famous actresses of the 20th and early 21st centuries. Yet, in October 2017, the New York Times published a lengthy article concerning allegations against Harvey Weinstein stretching over three decades. These allegations concerned Weinstein's sexual behavior towards women employed by him or seeking employment. According to the New York Times, and documented through interviews with current and former employees and legal records of all of Miramax and the Weinstein Company, Weinstein was cited in the Times for sexual harassment and unwanted physical contact with female employees. It was also disclosed that Weinstein reached at least eight settlements with women. Among these were a young assistant, an actress and another assistant in London, England, an Italian model, and others. All of this became known to the *New York Times* when Lauren O'Connor, a colleague of a sexually exploited female employee, sent a memo concerning sexual harassment by Weinstein to several executives at Weinstein's company. Weinstein evidently demanded that female applicants at his company had to meet him in his private hotel room.

All of Weinstein's employees signed a confidentiality clause in the contracts saying they will not criticize him or his company. The women who accepted payouts agreed to confidentiality prohibiting them from speaking about the deals or the events relating to Harvey Weinstein. Even Lauren O'Connor, who had sent the original memo concerning Weinstein's behavior, accepted a settlement with Weinstein and thanked him for the career opportunity he had given her.

The *New York Times* reporters who interviewed numerous women who had contacts with Weinstein said that many women in his company would not visit him alone but always brought someone else. That raises the question of how Weinstein could have continued his assault against women for 30 years before it all became public.

Even before the *New York Times* article recited most of his misconduct towards women, Weinstein was confronted by an Italian model who came to see him in his office, where he grabbed her breasts. She called the police, which made his behavior public.[329]

The article concerning Weinstein came to the attention of Tarana Burke, who had founded a "Me Too Movement," allowing women to complain about sexual harassment on the part of powerful men. That movement in turn led to the exposure of 201 powerful men accused of sexual misconduct. It also led to the indictment of Harvey Weinstein on an accusation of rape and to his dismissal from the Weinstein Company. Accused of raping a woman in a New York hotel room, he faces five felony charges for other kinds of sexual assault on as many women.[330] It is doubtful that his considerable contributions to Democratic politicians, including Barack Obama and Hillary Clinton, would help him in his defense.

The public denunciation of Weinstein and his several court appearances led to the denunciation of 201 men who lost their jobs or major roles in the filming industry. There can be little doubt that movie actors and actresses are role models in American culture, so that a good number of men may well have been influenced by their misconduct towards women. Those men who lost their jobs were given no opportunity to defend themselves, but were dismissed on the statements of one or more women alone.

One of the most prominent television hosts who was suddenly dismissed from his job is Bill O'Reilly. The official reason for his dismissal was the allegation by the *New York Times* that his employer, Fox News, had settled five harassment complaints brought by Fox employees over a 15 year period. The sexual harassment of which O'Reilly was accused was entirely verbal. O'Reilly may have said things which could be interpreted as harassment and /or could have been ignored. His ouster is a prime example of the hysteria which often accompanies social movements.[331]

Matt Lauer was 60 years old when he was suddenly fired from NBC for alleged sexual misconduct. Lauer had been a news anchor for many years and was hosting the Today show in November 2017 when he was suddenly dismissed because a woman claimed to have been harassed. Consequently, the network investigated other complaints alleging sexual harassment, and held nearly 70 interviews with current and former employees and 30 focus groups with 262 employees. One employee claimed that she was sexually assaulted by Lauer in his office. Lauer has denied the accusation of sexual assault.[332]

James Levine, 74, for 40 years the music director and conductor of the Metropolitan Opera Company, was dismissed March 12, 2018 on the grounds of having been "sexually abusive and harassing." Levine had the reputation of being the greatest American conductor since Leonard Bernstein. Because of American sexual obsession, the New York Times now seeks to revoke his musical achievements, despite the fact that these achievements cannot reasonably be disregarded by reason of his sexual offenses.

Evidently James Levine, like so many, has become the victim of an overall assault on male behavior, which is expected by women and their supporters to resemble that of females and not males.

It costs the Metropolitan Opera $300 million a year to run, so that it is highly reliant on the generosity of wealthy donors. These donations came into question when the New York Times reported that Mr. Levine sexually abused four men, an accusation James Levine denies. Levine was also accused by police in Illinois of sexually abusing a teenage boy. Evidently the New York Times went back decades to prove its arguments against Mr. Levine. James Lestock, a cellist, told the New York Times that he was abused by Mr. Levine when he was a student. Likewise, Albin Ifsich, a violinist with the New Jersey Symphony Orchestra, said he had been abused by James Levine for several years in Cleveland and in New York. Ashok Pai said that he was abused by James Levine he was 16 years old at a music festival in Illinois.

Levine conducted more than 2500 performances at the Metropolitan Opera.[333]

Brett Ratner, a successful film director in Hollywood, has been accused of sexual harassment and misconduct. Six women, including actresses Olivia Munn and Natasha Herstridge, accuse Ratner of aggressive, abusive, and unwanted sexual behavior. Brett was accused by a 19-year-old fashion model of being forced to perform oral sex. Ratner was further accused by another actress of masturbating in front of her in his trailer. Another woman, Jamie Ray Newman, told the LA Times that when sitting next to her on a plane, Ratner began loudly describing sex he wanted to perform on her. Actress Katherine Towne met Brett at a party in 2005, where he harassed her in a number of ways. Another actress claimed that at a party Ratner ran his index finger down her bare stomach and asked if she wanted to go into a bathroom with him. A survey by the LA Times of coworkers with Ratner found that all agreed that Ratner is a sexual predator.[334]

Leslie Moonves, 68, chairman of the Columbia Broadcasting System, was forced out of his job for numerous allegations of sexual misconduct. Moonves was considered the most powerful executive in America when he became victim of the "Me Too" movement. Six women accused Mooves of sexual misconduct and intimidation. Mooves was charged with forced oral sex, exposing himself, and committing violent acts between 1980 and 2000. He was also accused of pushing his organ into the mouth of a female lunch companion. This woman, Phyllis Golden Gottlieb, complained to the Los Angeles Police Department after the statute of limitations had run out. On another occasion, Moonves left his office and returned not wearing pants and then threw a woman against the wall. Other women described being forced to sing, groping and propositions all during working time.[335]

Drug addiction which kills is particularly widespread among popular musicians. These musicians receive wide acclaim among adolescents and are without doubt role models and culture heroes among young Americans. So many popular musicians have died over the years from the overuse of drugs that even a review of the most recent deaths among singers, rappers, and record producers leads to a long list of those who have died from drugs. Mac Miller, an American rapper, singer, and record producer, overdosed on fentanyl, cocaine, and alcohol. Dolores O'Riordan, musician, singer, and songwriter, drowned due to alcohol intoxication. Lil Peep, an American rapper and singer, overdosed on a fentanyl and Xanax prescription. Tom Petty, singer and songwriter, overdosed on prescription drugs including fentanyl and oxycodone. Scott Weiland, a musician, singer, and songwriter, overdosed on cocaine, alcohol, and MDA, an illegal drug. Corey Monteith, an actor and singer, died from a toxic heroin and alcohol combination, and Chris Kelly, a rapper, died from an overdose of cocaine and heroin. Jeff Hanneman, a musician, died from cirrhosis due to alcoholism, and the famous Whitney Houston, a singer and actress, drowned from the use of cocaine.

Amy Winehouse, a famous English singer, and songwriter, died from fatal alcohol poisoning, and Michael Jackson, a major pop singer and icon, suffered cardiac arrest as a result of acute propofol intoxication, as well as four additional illegal drugs. The American bass guitarist Howie Epstein died from a heroin overdose and the use of prescription antibiotics and the use of illegal drugs. Douglas Glenn Coleman, also known as Dee Dee Ramone, a singer and songwriter, died from a heroin overdose and illegal drugs. Chris Farley, a comedian, actor, and television personality, died from an overdose of morphine and cocaine complicated by heart disease. Margot Hemingway, an American actress, overdosed on phenobarbital and committed suicide. Likewise, Phyllis Hyman, an American singer-songwriter and actress, used a fatal overdose of phenobarbital to commit suicide. Chet Baker, a jazz musician, singer, trumpet player, and guitarist, fell from his hotel window and died, having used cocaine, heroin, and other illegal drugs. The famous actor Richard Burton died from a cerebral hemorrhage due to alcohol and alcoholism. John Belushi, an American actor, comedian, and musician who appeared on *Saturday Night Live* and other comedy shows, used speedball, and overdosed on a combination of heroin and cocaine.

The number of singers, musicians and other entertainers who have died from drug overdoses is so extensive that it has had a major effect on the drug use of Americans, leading to the epidemic of heroin deaths repeatedly cited by the president of the United States.[336]

This picture of role models and culture heroes in 21st century America has a number of consequences. Among these is the exaggerated and dangerous behavior of many men, sometimes referred to by the Spanish name macho. A good number of American men believe that aggression towards women enhances their masculine standing. This exaggerated masculinity is encouraged by high school sports, which emphasize aggression over academic success and football over algebra. American boys learn to have contempt for girls and women, an attitude leaving to violence and sexual misconduct.

Sexual assault, including rape and other violence, is also the outcome of opportunity. Prior to the emancipation of women in the 21st century, women were largely housewives who did not work outside the home and were therefore not available for aggression to which they are subject in the early 21st century. Many men have not yet accepted that women can "be there" in business and in the professions and that some women have become leaders in industry, politics, science, and scholarship. Undoubtedly the sexual mistreatment of women is related to the sex drive inherent in all. Nevertheless it is also competition for power which drives many men who mistreat women. Powerful women are still unusual and frequently resented by men. Therefore it is reasonable to assume that aggression against women by men is a power trip seeking to "put women in their place," which is no longer that of a follower but that of the leader, such as the president of General Motors or the speaker of the House of Representatives.

Chapter 9. Adolescent Sex

Human behavior is largely controlled by nature, including our drives, which are the product of biological imperatives. The sex drive, which is strongest in young people, is therefore a part of human development. In primitive societies which are not complicated by technology, there are numerous rules as to who may reproduce with whom. In some cultures, sex is entirely endogamous while in others it is exogamous. Both endogamy and exogamy are common in American life. Prior to the 21st century, sex was almost entirely restricted to adults and literally prohibited to children under the age of 18. The endogamy-exogamy concept was therefore age-related. Because birth control was primitive and not very effective, the effort to prevent the birth of unwanted children consisted of repressing sex among those too young to support any offspring. In addition, disease control was also ineffective, so that socially acquired diseases such as syphilis and gonorrhea could not be eliminated. In the 21st century, all of this has changed. Birth control is very much effective and at least some socially acquired diseases, but by no means all, are fairly well controlled. Therefore, sexual activity among adolescents is far more common than in past years. This means that young people in the United States in 2019 have sex for the first time at about the age of 17 and marriage has been postponed to the mid-20s. During the decade between the onset of sexual behavior and marriage, unintended pregnancy and sexually transmitted diseases have increased dramatically.[337]

Some Relevant Facts

Since 2010, 49% of unmarried 15- 19-year-old males and 44% of females have had sexual intercourse, although the proportion of those having sex before age 15 has declined in recent years. Between 2011 and 2013, about 13% of married females age 15 to 19 and 18% of married males in that age group had sex before age 15.[338]

The most common reason that adolescents aged 15 to 19 gave for not having had sex was that it was against religion or morals. The second reason for not having at sex was that they had not found the right person and the third reason was that they wanted to avoid pregnancy.

Among sexually experienced adolescents aged 15 to 19, 16% of females and 28% of males reported having had first sex with someone they had just met or who was "just a friend." All the others had a first sexual experience with a steady partner, a cohabiter, a fiancé, or a spouse.

3% of males and 8% of females age 18 to 19 said their sexual orientation was lesbian, gay or bisexual.[339]

Almost all births among women aged 15 to 19 occur outside of marriage. This was true of 89% in 2013, although in the last several years non-marital births among adolescents have declined from 52% in 1975 to 15% in 2013.[340]

One result of childbirths outside of marriage is that the youngest girls who give birth to babies cannot support these children because they do not have enough education and/or work skills with which to maintain themselves and their children. Therefore it is the taxpayer who has to pay the cost of maintaining these children and their mothers. According to *The Guide to Federal Temporary Assistance for Needy Families* published by The Department of Health and Human Services, federal expenditures for "Family Preservation" amounted to $797,624,580 in 2017.

The U.S. Census Bureau reports that in 2017 there were eleven million six hundred thousand (11,600,000) single parent families in the United States. 81.5% of these single parent families were headed by single mothers. 36% were poor and 28% were jobless in an entire year and 32% did not have enough food.

50% of single mothers were never married, 29% were divorced, and 21% were either separated or widowed. The median income for families led by single mothers in 2017 was about $35,400. The median income for married couples was $85,300. About 4,100,000 of the 10 million low income working families were headed by a single working mother. All of this means that single mothers are the poorest of Americans. The poverty rate for single mother families was 36%, which is nearly 5 times more than the poverty rate for married couples, which is 7%. 1/7 of all single mother families used food pantries and one third spent more than half of the income on housing. Families headed by single mothers are without doubt the poorest Americans and therefore the most likely candidates for homelessness. A majority of single mothers, that is 59%, received food stamps and 15% receive cash benefits. At least 15% of single mothers have no health coverage. Access to childcare is also difficult for single mothers, particularly in New York, Massachusetts, and Oregon, where single mothers with an infant would have to pay more than half of their income for daycare. About 15% of single mothers have not completed high school, although 36% hold a college degree.[341]

These statistics are an objective picture of the outcome of sexual activity for many young women. There are those who see no difficulty at all with the onset of sexual behavior at age 17, which is now common in the United States. Yet the pain and suffering of single mothers and children who have never met their father and who live in a family clearly supported by public assistance cannot be brushed aside by displaying the intact family, supported by at least one parent if not both. It is easy to say that sex at 17 is an indication of sexual liberation and freedom from constraint. Yet such slogans don't make the lives of single mothers and fatherless children any easier.

Sex in High School

Among some unwelcome conditions related to sexuality is sexual harassment in schools. It is unwanted and unwelcome behavior of a sexual nature that interferes with the right to receive an equal educational opportunity. Sexual harassment is regarded as a form of discrimination that is prohibited by Title IX, a federal law establishing civil rights in education. This law refers to harassing behavior that can interfere with one's educational opportunity, either by words, whether written or spoken, or by physical contact. Such behavior may also be a criminal act, such as assault or rape or child sex abuse.[342]

The Office for Civil Rights of the United States Department of Education recognizes two forms of unlawful sexual harassment in education. The first is the so-called quid pro quo (this for that) harassment, in which a school employee has to submit to sexual advances in return for participation in an educational program. This second form of sexual harassment in schools is called hostile environment harassment. This includes sexual advances, requests for sexual favors, or any other verbal or nonverbal behavioral of physical contact of a sexual nature by a student or employee or third-party. This form of sexual harassment is the most frequent in schools. According to a study by Louis Harris and Associates, Inc. there is a universal culture of sexual harassment with no significant racial difference flourishing in American secondary schools. 83% of girls and 60% of boys report sexual harassment in schools.[343]

Another unwelcome outcome of sexual behavior among high school students is the proliferation of sexually transmitted diseases. These diseases are passed from one person to another through sexual contact. They include chlamydia, gonorrhea, genital herpes, human papilloma virus, syphilis, and HTV. Although some sexually transmitted diseases can be treated and cured, herpes and HIV cannot be cured.[344]

Sexual Activity

According to The Youth Risk Behavioral Survey, 59% of students' grades 9 to 12 say that they have not had sex. However, 41% report having sexual intercourse. This constitutes a decrease from 54% to 41% of those who have had sex. Contraceptive use has increased among this cohort, so that the US reached its lowest teen pregnancy and birthrate in years.[345]

Three quarters of teen females and 5% of males had their first sex with a steady partner. 16% of females and 28% had their first sex with someone they had just met or was just a friend. About 4% of students report having had sex before the age of 13.[346]

Inexperienced young girls sometimes panic after delivering a baby. The birth of a baby can affect some single young mothers in a most unfortunate matter. There are some mothers who become so distraught by such an event that they kill their own child. This seems like a monstrous crime but is by no means unknown. For example, in July 2017, the remains of an infant were found buried in a backyard. The child had died more than two months earlier. It had been alive, not stillborn. The mother was Brooke Richardson, who was 18 years old at the time. She was charged with reckless homicide[347].

Likewise, a 14-year-old girl was charged with the death of her newborn baby boy in Highland Park, N.J. The 14-year-old was charged with an act of juvenile delinquency and indicted for murder in the first degree. The newborn child had been abandoned outside a residence at midnight.

New Jersey was also the scene of a body of a 10 month old baby girl which was found in a suitcase along the train tracks in Jersey City. Further, a baby boy of about two days was found alive and hospitalized.[348]

Teen Pregnancy Affects Graduation Rates

30% of all teenage girls who drop out of school say that pregnancy and parenthood is the major reason. This demonstrates how early pregnancy can have a lifelong effect on those unprepared to earn a livelihood. 36% of Hispanic girls who drop out of school are pregnant. Among African-Americans, 38% or more are so burdened.

Educational achievement affects the lifetime income of mothers. The evidence is that two thirds of families started by teens are poor and nearly one in four will depend on welfare within three years of the child's birth. Many of the children of teens continue this cycle of poverty. Only about two thirds of children born to mothers in high school earn a high school diploma, compared to 81% of the majority of high school students. Girls who give birth while attending a community college are 60% less likely to complete their degree as compared to women who do not have children during that time.[349]

Children of teen mothers are 50% more likely to repeat a grade and are more likely than children born to other mothers to drop out of high school.

Sex and Higher Education

Adolescence (ad lescere, Latin, meaning "toward growth") is by no means at an end on graduating from high school. In fact, it extends into the college years. Therefore it is appropriate to examining campus sexuality in America.

One feature of campus sex is the frequency of sexual assault. According to the Bureau of Justice Statistics, 11.2% of American female college students say they have experiences rape or sexual assault, violence, or incapacitation.

Among graduate and professional students, such as medical, dental or law students, 8% of female and 22% of male students experience rape or sexual assault through violence, force, or incapacitation. Male college students age 18-24 are 78%. Female college students are 20% less likely than non-students to be raped or sexually assaulted. Only one in six female victims of sexual violence received assistance from a victim service agency. 21% of transgender students have been sexually assaulted.[350]

31% of female college students do not report sexual assault to the police because they believe that the police cannot do anything about it. Others did not report sexual violence for fear of reprisals or because they did not want to be publically shamed.

College sex is often called "hook-up" sex. This consists of so-called "one night stands" in that the sexual activity is conducted with someone, possibly a "friend," but even with a stranger. As a result, 25% of college women report having been raped.[351]

Both college men and women report that their greatest fear concerning the sex culture in college is rejection. This sentiment was voiced by students at all colleges visited by New Yorker Magazine reporters, including New York University, Tulane, Dartmouth, Bard, and the so-called "Big Ten".

Alcohol and Sex

The presence of alcohol in American colleges is so widespread that it no longer receives any major attention. It is "taken for granted" that alcohol will be present at all student social gatherings and that those who want to enjoy the friendship of other students must drink alcohol with them. Therefore sex is also related to alcohol consumption by both women and men. Therefore sexual victimization and unsafe sex accompany the drinking bouts so common at college fraternities and sororities. The excessive use of alcohol also includes alcohol addiction as well as liver and cardiovascular disease. There is a difference between the sexes concerning the outcome of alcohol consumption. Women metabolize alcohol more slowly and reach high blood alcohol concentrations more quickly than men, thereby leaving women at risk of sexual assault.[352]

College women drink more than non-college women of the same age and they also drink more frequently. Collegiate culture is mainly responsible for the heavy drinking of college women and men. Moving away from home for the first time without parental supervision induces many first year female college students to try sex and alcohol.[353]

The college environment includes alcohol in all social situations and leads students to believe that alcohol facilitates friendship and relationships for the incoming freshman class and consequently for the next four years. College students and many other people also believe that drunkenness makes social relationships easier and eliminates fear of rejection. These beliefs motivate heavy drinking. The need for peer approval and close relationships with other students, and the anxiety to be popular with the opposite sex, contribute to increased alcohol intake.[354]

Not only among college students but among all Americans, there are those who seek to deal with stressful events in their lives by drinking alcohol. No human being is exempt from pain, disappointment, and defeat. Women even more than men are subject to psychosocial stress. Therefore many Americans drink to deal with painful events in their lives and to handle the emotionally upsetting situations which face college females, who exhibit greater interpersonal stress when managing the new college environment as freshmen. Academic pressure, an unfamiliar environment, and autonomy from parents all lead to excessive drinking and sexual behavior including lack of inhibition, increased sexual pleasure, and the discovery of sexual opportunities. Compared to students who abstain from both sex and alcohol, the sexually active are more likely to possess nonconformist personalities and therefore take greater risks drinking alcohol with more sex related activities.[355]

The Party School

Throughout the United States, there are colleges located in small towns. Most of these schools were founded in the 19th century or before, either by Christian or public supporters. These colleges taught the liberal arts to young men away from the influence of the big cities for the sake of maintaining morals and decorum. In the 21st century, the majority of college students are women, and party schools are preferred by many students, as sex and alcohol dominate the college scene. Since the students in small town colleges pay considerable tuition and have many other living expenses which become income to the college and to the small-town residents' businesses, partying, riotous behavior, and an anti-intellectual attitude cannot be criticized by those whose livelihood depends on income derived from students. Colleges depend on high retention rates and need students to return each year. Small-town merchants need the money students spend. Therefore, sex, alcohol, and drugs become the foundation of the party schools.

Small towns with colleges differ from other small towns in that they have in the population a highly educated faculty. These faculty members usually live in neighborhoods almost exclusively inhabited by academics. This comes about because of mutual interest and also because the income of professors is generally higher than that of people in the town. Sometimes labeled faculty row, the faculty members and their families occupy structures generally furnished in a manner approved by the upper-middle-class ethos. They all look the same. Family life in small town colleges differs from faculty life in large cities. Colleges located in cities allow professors a life outside of the occupation.

In small town colleges, however, everything that goes on the campus becomes fodder for gossip in town.[356] Who has been appointed, who has been promoted, and who did or did not receive tenure, all becomes part of the entertainment of the faculty community and their families. A play and movie, *Who's Afraid of Virginia Woolf*, captures these conditions well.

There is no other environment. Department chairs, deans, provosts, and a host of other sycophants dominate the social scene, as the wives of the male professors genuflect before the all mighty college presidents' wife at "the small town college."

Fraternities and Sororities

Student life centers mainly on fraternities and sororities at small town colleges. These organizations are also found on the campuses of large cities. They compete with many other recreational opportunities for students and with a considerable number of those who live at home. The student at the small college is dependent entirely on the friendship and camaraderie of other students, and therefore has little choice but to join fraternities and sororities.

The need to be associated with other students and to be popular is at least one factor in favoring a sex life in college. The so-called sexual revolution which has affected all Americans is another reason for unmarried youthful sexuality. Sexual expression on campus is often, therefore, in the form of a so-called "hookup," as men and women move from one to the other, having sex with people they barely know. Because this kind of sexual expression is so unsatisfactory, there are those students who reject all this and do not engage in sexual behavior. Furthermore, approaching someone for sexual purposes or not being chosen is frightening since it means rejection, which is the greatest fear college students have. Then there is coercion, which is feared by women. Coercion includes sexual assault on campus. As many as 25% of college women report having been raped.[157]

Because of these experiences, a good number of students choose no sex, so that about 40% of college students polled by *New York Magazine* claim to be virgins. These students did not want "backward dating," which puts sex first. There are even students who "hookup" regularly but find it unsatisfactory and seek more permanent relationships. This comes about because 70% of students polled say they have been in love at least once. Included in the sex scene in party colleges are also those students who will not drink alcohol nor have sex but participate in the party's activities. These students are also those who remain sober and drive the others home. As may well be expected there are students who had one or two sex experiences with one person with whom they finally associated permanently.

Homosexuality, both lesbian and gay, are well known on the party college circuits.

Here, the straight, the lesbian, the gay, and the transgender, claim that there are five genders, a policy which some colleges recognize.

Nearly 2000 students die from alcohol-related injuries each year. Every year, an estimated 1823 students between the ages of 18 and 24 died from injuries sustained by excessive alcohol consumption. This constitutes nearly 1 death for every two colleges in America. Almost 599,000 students are intentionally injured due to the effects of alcohol. Out of 4140 colleges in the United States, there are 145 injuries for every single campus. College drinking deaths were 26.7% from 1999 to 2015. In 2005 there were 1825 deaths, which were an increase of 27% from the 1440 deaths in 1998. Freshmen account for more than one third of college student deaths. The most dangerous year related to alcohol related deaths is the first year of college. While freshmen are only 24% of the total population of college students, they make up much more than their share of the number of deaths. Freshmen commit 40% of undergraduate suicides and have 47% of fatal accidents such as falling out the window or from a rooftop because of drinking alcohol. 53% of college students experience depression. The separation from family and familiar surroundings, the lack of sleep, leads college students to much of this destructive behavior. Some have estimated that 1.5% of students tried to commit suicide because of drinking or drug use.[358]

These are some real case histories of death by alcohol.

"Man Against Himself:" Alcohol, Sex, and Drugs

Dr. Karl Meninger's book *Man Against Himself* deals with self-destruction,[359] an inclination that is well illustrated by the numerous deaths of young college students at so-called party schools. Here sex and alcohol are dominant and little is learned and little expected from students; they are colleges in name only.

Because sex is an emotional experience, it — and lack of it — has consequences which the students like to drown in alcohol. Moreover, the party schools which promote sex also promote the use of alcohol, so that the two are joined together, often with gruesome consequences. Drinking alcohol facilitates sexual relationships by reducing inhibitions. In addition, many college students find it necessary to show off and exhibit themselves by binge drinking to the applause of other students. Lists of students who have died from drinking can be found on the computer. Those young folks who drink themselves to death usually do so in the company of friends of both sexes.

Some Case Histories

Michael Anderson, 19 years old, scaled an exterior wall of a 20-foot cooling tower at the University of Arizona. After reaching the roof, Anderson fell and died, having absorbed a considerable amount of alcohol prior to this adventure.[360]

Sierra Markee Winkler died on May 5, 2014, after falling off a cliff on an island beach close to the University of California Santa Barbara campus. Winkler had a blood alcohol content of 0.25 when she was found dead on the beach.

Thomas "Dulle" Brogan was found dead of an apparent suicide on May 27, 2014. He had been drinking with friends and his blood alcohol level was determined to be 0.19. Brogan was a University of Cincinnati student. He was 21 years old. For some time before he was found, he seemed to have disappeared and many fellow citizens were searching for him. He was finally discovered lying on the floor of a building next to his apartment.[361]

Ryan Uhre, 23, died on February 18, 2014. He fell from the second floor window of an abandoned building. He tested positive for cocaine, alcohol, and weed. He was enrolled in Florida State University at Tallahassee. Having recently graduated, he planned to go to law school. On February 7, 2014, his fraternity brothers reported him missing to Florida State police. On February 18, 2014, police discovered his body.[362]

Abram Sorek, 23, a student at St. Vincent College, was shot and killed by his best friend on February 13, 2015. His friend and he had been drinking beer and vodka for several hours. From the bar where they were drinking, they went to the home of another friend. They discussed buying a gun. His friend Michael Wilcko brought a handgun to a hot tub which they were using. The murder was not viewed as accidental by the district attorney because the shooter had absorbed a great deal of alcohol, including vodka. He pointed the gun at his friend and killed him because he was drunk. This meant that he was responsible for this death.

There are people who claim that they are not guilty of a crime because they were drunk at the time they injured others. The contrary is the case. A drunk person is responsible for his drinking and all its consequences.

On May 1, 2014, Stephen Guillermo, 26, a student at San Francisco University, drank a whole night then attempted to enter the wrong apartment in a building on a different floor than his. The owner of the apartment, Amisi Sudi Kachepa, shot Guillermo as he made an effort to force open the door early on the Saturday morning. Kachepa was arrested. According to Mark Guillermo, the victim's brother, Stephen was studying international business and worked driving for a ride sharing service and selling athletic shoes. This tragedy could have been avoided if the victim had not been drunk and if the shooter had not been aggressively willing to shoot first and think later. In this case, both the shooter and the victim were responsible for the death of the young man, who was looking forward to an entire life but had it cut short by alcohol.

Marissa Madrid, a student at Chico State University in California, died at the age of 22 when she fell from a tree in a recreational area in the early morning of April 23, 2013. She had climbed on a tree branch, about 20 feet off the ground, and struck her head on concrete. She died of her injuries. She had been drinking in downtown bars all evening, so that her blood alcohol level was tested to be 0.11.[363]

Evan Alexander Green pleaded not guilty in a San Louis Obispo County Superior Court to gross vehicular manslaughter while intoxicated, driving under the influence of alcohol causing injury, and driving without a license. Two men died in an accident caused by the intoxication of the driver. Those who died were Aaron Beaver, a 21-year-old student, and Marquis Nelson, also 20 and also a student. The driver Green showed a blood alcohol level of 0.245.[364]

Julia Catherine Gilbert, 21, a student at Oklahoma University, was found dead in her wrecked car on January 8, 2010. She had been at a party at a friend's house. Her car was upside down in the ditch when she was found after numerous residents searched for her. She had watched a football game but then was missing at about 3:30 A.M., the police said. She was last seen leaving a friend's house, driving to her parents' house in Edmont, OK. She was alone in her car when she struck a guardrail. Her alcohol concentration was 0.14% in her liver and 0.24 in her brain.[365]

On March 9, 2009, Noah Krolm, 22, died one week before graduating from the University of California at Santa Barbara. He was the victim of acute and chronic ethanol abuse. Toxicology reports show that his blood alcohol content was 0.257 at that time of his death. Noah jumped a fence at a cliff and fell to his death. In May, 2009, Sarah Tahmassebi, a second year student at the University of California at Santa Barbara, died after ingesting a number of intoxicants. It was reported that Sarah often "partied." On the day of her death she met with friends using cocaine as well as alcohol. On arriving home, Sarah fell to her bedroom floor. Several of her friends saw this and believed she had merely passed out, when in fact she had died. She had a blood alcohol level of 1.46% in addition testing positive for heroin, anti-depressants and muscle relaxants. The Santa Barbara University student community uses prescription drugs and anti-anxiety medication as a form of recreation. Like Sarah Tahmassebi, Chad Anderson Briner was found dead on the UCSB campus while sleeping on a recliner. Chad used prescription drugs. Nick Pancantoni, also a student at UCSB, died on March 9, 2009, after using heroin and a number of other intoxicants. It appears that the University of California Santa Barbara is so drug ridden that it is indeed a dangerous party school. Yet tuition at UCSB costs $12,250 or more per year.

Devin Arnold, 22, was found dead along a railroad track. Arnold was a student at Colorado State University studying mechanical engineering. He had attended a game in the company of his fraternity brothers and other students when he disappeared. He had left his companions several times and finally did not return to his seat. It appears that Devin Arnold committed suicide. While attending a game with his friends, Arnold was extremely intoxicated and was asked to leave the auditorium for that reason. He was hit by an oncoming train. His body was later found by a railroad employee. There is little doubt that Arnold was the victim of alcohol.[366]

Charles Terreni, Jr., 18, son of a prominent lawyer and a freshman at the University of South Carolina, died on April 8, 2015. He had a blood alcohol level more than four times the legal driving limit at the time of his death. His alcohol level was 0.375. Terreni was found dead at the campus house of Pi Kappa Alpha fraternity after an all-night party. As usual, that chapter's suspension was a measure which seldom makes any difference. For the family this is a horror caused by the irresponsible drinking, which is labeled "a good time."

Twenty year old University of Minnesota student Dylan Fulton died on September 12, 2018, in a fraternity house near the campus of the University. The cause of death was asphyxia with aspiration. At once the national organization of Alpha Gamma Rho suspended the University of Minnesota's chapter. Fulton was a sophomore majoring in animal science. His death was also related to ethanol intoxication. Fulton was a sophomore.[367]

These episodes plainly show that the alcohol culture in the United States is threatening millions of Americans who have learned that the ordinary pressures of everyday life cannot be faced nor resisted in a sober and rational manner. Innumerable young people learn from their parents and other adults that, faced with any difficulties or frustrations, we need to resort to the use of alcohol and other drugs in order to overcome or live with any frustration, any disappointment, any threat, or any loss. We are evidently also afraid to assert ourselves and to be independent. Therefore we are easily pressured to do things which are not in our interest but instead demonstrate how we can act against ourselves. Alcohol hazing related deaths have become far too common in fraternity culture. Students who engage in this kind of behavior ignore the dangers and even fail to understand its consequences. For example, those who see someone pass out usually claim that the target will sleep it off. Instead, many die. This leaves reasonable people to ask why this slaughter goes on and on when the tragedies that come from this behavior are predictable.

Alcohol and Drug Use in American Culture

Any attempt to explain the widespread abuse of alcohol and other drugs by college students must include a recognition of the alcohol and drug culture in the United States. Many college students come from families that drink alcohol to excess and/or use drugs other than alcohol.

The percentage of Americans drinking alcohol in general and in ways that are at high risk of probable cause of death has become a public health crisis. Indeed, a moderate amount of alcohol prevents disease and is beneficial. Exactly the opposite is true of excessive drinking, which can lead to cancer, stroke, heart disease, cirrhosis of the liver, diabetes, and a number of psychiatric problems and a high risk of death. Physicians estimate that about 16 million Americans have alcohol use disorder, also known as problem drinking. In a study published by the *Journal of the American Medical Association*, a team of researchers at the National Institute on Alcohol Abuse and Alcoholism found that having four or more drinks a day constitutes a high risk for women. For men, five drinks a day constitute a high risk. In the course of 12 months, researchers found that the percentage of people who consumed alcohol the previous year rose by 11.2%, particularly among women. This excessive use of alcohol leads to high risk driving. Some 30% of drinkers are drinking 4 to 5 drinks a day. The problem drinkers constitute 9.7% to 12.6%, representing 20.2 million people to 29.6 million Americans who drink too much. This means that one in eight Americans fit the diagnostic criteria for alcoholism. It is therefore not surprising that college students drink to excess, since they come from families who are also drinking and using drugs.[368]

Although these unnecessary deaths from alcohol and drug use are far too many, it is heartening to discover that since 2016 the use of illicit drugs other than marijuana has declined to the lowest level in 41 years. Alcohol use and binge drinking also declined. Misuse of prescription opioids also declined among high school and college students, from 8.7% to 4.8%. Heroin abuse also remained low.[369, 370]

Chapter 10. Sex Education

The earliest form of sex education in the United States was undertaken by Sylvester Graham (1794–1851). Graham was a Presbyterian minister who became a leading figure in the temperance movement. He was interested in dietary reform, but was also seeking to improve the moral character of his fellow citizens. He lectured that both sexes should wear loose fitting clothing to make them unisex. He also recommended taking cold baths, sleeping on hard beds, having three meals without snacks, eating unheated food, and exercising. He then dealt with sexual activity, claiming that eating only recommended food would decrease interest in sex. Because he spoke openly about sex, he was denounced by numerous Christian activists. Graham became the catalyst of what was to follow concerning sex education.[371]

In 1835, the Rev. John Todd published *Students Manual*, which asked young men to overcome this secret vice of masturbation because ejaculation decreased energy and productivity. This belief is reflected by an article in the *Boston Medical and Surgical Journal*, which warned that ejaculation leads to loss of energy. When Americans were still mostly living on farms, children saw the mating of family animals. This was no longer the case after more and more citizens moved into urban areas. Cities were viewed as including many temptations, which led boards of education to consider the possibility of classroom instruction about sex. The National Education Association discussed this in 1892 and passed a resolution asking for moral education in the schools. In 1913, Chicago became the first major city to introduce sex education in high schools. This did not last long, as the Catholic Church objected against this development and forced the superintendent of schools to resign.[372]

Therefore, sex education was given hardly any attention until, during the First World War, the federal government became involved. At that time (1917–1918) socially acquired diseases were rampant in the Armed Forces. Therefore in 1918 Congress passed the Chamberlain-Kahn Act, which allocated money to educate soldiers about syphilis and gonorrhea. This led to viewing sex education as a public health issue. The American Hygiene Association, founded in 1914, was the product of the so-called social purity movement. This organization sought to teach soldiers about sexual hygiene. The teaching consisted of showing soldiers microscopic slides of syphilis and gonorrhea organisms and of teaching about the symptoms of the diseases on the body of a soldier who actually had contracted either syphilis are gonorrhea are both.[373]

In 1919, a movie called *Damaged Goods* was released in Britain and the United States. This movie dealt with the subject of venereal disease and other aspects of sexuality. In this movie, a man has sex with the prostitute the night before his wedding. He develops syphilis and passes the disease onto his newborn baby and therefore commits suicide. This led to an effort by censor boards to suppress it, so that it became better known and achieved a level of notoriety.[374]

In that same year, 1919, the US Department of Labor Children's Bureau issued a statement to the effect that soldiers would've better off if they had received sex instruction in school.

After the First World War, during the 1920s, schools began sex education in their curriculum. At that time, the American Social Hygiene Association produced a movie called The Gift of Life. The purpose of this movie was to inform about sexuality and venereal diseases. It depicts a scientist who shows a boy the reproductive processes of plants and animals under a microscope and then uses diagrams to explain reproduction among humans.[375]

Sex Education in Public Schools.

The sexual revolution of the 1960s led to the ever increasing number of students, both in high school and in college, who participated in sexual activity. Because the consequences of this conduct led to an increase in unmarried motherhood and endangered many young people who contracted social diseases, the public schools of the United States were asked to teach sex education in an effort to prevent the negative outcomes of widespread sexual involvement. Therefore, all American states gradually introduced sex education for public school children.

In the 21st century, 24 states and the District of Columbia require public schools to teach sex education. Twenty-one of the states also require that students learn about HIV infection. 33 states and the District of Columbia also teach about AIDS. 20 states require that education about sex and socially acquired diseases must be medically factual and technically accurate. This means that the department of health in the states reviews the curriculum for accuracy and that the curriculum is based on published authorities by medical professionals.

In 38 states and the District of Columbia, school districts must allow parental involvement in sexual education programs, and four states require parental consent before a child can receive sex education. 35 states and the District of Columbia allow parents to opt out on behalf of their children.[376]

Sex education is taught in schools because the Centers for Disease Control and Prevention discovered that more than 47% of all high school students have had sex and 15% of high school students have had sex with four or more partners. 60% of students who have sex report using condoms and 23% report birth control pills during their last sexual encounter.

Reasons for Teaching Sex Education

In 2017, the United States had the highest teen birth rate in the industrialized world. Approximately one in four American girls becomes pregnant at least once by the 20th birthday. Teenage mothers are less likely to finish high school and are more likely than their peers to live in poverty and depend on public assistance and live in poor health. The children of teenage mothers are more likely than other children to suffer health and other disadvantages. Such children are more likely to come in contact with the child welfare and correctional system, drop out of high school, and become teen parents themselves. The National Campaign to Prevent Teen and Unplanned Pregnancy estimates that teen childbearing costs the taxpayer at least 9½ billion dollars each year.[377]

Transmission of Sexually Acquired Diseases

Adolescents are disproportionately affected a sexually transmitted infections. Although young people aged 15 to 24 represent only 25% of the sexually active population, they acquire one half of all the diseases, which amounts to 9.8 million new cases each year. About 3½ million adolescent girls are infected with social diseases. The most common of these diseases among teens is papillomavirus. It has been estimated that up to 35% of teenagers 14 to 19 have HPV. Girls 15 to 19 have the highest rate of gonorrhea and the highest rate of chlamydia. Boys also have many of these diseases, but are not very often diagnosed, because they are less likely than girls to have symptoms or seek medical care. It has been estimated that treating young people with sexually transmitted infections cost 6½ billion dollars each year. About 24% of HIV carriers are 13 to 24 years old.[578]

Sex Education in the States

Every state in the Union has legislation concerning sex education. Alaska requires local school boards to involve parents in sex education. Parents have the right to object to class activities of programs. Parents must be notified two weeks before a lesson about human reproduction or sexual matters is provided in a class. All materials concerning sex education must be approved by the school board and available to parents for review.

Colorado did indeed enact a law requiring schools to teach children about sexually transmitted infections, including reference to HIV and types of hepatitis. In Florida, public schools must offer a program regarding sex education, including family planning, pregnancy, and sexually transmitted infections. The instruction shall be developmentally and age appropriate. At a written request by a parent, a student may be excused from these classes. In Hawaii, sex education programs funded by the state shall provide medically accurate information that is age-appropriate and includes education on abstinence, contraception, and the prevention of unintended pregnancy. In Iowa, each school board shall provide age-appropriate and research-based instruction regarding human sexuality, self-esteem, interpersonal relationships, domestic abuse, and HPV.

In Maine, schools shall teach comprehensive family life education from kindergarten through the 12th grade. It shall include human development and sexuality education on family planning and diseases that are medically accurate and age-appropriate. In Michigan, the superintendent of the school district shall cooperate with the department of education and teacher training and provide medically accurate material instruction, which will prevent or reduce the risk of sexually transmitted diseases. In Missouri, sex education shall stress the moral responsibility and the avoidance of controlled substances whereby HIV can be transmitted. Students shall be presented with the latest medically factual and age-specific information regarding the effects and health benefits of all forms of contraception. In Massachusetts each school district is required to offer a medically accurate sex education which is age-appropriate and teaches the benefits of abstaining from sexual activity. Also included is information about contraceptives and understanding that there may be no violence, coercion, or intimidation concerning sex. The schools are required to ensure that parents are notified concerning the content of the sexual education so that parents can withdraw their child from all participation.

In Michigan, a law is pending subject to a House and Senate agreement which would require sex education to the effect that students learn that consent must be given by both parties to engage in sexual activity. Further, the information must be age-appropriate, medically accurate, and objective. In Missouri, any course materials related to human sexuality "shall be factually accurate. The Department of Health and Senior services shall prepare plans and programs for public schools concerning transmission and prevention and treatment of the HIV virus. The program shall stress moral responsibility and the avoidance of controlled substances." New Jersey requires that family life education "must be aligned with the most recent version of curriculum content standards, which requires that structural material be current and supported by extensive research."

In North Carolina, sex education shall be related to the human reproductive system. Materials used must be objective based upon scientific research that is "peer-reviewed and accepted by credentialed experts in the field of sexual health education."

New York State has an existing sex education law seeking to prevent sexual abuse. This is taught in all public schools. Instruction must be based on current medical information and it must recognize sexual abuse. The law also requires a standard for a type of teacher allowed to instruct in elementary schools.

In Ohio the Board of Education is required to include sexually transmitted disease information including prevention of HIV and AIDS. It provides that instruction should stress abstinence and that it shall be medically accurate. Parents may excuse a student from such classes. In Oklahoma, the state "Department of Education shall develop curriculum materials for sex education in conjunction with the state Department of Health. School districts shall teach about AIDS prevention. The curriculum shall be revised as new medical facts are discovered." In Oregon "each school district shall provide age-appropriate human sexuality education. Both in elementary and secondary schools, this shall be an integral part of the health education curriculum. It must be medically accurate, comprehensive, and include information about behaviors and hygienic practices that eliminate or reduce the risks of pregnancy, exposure to HIV, hepatitis B, hepatitis C, and other socially transmitted diseases."

In Rhode Island, the Department of Elementary and secondary education shall establish comprehensive acquired immune deficiency syndrome instruction with accurate information on transmission, and the course should also address abstinence from sexual activity."

In Tennessee, education agencies are required to develop and implement a family life education program. The curriculum "must be age-appropriate and provide factually and medically accurate information. Parents are to be notified in advance of the family life program, and are allowed to inspect materials and provide written consent for student to opt out of family life education."

In Texas, the department "shall develop model education programs be available to sex education. This shall include discussion of AIDS and HIV infection. The program must be scientifically accurate and factual."

In Utah, the state office of education "must approve all sexually education programs and programs must be medically accurate."

In Washington, schools have an AIDS prevention education program using a model curriculum approved for medical accuracy. "The curriculum shall be updated as necessary to incorporate new facts." Since September 1, 2008, every public school that offered sexual health education was required "to make certain that it is medically and scientifically accurate, age-appropriate, appropriate regardless of gender or race disability or sexual orientation, and included abstinence and other methods of preventing unintended pregnancy and sexually transmitted diseases."

In Wisconsin, a school board may provide a medically accurate and age-appropriate instructional program and human growth and development from kindergarten through 12th grade.

Wyoming does not require a sex education. Discussion of sex in Wyoming schools "shall deal with abstinence."

Opposing Public School Sex Education

Since the industrialization of the United States in the 20th century, the erstwhile responsibilities of parents have been placed more and more on the schools. It is therefore not surprising that sex education which was once purely a parental issue has become a part of the school curriculum. Nevertheless, all the states which mandate sex education allow parents to participate, to critique, or even to excuse the children from these lessons. Since not much is learned in sex education, it appears more reasonable to allow parents alone to introduce children to their biological functions.

Schools are age graded. This means that all children of the same age learn the same subjects. Yet it is obvious that children of the same age are not always at the same level of maturity. Therefore sex education in the schools will seem meaningful to some children in the same grade in which other children have never considered sex at all. It is therefore possible and in fact likely that many children who are confronted with sex education will now engage in sexual behavior because it has been brought to their attention in school. This would therefore mean that sex education would have the opposite effect of what is intended, in that now those who heard all about it will do exactly that which sex education is intended to prevent. Academic subjects are taught by giving children materials suitable to their level of readiness. But when it comes to the extremely sensitive area of sexuality, all children in the same grade level are given the same material, even if some are not yet physically or psychologically ready to understand that. Forcing boys and girls who listen to and view openly discussions of sexual functioning of the opposite sex's anatomy is embarrassing, confusing, and painful.

Teaching sex education may result in attitudes and beliefs concerning sex which come from teachers but which parents would not approve if they knew what was being taught. Children are taught things in sex education which parents may not want taught but which they cannot control unless they sit in the classroom alongside their children for each and every lesson. That is nearly impossible for most parents, who have to go to work or have other children at home.

The announced purpose of sex education is to reduce teen pregnancy and abortion. Yet there is no evidence that either pregnancy or abortion has ever been reduced by sex education. In an article in the March 2002 issue of the *Journal of Health Economics* called The Economics of Family Planning and Underage Conceptions, there is published evidence that the theory that providing contraceptives to teens will reduce underage conceptions and abortions is not true. Instead this study found that greater access to contraception is associated with an increase in underage conceptions.

It is not the role of the public schools to judge the quality of information on sexuality provided by parents. Some parents do a very good job of teaching this to their children, while others don't do this at all or do it poorly. School officials have no right to superimpose their sex education on parents who in their opinion do not do the job very well. In short, the school should stay out of the bedroom.

There is a good deal more to sex education then plumbing and birth control pills. Schools make a bad mistake when they send students the message that sex education courses teach how to do it and how not to get caught. Schools cannot substitute for the love of parents who can teach sex but also teach how one respects others and how sex is part of a loving relationship.

Children do not ask about sex past the level of their understanding. Telling children how to use condoms, the pill, the IUD, and how to get an abortion is far above the level of interest of almost all children. Abstinence seems not to enter into the discussion in schools, and children taught sex education don't really understand what it means to be pregnant or to have a social disease. This is best taught by parents in an intimate manner rather than in front of an entire class of children coming from different religious and ethnic backgrounds whose families do not necessarily approve of what is being taught.

There are those in schools who claim they can teach value free sex education. This is impossible. Teachers have values and these values enter into the discussion in class. It is important for children to learn that sex is not for them and that it is not in their interest to participate in sexual behavior. This means that students learn the values of the teachers, some of whom tell students to make up their own minds concerning sex and that there is no standard of sexual behavior but everybody makes his own decision. Sex education is based on the assumption that children will be sexually active and that the teachers don't expect students to control themselves. Many classes in public schools present birth control without telling students that it is wrong for them to use this. In short, no ethics are associated with teaching sex, and courts leading to all kinds of disasters which no child deserves. The religious faith of many a child is undermined by sex education. Jews and Christians both teach their children that premarital sex, birth control, and abortion are wrong, and yet these children sit in class and hear an authority figure contradict the beliefs of the parents and the family.[79]

The Abstinence Only Controversy

The First Amendment of the Constitution of the United States guarantees citizens the right to freedom of thought and speech and opposes censorship as an affront to constitutional principles: that government may not control what individuals read, see, hear, think, and say. This is particularly important in the educational setting of the classroom, which the Supreme Court has called the marketplace of ideas.

Publicly funded sex education programs may in some cases restrict students' information to limit learning to an approved measure about human sexuality. The stated goals of sex education programs are reducing non marital sexual activity and teen pregnancy. These goals should not be subject to government censorship but respect freedom of speech and access to information. There is in federal law an abstinence education provision which is a threat to First Amendment principles. Abstinence only education is censorship. According to that view, the exclusive purpose of sex education is to teach that a monogamous faithful marriage relationship is the standard of human sexual activity, and that sexual activity outside of marriage is harmful psychologically and physically. Students in abstinence only sex education programs receive only information concerning abstinence until marriage. In such sex education classes there is no discussion about contraception, safe sex practices, and sexuality. In fact, some in abstinence only programs provide false information claiming that contraceptives undermine romance. Homosexuality in such classes is presented as only having the outcome of contracting HIV/AIDS. Abortion in such classes is presented as morally wrong and physically dangerous and fetuses are labeled babies.

Abstinence only leads to widespread censorship of sexual information. Material about sexually transmitted diseases and central orientation is not presented in abstinence only textbooks. Articles about sexuality have been censored in the student press and teachers have been warned against talking about certain topics and cannot answer students' questions candidly. Some teachers have been threatened with lawsuits for teaching anything but abstinence.

Because the separation of church and state is so important a principal of American democracy, abstinence only education is promoted by religious groups and individuals hoping to impose their beliefs on students in public schools. Many of the curricula in abstinence only sex education classes were developed by religious groups whose opinions concerning non-marital sex, contraception, and abortion are not shared by other religious groups or by nonreligious people. As a result, children are often indoctrinated into beliefs which are contrary the parents' beliefs but which are presented as facts. The Constitution prohibits preference of one religion over another in public schools and therefore prohibits violating these principles.

The very existence of democracy depends on freedom of speech. However, abstinence only education excludes discussion of birth control, abortion, and homosexuality. In Montana, the Catholic diocese of Helena received $14,000 from the state's Department of Health and Human Services to teach classes in the Assets of Abstinence. In Louisiana, a group of pastors is preaching abstinence only to religious congregations with public funds and The Governor's Program on Abstinence is appointing regional coordinators and staff and members from numerous religious organizations such as the Baptist Collegiate Ministries.[380]

The school board in Franklin County, North Carolina, ordered three chapters literally sliced out of a ninth grade textbook because the material did not adhere to state law mandating abstinence only education. In Lynchburg, Virginia, school board members refused to approve a high school science textbook unless an illustration of a vagina was cut out.[381]

Sex Ed Teachers are disciplined for doing their jobs. In Missouri, a seventh grade health teacher was suspended when a parent complained that she had discussed inappropriate sexual matters in class. In Orlando, Florida, a teacher was suspended when he showed a student made video tape about preventing AIDS transmission.

Teachers are threatened with lawsuits. In Granite Bay, California, a student paper sought charges that a sex education teacher engaged in sexual misconduct. It threatened a lawsuit against the teacher because the abstinence only education was doing nothing to step sexual activity. In Santa Clara, California, a high school principal censored the student paper for printing an article entitled "Sex Raw and Uncensored" about gay and lesbian sexuality. Abstinence only education reflects hostility to same-sex relations and stigmatizes those who are gay or lesbian.[382] There really is that there is no need for censors because uncensored access does not promote sexual activity.[383]

Abstinence only sex education gives public funds to a religious institute for anti-sex education. Aside from the Montana and Louisiana programs, in California, Pennsylvania, Alabama, and other states, schools regularly host pledges and rallies on school premises during school hours.[384]

Students suffer from ignorance. Comprehensive sex education is becoming the exception rather than the rule. As a result more students lack basic information. In Granite Bay, a student asked where his service was and another asked if she could become pregnant from oral sex. Students in New York City protested that the increased focus on abstinence has curtailed access to education about HIV/AIDS. The Colorado Council of Black Nurses decided to return sixteen thousand dollars in abstinence only funding because the program was just too restricted. It did not teach responsible sexual behavior.[385]

Over a five year period, approximately five hundred million dollars in federal and state matching funds have been spent on abstinence only education. Because of the requirement that states match federal funds for abstinence only programs, state dollars that previously supported comprehensive sexual education had been diverted to abstinence only programs.[386]

The vast majority of American parents support comprehensive sex education. According to a recent study by the Kaiser Family Foundation, most parents want their children to receive a variety of information on subjects, including contraception and condom use, sexually transmitted diseases, sexual orientation, abortion, and emotional aspects of sexual relationships.[387]

In 1981, Congress passed the Adolescent Family Life Act, also known as the chastity law which funded educational program to promote self-discipline and other prudent approaches to adolescent sex. Grant applications to create such programs poured in and the dollars poured out to churches and religious conservatives nationwide. The ACLU challenged this in court as smuggling the values of the Christian right to public school children at public expense, a classic affront to the principal of separation of church and state.[388]

Does Sex Education Affect Adolescent Sexual Behavior?

In 1979, 47% of all seventeen year olds had taken a sex education course. By 1994, nearly 90% had been offered such a class. During the same time, the pregnancy rate of fifteen to seventeen year olds rose from 32.3 for one thousand women to 37.2 for one thousand women.[389]

Sex education is viewed as an informational policy designed to reduce the future cost of teen pregnancy as well as sexually transmitted diseases. Adolescents tend to imprecisely estimate the probability of teen pregnancy. Therefore, sex education is viewed as an informational policy.

The National Longitudinal Survey of Youth thought to explain how sex education affects teen sex choices and found that it increases the chances of losing virginity for females. There are five sex-related outcomes, namely virginity status, contraceptive use, pregnancy, intercourse frequency, and sexual transmitted disease infections. Approximately 16% of females and 17% of males reported they were no longer virgins, with more nonwhites than whites reporting having sexual intercourse at least once. One third of sexually active adolescents do not use contraception. A pregnancy was reported in one study but in another study 15% reported a pregnancy. Only a small percentage reported suffering from a sexually transmitted disease. This, however, is misleading, because many people will not acknowledge having syphilis, gonorrhea, or chlamydia. It is therefore of interest whether the adolescent had been offered sex education in school. The main determinants of risky teen sexual behavior include community disadvantage, family structure, economic disadvantage, peer and partner attitudes, characteristics of teens themselves, detachment from school, emotional distress, and sexual beliefs.[390]

Sex education is popular with parents. Several studies have shown that less than 2% of parents withheld students from sex education when it was offered. Schools that offer sex education usually refer students to family planning services, family planning counseling, or treatment for sexually transmitted diseases. Sex education courses are also likely to have contraceptive information.

It has been assumed that sex education provides the same information to all adolescents. This is not the case. A recent survey of secondary sex education teachers found that 23% had taught abstinence as the only way to avoid pregnancy.[391]

Adolescents living in families that attend religious services are less likely to engage in sex than those who never attend services. Adolescents who report drinking alcoholic beverages are more likely to have engaged in early sex. In sum, it is evident that sex education fails because it has no effect on the sexual behavior of students who had enrolled in it.

There are several reasons for the failure of sex education. The first is nature, which assigns to young adults so strong a sex drive that it is almost impossible to overcome by lectures or other sex education methods. Also, because sex has emotional aspects, sex education can hardly compete. Emotions differ from person to person, so that sex education affects different students differently. The culture of the student's family and community makes a good deal of difference as to the meaning of sex education.

Chapter 11. Old Age — Status and Role

I

American society is aging and later life is dominated by women, because after age 65, women constitute a majority of the population of the United States. It is, therefore, surprising that both gerontologists and feminist scholars have ignored the intersection of aging and gender. Consequently, very little has been done to comprehend the difference in aging experience between men and women and to recognize the separate implications of aging for both sexes.

Gender relations are, of course, not the same over a lifetime. This is true because physical changes create alterations in sexual expression. In addition, social strictures define appropriate sex roles for the young, the middle-aged and the old. Furthermore, class, ethnicity, and the age in which one lives determine much of what we experience with reference to age and sex.

Evidently, younger people are more concerned with sex and work than are old people. However, economic and state policies respecting gender affect old people more than young people. In addition, these policies affect women in a different fashion than they affect men. For example, women are more likely to be widowed and are therefore also more likely to be dependent on adult children. Women are more likely to live in an institution than is true for men and are also more likely to become the victims of elder abuse.[392]

Although old men are not as likely to be as dependent on others as old women, they are far less visible than old women. The reason for this "invisibility" is demographic. Because men's mortality rate is greater than that of women of the same age, men constitute only about 40% of Americans 65 years old or over. As age advances, men are increasingly in the minority. Thus, only 7% of men survive to age 85 even while one in every eight women, 12.5%, reach that age. This was not always so. Until the 1930s, the sex ratio of men to women in the United States was balanced at 1:1. During the next sixty years, however, this ratio changed dramatically, thus leading to the "feminization" of the old population. Consequently, there are now three women for every two men in the age group 65 years old or older. Indeed, the proportion of old men increased from 4% to 10% during this sixty-year period. However, almost 15% of women now reach that age. Meanwhile, the old-old, that is the population over age 74, is increasing at a faster pace than ever before.[393]

Another reason for the "invisibility" of old men as compared to women besides numbers is that the disadvantaged receive more attention from researchers and politicians than those who have more privileges.

Therefore, more effort and time has been spent on women's problems as old women are believed to be in "double jeopardy" by reason of gender and age.

A third reason for the "invisibility" of old men is the medicalization of their needs. Great emphasis is placed on the physical needs of old men who need pacemakers, bypass surgery, cardiac catheterization and other procedures, thus minimizing and actually making "invisible" the needs of healthy old men.[394]

One of these needs is sexual expression. That this is so may surprise many whose attitudes toward sexuality of the old rests on the most common American stereotypes relative to this common human need. The depth and prevalence of society's negative attitude toward sexuality in the old is not only evident in the attitude of the general public concerning this "taboo" topic, but can also be seen in the aged themselves. This is true in part because youth is preferred and old age is unpopular as we have repeatedly shown. Furthermore, many people view old age and aging as a disease rather than a normal process and therefore assume that persons suffering from that "disease" could not have the physical capacity to engage in sex. Next, it is obvious that the old are not attractively packaged, in that their bodies are not appealing. Many people assume that those not attractive are also sexless. This belief is enhanced by the fact that men are generally older than their wives and are therefore less likely to be capable of sexual performance. Consequently, women are deprived of sex at an earlier age than men, not because of their own incapacity, but because of the incapacity of their husbands. Finally, lower expectations lead to lesser performance. Since the whole American culture militates against sexual expression by the old, the old believe this themselves since they learned this opinion when they, themselves, were young. The "self-fulfilling prophecy" insures what belief presumes, and this deprives innumerable old people, and particularly women,, of this source of emotional satisfaction. Women are more victimized by these attitudes than men because older men can and do frequently associate with younger women, while older women are seldom able to attract younger men. This, too, is a cultural, learned attitude not dictated by any biological condition. It is condemnation, ridicule and repression rather than lack of sexual interest which inhibits the old in this regard and removes a very normal form of conduct into the realm of suspect and deviant conduct.[395]

II

While the word sex refers to physical attributes, gender refers to social standing. This is best understood with reference to economic differences between women and men. Thus, while there is no evidence that women cannot perform as well as men in most occupations now available in the United States, a large income difference between the genders persists in the United States. The differences in income are illustrated by a report by the United States Bureau of the Census which showed that American women earn on average 80% of the median income earned by men.[396]

While this discrepancy reveals that a considerable bias against American women continues to exist in the American economy, great changes in the position of American women have taken place in the past century, i.e., since 1901, and more can surely be expected. Thus, a century ago, husbands controlled the property of their wives; women were barred from most jobs; women could not vote and certainly none could hold an elected office.

Today, women not only work in innumerable occupations, but the economy actually depends on women as physical labor has come to a near end in industrial countries like the United States and talent and thought have made men and women equal in the workplace. This equality is not only the result of legal changes which insure that women are paid the same wages as men for the same work. This equality also results from the changed view of women's contribution to the work world. Heretofore, and traditionally, women's work was seen as voluntary and appeared to be compensated by the approval of family and public opinion.

Older women in particular were seen as "wise old grandmothers" whose duty traditionally was/is to give support and assistance to others. This view has changed somewhat in the United States, and is changing more and more as traditional views of women are changing all the time.[397]

Nevertheless, women still constitute a social minority in the United States in the 21st century, in that the word *minority* is here used to mean "a category of people distinguished by physical (or cultural) traits, who are socially disadvantaged."[398]

In view of what we already know about the status of the old in America, it is evident that the status of old women has been particularly precarious in the past and continues to be more distressing than is the status of old men. This situation has been called "The Double Jeopardy Hypothesis" in that American society values women less than men and the old less than the young.

Chappell and Havens have made a study of this "double jeopardy phenomenon" and found that old women exhibit a significantly worse mental health status than old men or any other group these researchers examined. Most significant is the finding that for old women, but not for men, contact with friends is directly related to mental health.[399]

It is, of course, nothing new that sex as well as age are two aspects of status-role which have been studied extensively by social scientists over the past fifty years. However, the effect of both of these statuses on the same persons at the same time has received far less attention than studies of each of these status-roles separately. Sex is fixed. But age changes all the time so that the status-role which age represents also changes all the time. The author defines status as the sum of privileges and role as the sum of obligations either ascribed to or achieved by an individual.

Men and women age differently. This is evident both in the physical and the social area. For example, women live longer than men. Average life expectancy is seventy-six years for both sexes, with 18% of white men and 38% of white women living to age eighty-five. White women can expect to live 79.8 years and non-white women can expect to live 75.7 years. White men have a life expectancy at birth of 73.2 years and non-white men can expect to live 67.7 years.[400]

These statistics indicate a widening gender gap as proportionately more women than men live longer. Thus, in the age group sixty-five to sixty-nine, there are eighty-one men for every one hundred women, a gender gap which drops to thirty-nine men to one hundred women over the age of eighty-five. Today (1997), there are nearly 900,000 men and 2.2 million women that age and older.[401]

According to the New York Times, men who survive to eighty-five or more are in better health than women who live that long.[402]

Achieving so high an age depends largely on the ability to function. That, in turn, underlies an older person's ability to remain independent and is "central to arguments about active life expectancy and the compression of morbidity."[403]

This means, for both women and men, that physical fitness and social contacts are both important in order to stay alive. This is true because longevity is not only related to inheritance but also to the ability to be independent in old age. This ability to be independent is not derived from the same sources for both sexes. Thus, for men physical exercise is a more important source of independence and continued health in old age than is true for women. For women, going out and meeting friends is more important to prolong life. This is not to say that physical activity is not also important for women. For example, Rakowski and More found that the number of days per week that women walked one mile or more is more strongly associated with mortality than a regular exercise routine which is more strongly associated with mortality for men. In short, old men should be encouraged to participate in regular exercise while family activities and community involvement serve women better.[404]

Regular exercise contributes not only to physical health, but also to psychological health. The study of this important issue has, however, been delayed and even prevented because there are so many activities which may be purely social, but are labeled "physical" even if the participants gain little physical benefits. The best example are golf players. Many people play golf for the sake of meeting people otherwise deemed important. Furthermore, many golf players make little if any effort at achieving physical exercise from playing golf. Those who ride in a cart from hole to hole are one excellent example. In this connection. Bennet and Morgan report that there are gender differences in the indoor and outdoor customary physical activities of women and men.[405]

Women participate more often in indoor physical activities such as housework and men in outdoor activities requiring flexibility and strength These differences, however, depend in part on marital status in that single, older women are more likely to also participate in outdoor physical activities than married women.[406]

III

Nearly five times more men than women are still married at advanced ages, in part because of the cultural directive which prompts women to marry men older than themselves. Including unmarried persons, it turns out that 70% of women, but only 36% of men over the age of sixty-five, live alone.

The social aspects of aging affect men and women equally despite the common belief that this is a concern of women only. Both sexes cling to youthful self-images in American culture because it is impossible to escape from the reminders of aging which are institutionalized everywhere. Birthday rituals, retirement benefits, entry into formal education and religious ceremonies all emphasize age. Willingness to accede to the cultural prescriptions pertaining to age are rewarded in American and all cultures. Deviation from these norms, or expected behavior, are penalized. This can be illustrated by viewing the consequences of dressing in a manner not considered appropriate to age. An old person, particularly an old woman, who dresses in a manner prescribed for the young is severely criticized. Likewise, sexual interests exhibited by those believed to be too old to have sexual interests are penalized in puritan America.[407]

Poverty visits old women more than old men. Thus, 23% of women age eighty-five or more live on or below the poverty level, a condition that is true for only 18% of men. The reason for this discrepancy lies in the earlier work history of women and men. In the age group now belonging to the old-old, there are many women who never worked in lucrative employment or who had an intermittent and sporadic work history leading to small pensions and few savings.[408]

Some observers say that women are better able to handle the physical and social losses associated with longevity because they have spent a lifetime developing intimate relationships with other women. Many men, however, relied on their wives for all their emotional needs or had only superficial relationships with their male friends.[409] Furthermore, as we have already seen, widowed men will find fewer widowed friends than will be true among women, as men remain married so much longer than is true of women.[410]

Traditionally, women have been less active, less often employed, and less aggressive than men. Assuming a domestic role, traditional women had a better opportunity to lead the same life in old age as they did in their middle-age or youth. This is not so for men and will not be so for working and career-oriented women. In short, men and women who were employed for many years need to find a transition to retirement that leaves them satisfied relative to income, status, and personal, as well as social worth. Matthews and Brown have found that for men, the critical factor relating to retirement had to do with occupation, while women were more concerned with health and financial resources than were men. [411]

While similar numbers of old women and old men have children in proximity, twice as many women as men receive some support from their adult children. In a study by Barer, 47% of women but only 11% of men over age 85 had a child functioning as caregiver. The explanation for this difference may lie in the greater needs of women or in the fact that more old men are still married than is true of women. It can also be that even needy men will not admit to this need, because of the cultural imposition of a "macho" attitude which dictates that men must not permit themselves to use the help of others, not even their children.

Women not only receive more help from children, they also maintain more contact with them. This means that over two-thirds of old women reported weekly or more contacts with a child compared with less than one-half of men. Furthermore, these contacts are closer because women are more likely to name a child as a confidant. Women are also more likely to name a friend as a confidant than is true of men, thereby exhibiting a greater capacity to maintain intimate relationships outside the family. This is true of old-agers but is also true of women of younger years.[412]

The same study by Barer found that men are more active in their old age than is true of women. Men, having more money and fewer physical problems than women, sustain their hobbies more often into old age than is true of women. Men also move about outside their home much more than women because among women who are old now, there are many who also stayed at home throughout their lifetime and are therefore more accustomed to a sedentary life than are men.[413]

The loss of a spouse is also a different experience for women than it is for men. Thus, "recently widowed men often feel out of their element when it comes to cooking, shopping, cleaning, washing and mending routine functions formerly handled by their wives."[414]

Men are usually unaccustomed to establishing social relations, not only because men are widowed for a shorter time than women are, but also because American culture demands that women, not men, make social arrangements among married couples. Men, then, are widowers for about ten years; women are widows for twenty-five years. During their widowed decade, many men never make friends again because they relied entirely on their wives to do so for them and they feel too old to start over. Women, having been involved in fostering social contacts for years, and dealing with widowhood much longer than men, are both encouraged and coerced by circumstances to continue old friendships and to make new ones. Thus, many widowed men are almost helpless in their widowed condition and are extremely lonely and alone, particularly if they are among the old-old, i.e., those eighty years old and over.[415]

IV

The progress of life may be seen as a series of status changes. The first of these is birth and the last, death. Between these changes are such major events in the life cycle as the attainment of physical maturity, usually celebrated by such ceremonies as First Communion or Bar Mitzvah. Graduation from high school and the assumption of economic independence is another status change receiving a great deal of attention in American society. Marriage, college graduations, promotions, birthdays, and most certainly retirement can all be listed as important status changes. We are here concerned with retirement which affects such basic life issues as self-identity, self-worth, relationships with others, financial status, and daily activities. Now, sociologists have shown that occupation is the most important criterion of social standing in the United States because American society places such a great deal of emphasis on work and income.[416]

Therefore, it is evident that for many Americans, retirement poses a terrible threat because of all these issues. Yet, even as retirement is dreaded by some, it is welcomed by others. One means of studying different attitudes toward retirement is to investigate these differences by gender. Hanson and Wapner undertook such an investigation, and found that retirement "can be categorized into four modes of experience."[417]

The first of these modes of experience is called "transition to retirement." Hanson and Wapner found that formal roles have relatively less importance for women than for men and that therefore women find it easier than men to adjust to retirement. Women are said to experience more continuity in their lives than men because women derive their identity more from informal roles and interpersonal relationships than men. Men derive their status mainly from formal roles. Therefore, a woman who retires is more often able to continue her status-role as "friend" or committee member despite retirement. Men, however, are more likely to have based their entire status on their work relationships and become truly "disconnected" when they have lost their occupation.

There are three other experiences involving retirement as discovered by Hanson and Wapner. These are corroborated by the findings of other researchers and assert that women 's relationships with their female friends are closer than is true of men; that women retire at a younger age than men because women are usually married to older men but retire simultaneously with them and that old and retired women have greater financial worries than men because they earned less and live longer than men. It is for these reasons that women are more often recipients of public assistance programs in the United States than is true for men.[418]

The principal public assistance program supporting the retired in the United States is called Social Security. It covers almost all workers, their spouses and dependents. It is not means tested, except for taxation of benefits, and it is indexed for inflation. In addition, the United States has a Supplemental Security Income program which may be called a "safety net" for those whose poverty also makes them eligible for the Food Stamps program. Medicare is another United States government program of benefit to the old. This program is neither means nor asset-tested although it requires insurance premiums and co-pay from the patient. Therefore, the United States also has a Medicaid program which is administered by the states at each state's discretion. All of these programs and others are of considerable help to the poor and old and help women ;more than men because women need these services more than men.[419]

All of this is called the "feminization of poverty" which is visible both among those women young enough to bear children and among the old and retired. It must be understood, in this connection, that factors other than age also bear on this "feminization." Race is at least as powerful in promoting poverty as old age is, and education, employment history and the receipt of private pensions must not be overlooked in this connection. This means that if we compare the Social Security and other public benefits given old women among whites and blacks, then it seems that income is about the same for both races. However, few blacks have private pensions. Therefore, race cannot be omitted as a major factor in the production of old age poverty in this country.[420]

The "feminization" of poverty is however gradually declining. The reason for this has been and continues to be the changes in the American economy which permit women greater work opportunities than ever before. Thus, finance, realty, banking, publishing have all created new opportunities for women since about 1980. At the same time, men have been pushed out of traditional male occupations having mostly to do with manufacturing skills. As a consequence, it can be anticipated that women will retire with much more money in future years than was ever true before. In short, opportunity will increase female participation in the labor force at good wages and high salaries will therefore countermand the inequality of income from which women have always suffered. This will mean that the so-called "dual labor market" which permitted men to earn well, receive good benefits including pensions and job security while women received none of this, is about to come to an end. Hence, we can anticipate that as women achieve more education, are paid more and earn higher pension benefits, old age poverty will not be as gender-bound as it is now. In short, convergence and similarity are possible and even probable among the old of both genders in the foreseeable future.[421]

At this writing, this convergence has not yet been achieved. Instead, old women are particularly vulnerable in our major cities and are frequently so isolated that their lives are seldom recognized or their problems alleviated. An example of the loneliness suffered by many such women is the following letter written to the *Los Angeles Times*:

"I'm so lonely I could die. So alone. My hands and fingers pain me. I see no human beings. My telephone never rings. I'm so very old, so very lonely. I hear from no one — way past eighty years. Should I die? Did you ever feel sure the world ended? I'm the only one on earth. How else can I feel? All alone. Here, no one. Oh, dear God, help me. Am sound of mind. So lonely, very, very much. I don't know what to do." Enclosed in her letter was a dollar bill to be paid to anyone willing to call her so that she could hear the sound of a human voice.[422]

In view of the greater and greater longevity of women, there are more and more old women in our cities who have lost those principal attributes that were erstwhile associated with a sense of social worth and made old age a positive experience, as it still is in some non-American cultures. These attributes are first, control over resources such as money or land. Of course, current adult American children do not need to wait for the death of their parents in order to earn their own livelihood by inheriting land because they generally gain their own income by non-farm occupations. It needs to be remembered, however, that even when the United States was mainly an agricultural society, women did not own or inherit land, but needed to bargain for their livelihood by appealing to their son's sense of obligation and filial piety. A second attribute of old age was at one time knowledge, which could be transmitted to the younger generation, such as farming. Now, currently important skills such as computer operations are known better to the young than the old and the old are not needed any more. Again, these skills were at one time known mainly to men while women performed tasks having to do with the household. Important as links to the past or important as those nearest to being ancestors, the old were once held in high esteem by those younger than themselves. There is however, hardly any room for such beliefs in the United States in the 21st century. Except for some immigrants living in a subculture, Americans do not pay much attention to ancestry, including their own.

A fourth attribute associated with a sense of social worth was at one time membership in an extended family bound by mutual obligations. These obligations are indeed recognized among American families. However, those old parents who move into the home of an adult child soon may find that they are "guests" in a strange house and that they can do nothing about this.

While membership in a small community with stable, sacred values was at one time commonplace, this function has almost entirely disappeared in urban societies today, as has an economy in which the contribution of each person is important. This, the sixth attribute of social worth, has utterly disappeared in face of automation so that neither old men or old women are now needed in the labor force. Those among the old who keep working after age 65 do so either because they need the money or because they need the social network that employment provides. Finally. Membership in a small group in which it is the duty of everyone to take care of everyone else is frequently not available to old city dwellers. This is true because innumerable relatives move from the place of their birth each year and also because such groups hardly exist in industrialized, urban environments even for the young.[423]

The unavailability of meaningful small groups has a direct effect on self-perception. George Herbert Mead in his epochal work Mind, Self and Society, showed conclusively that the self is developed through social interaction. This means that all of us learn to view ourselves from the perspective of others in that the "I" is the creative and acting aspect of the self, and the "me" is the internalized attitudes of others. The mental dialogue which results from this interaction is the self-concept. Evidently, then, those who have lost opportunities to interact with others, or do so only rarely, or in an unsatisfactory manner, will develop a less and less meaningful memory in connection with the social roles gender imposes on us.[424]

Elizabeth Markson has shown that as group affiliation declines in old age, and as this becomes a more female problem than a male condition, those who are more and more isolated demonstrate an excessive self-preoccupation, leading to memory loss. In other words, references to other people decrease for the isolated and memory loss increases in proportion. Finally, a narrowing and constricting of experiences leads to a lack of identity and a sense of despair.[425]

V

Surely entrance into a nursing home is an experience which can seriously affect a sense of identity and lead to despair, although it strikes men and women differentJy. Both genders, of course, are faced with a most profound status change upon entering such a home. This means that nursing homes, unlike hospitals or even prisons, are usually the last way station before death and that those who enter there know that they will probably never be an independent individual again.

The average age of nursing home residents is over eighty-two and it is not uncommon to have patients in their high nineties and even centenarians included in the nursing home population. Because so many nursing home patients are ill or unable to deal with the needs of daily life in an adequate manner, nursing home patients, by definition, are dependents. However, the lack of control over one's self is somewhat alleviated for those who have some money, interested relatives, and friends, and the help of other outsiders willing to intervene. Men are more likely to have some financial resources than women and are therefore more often the beneficiaries of outside contacts, extra food or amenities or even legal help than are old women[426]

Nursing home patients who enter the home with some possessions that mean a great deal to them find the experience somewhat easier to accommodate than those who arrive with nothing. "Common sense suggests," say Wapner et al., "that cherished objects or possessions may be associated with adaptation to new environments." This is true because possessions are an extension of the individual and serve as aids in defining who we are. Possessions are indications that the owner has control over his environment.

Possessions thus have two types of meaning. One of these is called the general meaning and include memories, experiences, style, utility, personal value, intrinsic qualities, and associational context. The second meaning is the person-related meaning and refers to possessions identified with self, immediate family, relatives and friends. Possessions make it easier for old women and men to deal with the transition from independent living to becoming a nursing home patient. This means that cherished possessions permit the new nursing home resident to establish a "home base" from which to then explore the new environment. Goffman has shown that in a total institution, such as a nursing home, the presentation of self is dependent on using one's "identity kit." This "identity kit," according to Goffman, consists of objects, or possessions, that can be used to present an image of the self to others. Furthermore, the most cherished possessions are used to maintain a connection between the present world of the nursing home and the past world which the nursing home patient will most probably never experience again. Locating familiar objects in the new environment of the nursing home also makes it easier for the new patient to connect to the new environment because the prized possessions become a part of the nursing home and therefore allow the patient to accept his new status and identity. Such possessions also meet some of the most immediate needs of the patient, such as the use of a prayer book or a means of artistic expression. Finally, possessions such as a gold ring reflect a patient's social status.[427]

All of this is much more important to women than to men because men are far more often retired from occupations and professions that are sources of social status, ipso facto. This is so because in American culture, men's work and career success are viewed as measures of their masculinity. Self-definition, self-respect and personal worth among men are primarily established through achievements on the job and to a far greater extent than is true for women. These differences persist into old age and into retirement, so that men's gendered behavior and identity do not change throughout life. Even an increase in the desire to retire or actual retirement does not imply a decrease in the work ethic or a lack of motivation.

According to the research of Lorence, retirement may be an economically rational decision or be the consequence of illness but is seldom the result of a change in men's perception of the masculine role.[428]

Thus, old men do not change their behavior because men's identity is usually synonymous with their occupational role and becomes part of their so-called "ego structure." It is for this reason that many men who do not need the money choose to continue to work because they believe that the traditional masculine role requires involvement in work. Work, success and power are an integral part of masculinity dependent on the completion of task-oriented behavior. Solomon and Szwabo have called this "generativity," maintaining the ability to "create and use options for continued successful behavior." All of this is more likely to be the province of those old men born before the Depression decade 1929–1939, who are found in nursing homes now.[429]

The belief that successful behavior depends on performance of tasks is visible throughout the lifetime of men in Western civilization. Thus, men in their "middle adulthood" dominate almost all segments of society from religion to politics, business and education. They are the decision-makers and have great impact on events outside the home.

In popular culture, however, old men play no such role. Classified as "senior citizens" or just "old," they are viewed as deprived of their masculinity by old age; they are seen as sexless or asexual and in the end, not men at all. This popular view of old men contrasts sharply with the view old men like to maintain about themselves. For that view reflects the work tradition which the old have used as a source of self-identification all their lives. It, therefore, remains yet to be seen whether those men born after the 1930s will be able to shed the older men's "masculine mystique" and assume a role more sensitive to feelings and be more willing to give up the work-oriented roles of their youth and middle years and seek closer relationships with others as a source of self-identity as women have done successfully both in nursing homes and outside. There are some students of gerontology who claim that aging ipso facto emasculates men and that, therefore, there is a gender convergence in later life which makes men and women almost indistinguishable in old age. Others argue that changes in the perception of the masculine or feminine role are the result of historical forces and are not automatically the result of chronological aging. For example, men who are familiar with the Depression may be more willing to accept the concept of a two-income family than is true of men who were raised to believe that their masculinity is diminished by their wife working outside the home.[430]

Women are less likely than men to have retired from long work careers or prestigious occupations and therefore depend more on the presence of prized possessions for a sense of continuity and power than is true of men. As a consequence, significantly more female nursing home patients than male patients have cherished possessions. Women view these possessions much more as a source of comfort than is true of men and also view these possessions as associated with self-other relationships. These closer relationships experienced by women are visible in the fact that female nursing home patients receive more phone calls and letters than men, are invited more often to friends' and relatives' houses than men, were judged more realistic than men, and were judged as more motivated to deal with conflict situations.[431]

VI

Access to social benefits, such as pensions and insurance, are of vital concern to the old, although by no means ignored by younger persons. It is, therefore, significant relative to gender discrimination that old women in the United States and elsewhere do not receive the same opportunities to collect benefits equal to those of men. The reasons for this discrepancy lie once more in the differential status between the genders.

One reason for this difference lies in the many work-related insurance schemes. Alone the fact that the proportion of women who work less than the proportion of men who do so, guarantees that men will be more often eligible for insurance and pension benefits than women. Thus, there are about 53 million women and 63 million men in the United States labor force. This, despite the fact that there are only 95.1 men in the United States for every one hundred women. Evidently, then, women are less frequently employed than men and consequently are less often eligible for benefits tied to the labor market.[432]

Furthermore, women are frequently disqualified from insurance benefits because of their patterns of employment, such as part-time or intermittent work and, most of all, low earnings. Because women are so many times needed to supervise children, many women cannot meet the benefits requirement that they be available for work at all times. Entitlement for many benefits depends on contributions. This is again a hurdle for many women because their lower earnings make their contributions less. This means that women's labor market participation does not automatically lead to their equal participation in the benefits accruing to men. Evidently, gender inequalities in earnings are perpetuated as inequalities in benefits. In fact, inequalities in benefits can be even more pronounced than inequalities in earnings.[433]

Earnings, or income of the old are, of course, not monolithic or uniform. Nevertheless, a popular stereotype exists which views all old people as greedy, affluent and politically powerful. This stereotype also supports the view that the old are receiving too many benefits and do not adequately share the tax burden. This is, of course, the opposite of the beliefs that all who are old are poor, infirm, frail, poorly housed, and without power. Both views are, of course, wrong because there are millions of old Americans and the differences between them are very great. Some are quite poor and others are very wealthy. This is, of course, also true of all Americans. Therefore, no label fits all the old. We can say however, that changes have occurred in the economic position of the old. This is best understood if we consider that in 1959 the United States Census considered about 35% of the old "poor" as compared to 20% of the general population. In 2017, 12.2% of the old were labeled poor as compared to 13.5% of the general population. Evidently, then, all the old were neither poor nor rich nor middle class at any time.[434]

The main reasons for the decline in the number of the poor among the old have been government income maintenance programs. These programs, however, are not equally distributed among the old population. Thus, the United States Government General Accounting Office has shown that 8% of women 65 years old or older are poor, but only 5.2% of men in that age group are among the poor. If we refine these numbers to deal with those age 65 to 74, we find that 6.1% of women, but only 4.7% of men are among the poor. Among those 75 years old or older, the differences are 10.7% and 6.0% respectively.[435]

The four factors which contribute most to poverty among the old are longevity, widowhood, living alone, and working in the "secondary" labor market. All of these are attributes of women much more than of men. In fact, women have been forced to rely more and more on service occupations which pay low wages even as men have lost their jobs due to industrial downsizing, plant closings and declining unionization. Women, in the meantime, have found employment opportunities in service occupations which pay low wages.[436]

"Men as a whole have typically experienced greater gains from enacted programs than have women." So says Gonyea. This does not mean that all men benefit equally. In any case, however, women have received fewer benefits than men because of the assumptions made by the Social Security Act of 1935. These assumptions are first, that only a small percentage of Americans would survive to collect benefits at age sixty-five. Second, that Social Security would be only one source of support in old age and that personal savings, pensions and dividends would add to the support of the old, and third, that the family would be an economic unit receiving the Social Security benefit in a world in which women kept house, men alone went to work and women received half of their husbands' income in Social Security benefits. Today, these assumptions are no longer true, as longevity, lack of income or lack of frugality, and a high divorce rate have defeated all of these beliefs.[437]

Thus, before the 1960s, both sexes faced a 33% chance of living in poverty in their old age. Today, old men enjoy a four-fold reduction in poverty even as the reduction in women's poverty is only two-fold. Among the married, the risk of poverty is 5.3% for women and 5.7% for men. However, the poverty risk for unmarried women is four times as great while that for men is only double among the unmarried. This is true because both Social Security and SSI, i.e. supplemental income payments, reward couples and penalize singles, who are 80% female in old age.[438]

VII

Crime against the old is less frequent than it is against the young. This may be a surprise to some who believe the old to be more vulnerable and hence more victimized by crime. However, the Bureau of Justice Statistics shows that the rates of robbery, for instance, is 10 per hundred thousand among victims 12–15 years old, 8.3 per hundred thousand among victims 15–19 years old, 13.9 per hundred thousand among victims 20-24 years old, but only 1.9 per hundred thousand among people 65 years old or older. The greater number of old women compared to old men in the population makes women more frequently the target of such crimes.[439]

There are some crimes which victimize women and rarely men, such as rape and purse snatching. While purse snatching is a crime which may rank low among the concerns of the police, it should nevertheless be given more prominence than it now receives because it not only deprives the poor and old of resources they need, but because it also leaves a terrible sense of vulnerability in its wake which tends to lock the elderly in their homes in fear of going out into a dangerous neighborhood.[440]

Thus, while the old are actually less likely than the young to be victimized by street crime, it is the fear of crime which victimizes old people and particularly women. The reasons for the low rate of actual victimization compared to the fear of victimization lies in the difference in life-style between the old and between women and men. Thus, the old do not go to work as much as do the young, and old women are even less likely to go to work than is true of old men. Furthermore, the old often live in segregated housing, including nursing homes, even as infirmity confines more women than men to both nursing homes and their own homes. If, therefore, we calculate the consequences of crime in terms of the restrictions crime imposes upon the old, and in particular upon old women, then it may well be that the old are far more victimized by crime than the young.[441]

While street crime is fairly visible and is viewed with special disgust by the public, there is a form of violence against the old which is not very visible and which victimized old women more than men because women are even more defenseless than men. That crime is "parent bashing," also known as "the battered parent syndrome." Physical as well as verbal abuse of the old coupled with shame is the principal reason for these attacks. Like small children, those old victims who depend on middle-aged children and other adults are also unwilling to complain to police or visiting nurses and social workers that their own children are abusing them. Furthermore, their dependent status often leads them to keep quiet about such abuse for fear of being abandoned altogether. Since women, as we have seen, exhibit greater dependency needs than men, and are in the majority of those surviving to an age when they need special care, they are again more victimized by parent abuse than are men.

Physically violent crimes are not _the only crimes perpetrated against the old. Many old people are the victims of various kinds of fraud. Among these are social referrals luring widows into so-called introduction services for big fees to meet new friends when this can be done free at any church or senior citizens center. Land fraud is also very common. Real estate developers will claim to sell developed land in developed communities, when in fact the land is a swamp or has no facilities. Mail-order fraud will advertise innumerable products for excessive money or by claiming miracle cures. There are door-to-door salespeople who prey on lonely old women and men who are eager for conversation. Some contractors scare lonely old people into having repairs made to their house when these repairs are not needed. Investment fraud is practiced against old people seeking to hedge against inflation while mail-order health insurance often include so many "ifs" and "buts" that the insurance is in fact worthless when the insured's health is failing. These and a host of other "white collar crimes" victimize old women much more than old men because there are so many women who live alone.[442]

VIII

We have seen that women and men age differently, because they not only differ biologically, but also with respect to the status role each gender must accept. Thus, old men are less visible than women because life expectancy permits more women to arrive at an old age. Physical activities, including sexual expression, also differs between the genders. The greatest differences between old women and old men, however, lies in the economic sphere, including pensions and insurance payments, because these are so heavily tied to earnings during the younger years.

We have explored the relationship of women and men to their adult children and to such status changes as entrance into a nursing home. Finally, we have briefly dealt with the crime issue.

ENDNOTES

1   United States Census Bureau. "Women by the Numbers." https://www.infoplease.com/women-numbers, accessed March 26, 2019.

2   Thomas Pearls and Ruth Fretts, "Why Women Live Longer Than Men," *Scientific American*, (June 1998):1-9.

3   Ibid. :2.

4   *Fortune Magazine*, no author, no date.

5   Medical Group Management Association, "Provider Compensation 2016,":2.

6   Medscape "Female Compensation Report" (2016). https://www.medscape.com/features/slideshow/compensation/2016/female-physician, accessed March 26, 2019.

7   In a Spirit of Caring, "The Gender Shift," http//www.spiritofcaring.com.

8   Heidi Chumley, M.D. "The Importance of Female Role Models," https://medium.com/@DrHeidiChumley/the-importance-of-female-role-models-in-medicine-f0e1538933e0, posted April 17, 2016, accessed March 26, 2019.

9   J.F. McMurray, "The work life of women physicians." http:www.ncbl. nlm.niih.gov/pubmed.

10   Analyn Kurtz, "Pharmacists: Most Equal Job for Men and Women," *Money*, (February 11, 2013):1.

11   Staci Zaretsky, "Women in the Legal Profession Continue to be Treated Like Crap," *Above the Law*, (December 1, 2015).

12   Joan M. Hall, "Reflections on Women Lawyers etc." *The Capitalist*, vol.vll, no.l, (September 2017)

13   Ibid. 7-15.

14   No Author, New Brunswick, NJ, Rutgers University. *History of Women Governors*, Center for American Women and Politics, 2017. No page.

15   Zachary Cole, "Bay lawmakers among the wealthiest," *San Francisco Chronicle*, (June 26, 2004):4.

16   U.S. Department of Labor, Bureau of Labor Statistics, "Labor Force Statistics from the Current Population Survey," :1-20.

17   McDonald, A., Postle, K. and Dawson C., "Social Workers in Unity, Care Practice: Ideologies and Directions: Older People," *British Journal of Social Work*, (May, 2008):1-20

18   Harry Wasserman. "The Professional Social Worker in a Bureaucracy," *Social Work*, Vol. 16, No. 1 (January 1971), pp. 89-95.

19   United States Department of Labor: Bureau of Labor Statistics-healthcare/dental assistant.

20   "Women in architecture and engineering occupations in 2016." TED: The Economics Daily. US Dept. of Labor, Bureau of Labor Statistics.

21   "Same occupation, different pay: How wages vary," TED: The Economics Daily. *US Dept. of Labor, Bureau of Labor Statistics.*

22   Mark Ferenchik. "Why are men more likely to take dangerous risks?" *The Columbus Dispatch.* Jun 3, 2018.

23   C.J. Kahane, "Injury Vulnerability and Effectiveness," Washington, DC: *National Traffic Safety Administration,* (DOT HS -811-766).

24   Washington, DC: US Department of Justice, Federal Bureau of Investigation. *Uniform Crime Report (2015).* Table 2 21A.

25   Jack P. Gibb and Walter Martin, "A Theory of Status Integration and its Relationship to Suicide," *American Sociological Review,* Vol. 23, No.2, (1958):140-142.

26   Robert Maris, Aaron Berman, Morris Silverman, *Comprehensive Textbook of Suicidology,* (New York: The Guilford Press, 2000).

27   Andrew F. Henry and James F. Short, *Suicide and Homicide,* (The Free Press, 1974).

28   William H. Courtnay, "Construction," Consruction of masculinity and their influence on men's well-being," *Social Science and Medicine, vol.50,* (2000): 1385-1401.

29   Stephen Dinan, "Illegals commit crimes at double the rate of native born." *The Washington Times,* Janury 26, 2018.

30   United States Department of Justice, Federal Bureau of investigation, Uniform Crime Report," Murder Victims by Sex," (2015), Table 1.

31   Kelly Cohen, "FBI: violent crime falls, but murder rises during first half of 2017," *The Washington Examiner,* January 26, 2018.

32   Washington, DC, United States Department of Justice, Federal Bureau of Investigation, "Homicides by Gender", Expanded Homicide Table 5.2017.

33   Bureau of Labor Statistics, "Occupational Outlook Handbook," https://www.bls.gov/ooh/management/top-executives.htm#tab-5, accessed March 28, 2019.

34   Bureau of Labor Statistics, "Weekly and Hourly Earnings Data from the Current Population Survey," https://data.bls.gov/pdq/SurveyOutputServlet, accessed March 28, 2019.

35 Kim Parker and Renee Stepler, "Americans see men as the financial providers, even as women's contributions grow," FacTank, https://www.pewresearch. org/fact-tank/2017/09/20/americans-see-men-as-the-financial-providers-even-as-womens-contributions-grow/, Pew Research Center, posted September 20, 2017, accessed March 28, 2019.

36 Rich Morin, "Study: More men on the 'daddy track'," FacTank, https:// www.pewresearch.org/fact-tank/2013/09/17/more-men-on-the-daddytrack/, Pew Research Center, posted September 17, 2013, accessed March 28, 2019.

37 Robert Franklin, "Pew Research Shows Gender Roles Have Changed, But Not Much," https://nationalparentsorganization.org/recent-articles?id=22855, National Parents Organization, posted March 21, 2016, accessed March 28, 2019.

38 Belinda Luscombe, Men Without Full-Time Jobs Are 33% More Likely to Divorce, Time, http://time.com/4425061/unemployment-divorce-men-women/, posted July 28, 2016, accessed March 28, 2019.

39 Kerry Close, "The Average U.S. Household Owes More Than $16,000 in Credit Card Debt," Money, http://money.com/money/4607838/householdcredit-card-debt/, posted December 20, 2016, accessed March 28, 2019.

40 Gallup Research, "State of the American Workplace," https://www.gallup. com/workplace/238085/state-american-workplace-report-2017.aspx, accessed March 28, 2019.

41 Anna Robaton, "Why so many Americans hate their jobs," CBSNews.com, https://www.cbsnews.com/news/why-so-many-americans-hate-theirjobs/, posted March 31, 2017, accessed March 28, 2019.

42 Steve Crabtree, "Worldwide, 13% of Employees Are Engaged at Work," Gallup, https://news.gallup.com/poll/165269/worldwide-employees-engaged-work.aspx, posted October 8, 2013, accessed March 28, 2019.

43 Michael Knoll and Rolf van Dick, "Do I Hear the Whistle…? A First Attempt to Measure Four Forms of Employee Silence and Their Correlates," *Journal of Business Ethics*, Vol 113, No. 2 (March 2013), pp. 349-362.

44 Federal Bureau of Investigation, "Law Enforcement Officers Killed and Assaulted (LEOKA) Program," https://www.fbi.gov/services/cjis/ucr/leoka, posted March 1, 2019, accessed March 28, 2019.

45 Kaitlyn Schallhorn and Madeline Farber, "Officers killed in the line of duty in 2018," Fox News Channel, https://www.foxnews.com/us/officers-killedline-of-duty-2018, posted December 30, 2018, accessed March 28, 2019.

46 Federal Bureau of Investigation, Uniform Crime Reports, "2019 Law Enforcement Officers Killed & Assaulted," https://ucr.fbi.gov/leoka/2016/officers-assaulted/assaults_topic_page_-2016, accessed March 28, 2019.

47 U.S. Department of Veterans Affairs, "America's Wars Fact Sheet," https://www.va.gov/opa/publications/factsheets/fs_americas_wars.pdf, posted May 2017, accessed March 28, 2019.

48 Ibid.

49 American Psychological Association, "By the Numbers: Men and Depression," *Monitor on Psychology*, https://www.apa.org/monitor/2015/12/numbers, posted December 2015, accessed March 28, 2019.

50 Marc Freedman and Trent Stamp, "The U.S. Isn't Just Getting Older. It's Getting More Segregated by Age," *Harvard Business Review*, https://hbr.org/2018/06/the-u-s-isnt-just-getting-older-its-getting-more-segregated-by-age, posted June 6, 2018, accessed March 28, 2019.

51 Anita Bernstein, "For and Against Marriage, *102" Michigan Law Rev, 129.*

52 Stephanie Koontz, *Marriage: A History.* New York: Penguin Books, (2006).

53 Ibid.p.190.

54 John L McCormick," Title to Property, Title to Marriage to Marriage" Valparaiso, Law Review, v.42. no.2, (Winter 2008):461-502.

55 Leslie J. Harris et.al. *Family Law,*(New York: Wolters Kluwer, (2014)p.172.

56 King v. Smith, 392 U.S. 309 313-314(1968).

57 Utah Code 30-1-4.5(2007).

58 Theda Sokol, *The Political Origins of Social Policy in the United States,* Cambridge, Mass. (Harvard University Press, 1995)p.66

58 Abigail Geiger, "8 facts about love and marriage in America," *Pew Research Center*, (February 13, 2018:1.

58 Ibid.:1.

58 Ibid:1.

58 Ibid.:1.

58 Abigail Geiger, "Americans increasingly looking for love online," *Pew Research Center,* the (February 13, 2018):7.

58 Abigail Geiger, "8 facts about love and marriage in America," *Pew Research Center*, (February 13, 2018:1.

58 Ibid.:1.

58 Ibid:1.

58   Ibid.:1.

58   Abigail Geiger," Americans increasingly looking for love online," *Pew Research Center*, the (February 13, 2018):7.

59   Abigail Geiger, "8 facts about love and marriage in America," *Pew Research Center*, (February 13, 2018:1.

60   Ibid.:1.

61   Ibid:1.

62   American Religious Identification Survey New York, The Graduate Center, City University of New York,(2001).

63   Darren Sherkat, "Tracking the Restructuring of American Religion", *Social Forces*, vol.79, no.4,(2001):1459-1493.

64   W. Bradford Wilcox, "Family," In *Handbook of Religion and Social Institutions*. Helen Rose Ed., New York : Springer (2005).

65   Rosemary Radford Ruether, *Christianity and the Making of the Modern Family*, Boston, Beacon, 2000.

66   Wade C Roof, *Spiritual Marketplace*, Princeton New Jersey, Princeton University Press, (1990).

67   Darren Sherkat, "Religious Intermarriage in the United States," *Social Science Research*, vol.33, no.4 (2004):606-625.

68   Ibid.:1.

69   Abigail Geiger," Americans increasingly looking for love online," *Pew Research Center*, the (Februaru 13, 2018):7.

70   US Census Bureau (2010) "America's families and Living Arrangements."

71   Kay Williams, et/al. "Marital status and mental health," In: Theodore Scheid, *A handbook for the study of mental health*, (Cambridge, UK(2010)pp.306-320).

72   Pamela Schmock, Wendy Manning and Meredith Porter, "Everything was there except money," *Journal of Marriage and the Family*, vol.67, (2005) :680-696.

73   Bernice L. Neugarten, "Time, age and the lifecycle. *American Journal of Psychiatry*, vol. 136, (1979):887-894.

74   Peggy A. Thoits, "Personal agency and the stress process," *Journal of health And Social Behavior*,vol.47, (2006):309-323.

75   Leonard I. Pearlin, "The sociological study of stress," *Journal of Health and Social Behavior*,vol.30, 91989):241-256.

76   Adam Thomas and Isabel Sawhill, "For love and money," *The Future of Children*, vol.15, (2005):57-74.

77 Susan L. Brown, "Marriage and child well-being," *Journal of Marriage and Family*, vol.72, (2010):1050-1077.

78 Austin Nichols, Explained the changes in poverty over the past four decades," Washington DC, *The Urban Institute*, 2013):1.

79 David Lichter and Martha Crowley, "Welfare Reform and Child Poverty," *Social Science Research*,vol.3, (2004):385-408.

80 Pub L. 104-193 Washington DC. 104th United States Congress 9 August 1, 1996).

81 United States Department of Labor, Bureau of Labor Statistics,(2012).

82 Michael L. Norton and Dan Ariely, "Improving Online Dating" *Journal of Interacting Marketing*, vol.22, no.1, (Winter 2008) :51-61).

83 Shei Spiritof, "How Long has the institution of marriage existed?" *The Spruce*, (February 18, 2018) no page number.,

84 Ibid.

85 Claudia Goldin and Laurence Katz, "The Power of the Pill," *National Bureau of Economic Research*, Cambridge, MA. (2000).

86 George Akelof, Janet A. Yellen and Michel Katz, "An analysis of out-of-wedlock childbearing in the United States," *Quarterly Journal of Economics*, vol. 17, no.2 (May 1996):277-317.

87 Bruce C. Daniels, "Puritan Ambivalence Toward Leisure and Recreation," *American Studies*, vol.34, no.1 ((1993):121.

88 Brenner, *The Puritan Experiment*, p.92.

89 Edmund S. Morgan, *The Puritan Dilemma*, London: Pearson (2006).

90 John Calvin, *The Institutes of the Christian Religion*, Translated by Ford Lewis Battles, (Philadelphia. Westminster Press, (1960):vol.2, 1270.

91 Cotton Mather, *The Diaries of Cotton Mather*, Worthington C. Ford, Ed,. American Classics, (New York: Frederick Ungar, (1911-1912): n.d.:1270.

92 David D. Hall, *The Antinomian Controversy*,(Middletown, T. Wesleyan University Press, (1968):362.

93 Samuel Sewall, M. Halsey Thomas, Ed., *The Diary of Samuel Sewall*, New York: Farrar, Strauss and Giroux, (1973):158.

94 Kai Erikson, *The Wayward Puritans*, New York: Pearson, Allyn and Bacon, 1966.

95 Anna Menta, "An Updated List of Men Accused of Sexual Harassment, Misconduct and Assault," *Newsweek*, (January 12, 2017).

96   Emily Street and Michael Schmidt, "Bill O'Reilly Is Forced out of Fox News," *The New York Times* (April 19, 2017), Business.

97   Sheryl Gay Stolberg, "Kavanaugh's Nomination In Turmoil as Accuser Says He Assaulted Her Decades Ago," *The New York Times*, (September 18, 2018):1.

98   Clair Cain Miller, "Unintended Consequences Of Sexual Harassment Scandals, *The New York Times*, (October 2, 201):B1.

99   Terrence Diggory, "Race, Gender, and Liberal Fallacies," *The New York Times*, (October 20, 1991):E15.

100 In 1983 the Minneapolis City Council passed an ordinance called the Dworkin McKinnon ordinance. This ordinance was found unconstitutional by the United States Supreme Court in American *Booksellers v. Hudnut* and in *Hudnut v. American Booksellers. versus*

101 Catherine MacKinnon. *Feminism Unmodified.* Cambridge: Harvard University Press, (1987).

102 Jacobellis v. Ohio 378 U.S. 1841 (1964).

103 Stanley v. Georgia, 394. U.S. 557 (1969).

104 Miller v. California, 413 U.S. (1973).

105 Eric Holder, Speech 1 The National Strategy Conference on Combating Child Exploitation. (May 19, 2011).

106 United States Department of Justice, Citizen's Guide To Federal Law On Child Pornography, https://www.justice.gov/criminal-ceos/citizens-guide-us-federal-law-child-pornography, accessed 4/1/19.

107 Butler v. State of Michigan, 332 U.S.380 (1957)

108 Feminist Anti Censorship Task Force. *Hudnut v. American Bookseller*, 771F.2nd 323 (7th Ctr. 1985).

109 Dolf Zillman, "Effects of Prolonged Consumption of Pornography," Hillsdale, NY: Lawrence Erdman, (1989).

110 Ibid.:29.

111 American Psychiatric Association, *Diagnostic and Statistical Manual Of Mental Disorders*, Arlington, Virginia, American Psychiatric Publishing, (2013):797-798.

112 M. G. Weiss and C.M. Earles, "The effects of exposure to film sexual violence on attitudes toward rape," *Journal of Interpersonal Violence*, v.10, (1995):71-84.

113 Malamuth G. Hald and C. Yuen, "Pornography and attitudes supporting violence against women," *Aggressive Behavior*, vol.36, (2010):14-20.

114 Nicholas Gage, "Organized crime reaps huge profits dealing in pornographic films," *the New York Times*, (October 12, 1975):1.

115 Ibid. :2.

116 Ibid.:3.

117 Paul Cheyney, "The XXX crisis: Is pornography out of control?" *The Globe and Mail*, (December 21, 2000):F4-F5.

118 Dolf Zillmannn and L. Bryant, "*Pornography: research advances and policy considerations*,(1989) Hillsdale and Erdbaum, :150-184)

119 Martin Barron and Michael Kimmel, "Sexual Violence In Three Pornographic Media" *Journal Of Sex Research,*

v.37, (January 17, 2010):161-168.

120 N.M. Malamuth, et.al. "Pornography and Sexual Aggression." *Annual Review of Sex Research*, v.11, (2001): 26-91.

121 Joe Pinsker, "The Hidden Economics of Porn," *The Atlantic*, (April 2, 2016):n.p.

122 No author, "12 celebrities who started out in the adult film industry," *emgn. com/s/12-celebrities-who-started-out-in-the-adult-film-industry/4/*, accessed July 17, 2018.

123 Jack Rear, "The Amount Of Scenes Porn Stars Have to Film in a Day is Staggering." *Pretty*, (July 14, 2016):1.

124 James D. Griffith, et.al. "Why Do Women Become Porn Actresses?" *The International Journal of Sexual Health*, (July 202):1.

125 No author. "Catholic Church Sexual Abuse Scandal," *The New York Times*, (August 14, 2018).

126 Henry David Thoreau, "Civil Disobedience" in *United States Magazine And Democratic Review*, (1849).

127 Robert Caro, *The Years of Lyndon Johnson*, vol. 1. *Path to Power*, (New York: Alfred Knopf, 1982) p.3.

128 Gr3egory Claes, "Individualism, Socialism and Social Science," *Journal of the History of Ideas*, vol.46, (1986):81-93. See also: George Stiger, "*De Gustibus non esr disputandom*" (With taste there is no argument) *American Economic Review*, vol.67, no.2, (19777):76. It shows me:

129 David K. Dunaway, *Making Hay with Huxley*,New York, Harper and Row, (1990):

130 Nancy Polikoff, *Beyond Straight and Gay Marriage*, Boston, Beacon Press, (2008):38.

131 Craig A. Rimmtman, *Gay Rights, military wrongs.*" New York: garland Pres, (1996):249.

132 Donald P. Haider-Markel, "Beliefs about the Origin of Homosexuality, "*Public Opinion Quarterly*, vol.72, ((2008):259-310.

133 Samantha Allen, "just how many LGBT Americans are there? *The Daily Beast*, January 14, 2017) :1.

134 Ibid. :238.

135 Judith Treas, "How cohorts, education and ideology shaped a new sexual revolution on American attitudes toward nonmarried sex." *Sociological Perspectives*,vol.45, (2002):263-283.

136 Alan Binder and Richard "Kentucky clerk denies same-sex marriage licenses, defying Court" (*The New York Times*) (*September1, 2015):1.*

137 Meehan, W. and J. Ranch,, Gay Marriage, Same-Sex Parenting And America's Children," *The Future of Children*,v.15, (2005):97-115.

138 Ibid.:558.

139 Sarah Lyall and Richard Bernstein, " The Transition of Bruce Tanner: a shock to some, visible to all." *The New York Times*, (February 6, 2015):Sports 1.

140 Alan Soble, "Bisexuality: *Sex from Plato to Paglia-a philosophical encyclopedia* New York, Greenwood Publishing Group, (2006):115.

141 Amethyst Tate, "Angelina Jolie's bisexual desires to her and Bad Pitt," *Okay Magazine*, September 1, 2016).

142 Beth A Fierstein, *Becoming Visible: Counseling Bisexuals across the Lifespan.* New York: Columbia University Press, (2007):9-12.

143 Mike Szymanski, "Moving Closer to the Middle: Kinsey, the movie and the rocky road to bisexual acceptance," *Journal of Bisexuality*,vol.8, (2008):287-308.

144 Simon Le Vay, "Queer science: The use and abuse of research into homosexuality," Cambridge, The MIT Press, (1996):22.

145 Benedict Carey, "Straight, Gay or Lying?:Bisexuality Revisited," *The New York Times*, (July 5, 2005):Health Section.

146 Francis Lemola and Ciani Camperio, "New Evidence of Genetic Factors influencing sexual orientation in men" *Archives of Sexual Behavior*, vol.38, (June 2009):393-399.

147 L. Ellis and S. Cole-Harding, "The effects of pre-natal stress......on human sexual orientation," *Physiology and Behavior*, vol.74, (2001):213-226.

148 Michael Ruse, *Homosexuality: A Philosophical Inquiry.* Ox ford. Basil Blackwell,(1988):22.

149 Edmund Bergler, *Homosexuality: Disease or Way of Life?* New York: Hill and Wang, (1957):8.

150 Alan P. Bell, Matin S. Weinberg and Susan K. Hammersmith, *Sexual Preference: Its Development in Men and Women*, Bloomington, Indiana University Press, (919810:200-201.

151 Bob Greene, "She Was an Original, Not A Photocopy," *The Chicago Tribune*,(July 24, 1997)::2.

152 D.W. Black, L. Kehrberg, D. Flumrtfelt, and S. Schlosser, "Characteristics of 36 subjects reporting compulsive of sexual behavior. " *American Journal of Psychiatry*, vol. 154, (1997):242-249.

153 S.C. Kalichman and D. Rompa, "Sexual sensation seeking and sexual compulsivity scales" *Journal of Personality Assessment*. Vol.65, (1995):370-395.

154 F.H. Taylor, "Observations on some cases of exhibitionism" *Journal of Medical Science*, vo volume.93, (1947):631-633.1

155 S. Hugh-Jones and B. Gough, "sexual exhibitionism as sexuality and individuality." *Sexualities*, vol. 8, (2005):259-281.

156 W.R. Avison, J. Ali and D. Walters, "Family Structure, Stress and Psychological Distress," *Journal of Health and Social Behavior*," vol.48, (2007):306.

157 Duncan Cramer, "Living Alone: Marital Status, Gender, and Health, "*Journal of Community and Applied Social Psychology*, vol. 3, (1993):3.

158 Renee Stepler, "Number of US adults cohabiting with a partner continues to rise, especially among those 50 and older," Washington DC, the Pew Research Center, (April 6, 2017):1-7.

159 Ibid.pp:2-7.

160 S.A. Kennedy and L. Bumpas, "Cohabitation Children's Living Arrangement. New estimates from the United States," *Demographic Research*, vol.19, (2008):1663-1692.

161 A. Jose, D.K. O'Leary, and A. Moyer, "Does premarital cohabitation predicts subsequent marital stability and marital quality?" *Journal of Marriage and the Family*, vol.72, (2010):105-116.

162 Ibid. :116.

163 Rhodes, et.al. "The pre-engagement cohabitation effect." *Journal of Family Psychology*, vo.23, (2009):107-111.

164 National Survey of Family Growth, https://www.cdc.gov/nchs/nsfg/index.htm, accessed April 3, 2019.

165 Wendy D. Manning, "Childbearing Co-habiting Unions," *Family Planning Perspectives*, vol.33, no.5, (September-October 2001)::220.

166 Myra Fleischer, "State of the Divorce Rate in the United States, 2017" *Community Digital News* (February 3, 2017):1.

167 Nicholas H. Wolfinger, "Parental Divorce and Offspring Marriage::Early or Late?" *Social Forces*, vol.82, he (2003):337-354.

168 Andreas Diekmann, "Is women's labor force participation caused by increasing divorce risk?" *Social Work*, vol.45, (1994):83-97.

169 Shelly Lundberg and Robert Pollak, "Bargaining and distribution in marriage," *Journal of Economic Perspectives*, vol.10, (1996):130-158.

170 P.R. Amato, "Consequences of Divorce for Adults and Children," *Journal of Marriage and the Family*, vol.62, (2000):1260-1287.

171 J.D. Teachman and K.M. Paasch, "Financial Impact of Divorce on Children and the Family," *Future of Children*, vol.4, (1994):63-83.

172 E.M. Hetherington and W.C. Clingenpeel, *Monographs of Society in Child Development*, Chicago, University of Chicago Press,vo.57, (192)p.2-3.

173 M. Lamb, "Noncustodial fathers and their impact on divorce," In: R.A. Thompson, et.al., *The Post Divorce Family*, Sage, Thousand Oaks, CA (1999):105-126.

174 J.M. Gottman, *What Predicts Divorce?* Hillsdale, NJ, Erdman (1994).

175 P.T. Davies and E.M. Cummings, "Marital Conflict and Child Adjustment," *Psychological Bulletin*, vol.116, (1994):387-411.

176 D. Doumas, G.,Margolin, and R.S. John, "The intergenerational transmission of aggression across three generations" *Journal of Family Violence*,vol.9, (1994):157-175.

177 U.S. Department of the Census Washington DC "Current Population Reports, ":70-80.

178 C. Shammas, "Reassessment of married women's property acts," *Journal of Women's History*, vol.6, (1994):9-30.

179 Stephanie Coontz, "Divorce-no-fault style," *The New York Times*, (June 16, 2010):1.

180 Divorce Writer, "New York On-line Divorce," https://www.divorcewriter.com/NewYork, accessed April 3, 2019.

181 Chabad org, "Jewish Divorce 101," https://www.chabad.org/library/article_cdo/aid/557906/jewish/Divorce-Basics.htm, accessed April 3, 2019.

182 Catechism of the Catholic Church. "Offenses against the Dignity of Marriage".

183 Kate Mouleno, "America's abandoned children," *Huffington Post*, (May 2, 2011)::1.

184 No author, "The Proof Is in: father absent arms children," *National Fatherhood Initiative*, n.d.

185   Canon Law Society of America. *Proceeding of the Thirty-First Annual Convention* (1969).

186   The Diocese of Harrisburg, "Twelve Myths About Marriage Annulments in the Catholic Church," https:www.hbgdioese.org/tribunal, *Harvard Law Review*, (June 2006):2469-2470.

187   New York City Bar, "Annulment," New York, 2017.

188   Ashely Coleman, "North Carolina Mother, 44, married 25 year old son," *Daily Mill*, (September 12, 2016):1.

189   No author, Washington, DC "U.S. Department of Homeland Security, Immigration and Customs Enforcement, ICE dismantles organized crime visa scheme," (11/20/12).

190   PACER 2:12-cv01795-APG-CWH.

191   Jeff Reinitz,"Two from Waterloo Indicted on Marriage Fraud Charges," *The Courier*, (October 8, 2018):1.

192   No author," "Bigamy Law ad Legal Definition,"*U.S. Legal*, no date:1.

193   Robert B. Riggs, "Reynolds v. United States," In: Daniel H. Ludlow, *The Encyclopedia of Mormonism*, New York, MacMillan(1992):1229-1230.

194   Gustav Larson, *Federal Government Effots to 'Americanize' Utah.* "Government, Politics and Conflict," :250-254.

195   Chris Baynes, "More than 200,000 children married in US over the last 15 years," *Frontline*, (July 8, 2017)::1.

196   Nicholas Kristoff, "An American 13 year old Pregnant and Married to her Rapist" *New York Times* (June 1, 2018)::5

197   Legal Information Institute, "Marriage Laws of the Fifty States," (September 17, 2018):1.

198   Perspective: Washington Post (February 12, 2017).

199   Amanda Parker, "Worse than Weinstein is the exploitation of Florida girls," *Sun Sentinel*, (October 24, 2017):1.

200   No author, "Why can 12 year olds still get married in the United States? *Washington Post*, (February 21, 2017):1.

201   Engy Abdelkader, "Force or Choice: American Muslim marriages." *The Huffington Post*, December, 2017).

202   Liz Welch,, "My Mom Took Me Overseas and Forced Me into Being 18 Bride," *Seventeen*, (September 28, 2018):1.

203   Danielle Selby, "This American girl was forced to marry a stranger in a religious cult at age 15." *Global Citizen*, (June 28, 2016).

204 R.K. Jones and J.J. Jerman, "Population group abortion rates and lifetime incidence of abortion," *American Journal of Public Health.* (2017):1

205 Barber Goldberg, "Abortion Rate In US Fell Sharply in Decade ending 2015." *Health News,* November 21, 2018):1.

206 J. J. Jerman and R.K. Jones, "*Characteristics of United States abortion patients,* New York: Guttmacher Institute, (2006):1.

207 Ibid.2.

208 Ibid. 2

209 17 Stat 598.

210 Judith Walzer Leavitt, *Brought to Bed: Childbearing in America 1790-1950.* New York: Oxford University Press (1986).

211 Martha Vicinus, "Sexuality and Power: a review of current work in the history of sexuality." *Feminist Studies,* vol.8 (Spring 1987):153-156.

212 G. Wiehl, "Abortion and Public Health," *American Journal of Public Health.* Vol.24 (May 1938):63.

213 James Foster Scott, "Criminal Abortions," *American Journal of Obstetrics and Diseases of Women and Children. Vol.53* (January 1896).

214 William D. English, "Evidence, dying declaration, preliminary questions of fact." *Boston University Law Review,*

Vol. 15, (April 1935):382.

215 White House Conference on Health and Protection, Washington, DC *Fatal Newborns and Maternal Mortality and Morbidity,* New York, (1940).

216 No author, "End murder by abortion," *The Chicago Tribune,*(June, 1915):1.

217 Inquest on Petrovitis, "case 254-255, (1916). *People v. Hobbs* 297 Ill. 399 (121).

218 People v.Patrick 2120 (1912), 272 Ill.

219 Sheila M. Rothman, *Women's Proper Place.* New York, (1978):203.

220 Deborah A. Dawson, "Fertility control in the United States before the contraceptive revolution," *Family Planning Perspectives,* v.12, (1980):76-86.

221 Norman E Hines, *Medical History Of Contraception,* New York: Viking (1970):309.

222 Frederick S. Jaffe, "Knowledge, Perception and Change," *Mount Sinai Journal of Medicine,* vol. 43, (1975):243-345.

223 John Frith, "Arsenic: the Poison of Kings," *Journal of Military and Veterans' Health.*vol.21,no.4, (January 2017):1.

224 Paul M. Wright, "The evolutionary role of chemical synthesis in antibacterial drug discovery," *Anfewandte Chemie*, Vol.53, no.34, (August 2014):8840-8869.

225 410 U.S. 113 (1973).

226 Jane Atkinson, "The Law and Henry Wade," *D Magazine*, (June 1977):1.

227 No author, "Anti-abortion violence," Anti-Defamation League, no date.

228 Ron Sylvester, "Scott Roeder gets hard 50 in murder of abortion provider George Tiller." *The Wichita Eagle*, (April 2, 2010):1.

229 Jim Yardley and David Rhode, "Abortion Doctor in Buffalo Slain: attack fits violent pattern." *The New York Times* October 25, 1998) '

230 Ichal E. Miller and Yanan Wang, "The radical, unrepentant ideology of abortion clinic collects," *The Washington Post*, (September 30, 2015):1.

231 Abby Goodnough, "Florida executes killer of abortion provider," *The New York Times*, (September 4, 2003):1.

232 Dalia Lirwick, "The murderer who started a movement," *Slate*, (October 31, 2017):1.

233 No author, "Rachelle 'Shelley' Shannon, activist who shot abortion Dr. George Tiller, released," Kansas City Star, May 22, 2018.

234 Donald Golen and Brian McGrory, "Clinic shooting suspect, John Salvi captured." The Boston Globe, (January 5, 1995):1.

235 William E Dyson, *Terrorism: An Investigators' Handbook*, New York: Routledge, (2008)*p.479*.

236 Eric Rudolph, "Statement," *Army of God*, (October 26, 2006).

237 Maryanne Voller, *Eric Rudolph: Murderer, Myth, and the Pursuit of an American Outlaw*. New York, Harper, (2006).

238 No author, "Accused Planned Parenthood shooter found incompetent to stand trial," https://www.kktv.com/content/news/Accused-Planned-Parenthood-shooters-mental-competency-up-for-debate-378888511.html, posted May 10, 2016, accessed April 4, 2019.

239 Karen Lowenthal, "Donald Cooper Dale off Violence," *Choice Magazine*, (December 21, 2014).

240 No author, "Army of God claims responsibility for clinic bombing," CNN (February 2, 1998).

241 Richard Perez Pena, "Anti-abortion activists charged in Planned Parenthood video case," *The New York Times*, (March 29, 2017)."1.

242 Patricia B. Windlee, "Targets of Hatred," New York: St. Martin's Press, (2001):23.

243 Winfried Turnwer, J"urors convict Marley," *Tines Daily*, (December 11, 2015):1-3.

244 Code of Canon Law 1398.

245 Alexander Cooperman, "Eight Facts about Orthodox Jews," *Pew Research Center*, (October 17,2013):1.

246 David F. Kelly, Contemporary Catholic Healthcare Ethics, Washington, *Georgetown University Press*, (2004);111-113.

247 Barbara Karkabi, "Abortion no main issue for Catholics," *Houston Chronicle*, (October 31, 2008):1.

248 No author, "Obama, Catholics, and the Notre Dame commencement, *Pew Forum On Religion and Public Life* (August 30, 200)0:1.

249 No author, "Religious groups' official position on abortion, *Pew Research Center*, (January 10, 2013).

250 Pew Research Center, "Public Opinion on Abortion," https://www.pewforum.org/fact-sheet/public-opinion-on-abortion/, posted October 15, 2018, accessed April 4, 2019.

251 *Planned Parenthood of Southeastern Pennsylvania v. Robert C. Casey*, 505 22U.S. 833.

252 Robert K Jones and John Jerman, "Abortion incidents and service availability in the United States." *Perspectives on Sexual And Reproductive Health*, v.49, no.1, (2017):17-27.

253 Ibid.:3.

254 Ralph K. Jones, "Reported contraceptive use in the month of becoming pregnant among US abortion patients," *Contraception*. (December 18, 2017):1.

255 Susan Morrissey, "RU486," *Chemical and Engineering News*, vol.96, no. 68. (December 3, 2018):1.

256 Ibid: 3.

257 No author, "Robert Lewis Dear –The Colorado shooter," CNN (May 11, 2016).

258 John M. Murtagh and Sara Harris, Cast the First Stone (New York: McGraw-Hill, 1957), p. vii.

259 James G. Frazer, The Golden Bough: A Study in Magic and Religion (London: Macmillan, 1924), p. 385.

260 Mary Beard and John Henderson, "With This Body I Thee Worship: Sacred Prostitution in Antiquity," Gender and History 9, no. 3 (November 1997): 480.

261 Will Durant, *Our Oriental Heritage* (New York: Simon and Schuster, 1954), p. 491

262 Beard and Henderson, "With This Body," p. 480.

263 Nicki Roberts, Whores in History: Prostitution in Western Society (London: HarperCollins, 1992).

264 Alex Thio, Sociology (New York: Longman, 1998), p. 214

265 Kingsley Davis, "Sexual Behavior," in Contemporary Social Problems, ed. Robert Merton and Robert Nisbet (New York: Harcourt Brace Jovanovitch, 1971).

266 Gerhard Falk, Sex, Gender and Social Change: The Great Revolution (Lanham, Md., and New York: University Press of America, 1998).

267 Monica Prasad, The Morality of Market Exchange: Love Money and Contractual Justice," Sociological Perspective, 42, no. 2 (summer 1999): 183.

268 Ibid., p. 194.

269 Ibid., p. 203.

270 Carole Pateman, "What's Wrong with Prostitution?" Women's Studies Quarterly 27 (spring/summer 1999): 53.

271 Simone de Beauvoir, The Second Sex (New York: Vintage Books, 1974), p. 619.

272 Cicely Hamilton, Marriage as a 71-ade (London: Women's Press, 1981), p. 37.

273 M. Macintosh, "Who Needs Prostitutes? The Ideology of Male Sexual Needs," in C. Smart and B. Smart, Women, Sexuality and Social Control (London: Routledge and Kegan Paul, 1978), p. 54.

274 Eileen McLeod, Women Working: Prostitution Now (London: Groom Helm, 1982), p. 84.

275 Jody Miller, "Feminist Theory," in Alex Thio and Thomas Calhoun, Readings in Deviant Behavior (New York: HarperCollins, 1995).

276 Kathleen Barry, The Prostitution of Sexuality (New York: New York University Press, 1995).

277 Alex Thio, Sociology, p. 215.

278 Vern L. Bullough and Bonnie Bullough, Women and Prostitution; A Social History (Amherst, N.Y.: Prometheus Books, 1987), p. 299.

279 Studs Terkel, Working (New York: Pantheon Books, 1974), p. 57.

280 Valerie Jenness, Making It Work: The Prostitutes' Rights Movement in Perspective (New York: Aldine De Gruyter, 1993), p. 1.

281 Sydney Biddle Barrows, Mayflower Madam (New York: Ivy Books, 1986), p. 171.

282 Ibid., p. 72.

283 Gail Pheterson, A Vindication of the Rights of Whores (Seattle: Free Press, 1989).

284 Philip Alston, The Best Interests of the Child (Oxford: Clarendon Press, 1994), p. 1.

285 Barbara Meil-Hobson, Uneasy Virtue (New York: BasicBooks, 1987), p. 217.

286 Graham Scambler and Annette Scambler, Rethinking Prostitution: Purchasing chasing Sex in the 1990 (London and New York: Routledge, 1997), p. 188.

287 Diane Post, "Legalizing Prostitution: A Systematic Rebuttal," Off Our Backs 24 (July 1999): 8.

288 Linda L. Lindsey and Stephen Beach, Sociology: Social Life and Social Issue (Upper Saddle River, N.J.: Prentice-Hall, 2000), p. 75.

289 David Knox, Human Sexuality: The Search for Understanding (New York: West Publishing Co., 1984), p. 460.

290 Barbara Serman Heyl, The Madam as Entrepreneur: Career Management in House Prostitution (New York: Transaction Publishers, 1979), chap. 5.

291 Barrows, Mayflower Madam, p. 367.

292 Paul Goldstein, "Occupational Mobility in the World of Prostitution: Becoming a Madam," Deviant Behavior 4 (1983): 267.

293 Nils Christie, "Conflict as Property," British Journal of Criminology 17 (1977): 1-15.

294 Lisa Maher and Kathleen Daly, "Women in the Street-Level Drug Economy," Criminology 34 (1996): 465-91.

295 Neil McKeganey and Marina Bernard, Sex Work on the Streets (Philadelphia: phia: Open University Press, 1996), p. 72.

296 Knox, Human Sexuality: The Search for Understanding, p. 463.

297 D. Kelly Weisberg, Children of the Night: A Study of Adolescent Prostitution (Lexington, Mass.: Lexington Books, 1985), p. 22.

298 Donald M. Allen, "Young Male Prostitutes: A Psychosocial Study," Archives of Sexual Behavior 9, no. 5 (1980): 400.

299 Cameron Forbes, "Child Exploitation in the Philippines," in Caroline Moorehead, A Report on Violence Toward Children in Today's World (New York: Doubleday, 1990), p. 236

300 Weisberg, Children of the Night, p. 56.

301 Scambler, Rethinking Prostitution, p. 181.

302 Bullough and Bullough, Women and Prostitution, p. 291.

303 Kit Roane, "Gangs Turn to New Trade," New York Times, July 11, 1999, p. 123.

304 Edward O. Wilson, *Socio-biology*, Cambridge,Mass. Harvard University Press, 2000.

305 James Bennett, "Despite intern, president stays in good graces," *The New York Times*, (February 4, 1998):1.

306 Stanley Renshon, *The Clinton Presidency and the Public Audience*. New York: Routledge, (1998).

307 Nancy Gibbs, "Tick,Tock, Tick...Talk" *Time*, (August 10, 1998).

308 Nigel Cawthorne, *Sex Lives of the Presidents*, New York: St. Martin's Press,(1996), p.236.

309 Molly Olmstead, "Representative Collins, Charged with Security Fraud, Re-elected in New York," *SLATE*, (November 7, 2018)::1.

310 Laura F. Bischoff, "Anothee Ohio Lawmaker resigns, cites inappropriate behavior." *Dayton Daily*, (November 16, 2017):1.

311 Alia B. Rau et.al. "State Senator Scott Bundgaard resigns from legislature," *The Arizona Republic*, (January 6, 2010:1

312 Rob Davis and Adam Nagourney, "Ex-mayor of San Diego, pleads guilty to charges of sexual harassment, *The New Yok Times*, (October 16, 2016):1.

313 George Prentice, "John McGee, who left Idaho Senate following sex scandal, emerges as vice president of development for Boise rescue mission, *Boise Weekly*, (July 11, 2017)."

314 Mike Donahey, "Ex-Lawmaker Keith Fanham dies in prison serving time for child pornography," *(March 19, 2015)*.

315 Elisha Anderson, "Sen. Virgil Smith goes directly to jail, collects 71k." *Detroit Free Prss*, March 21, 2018):1.

316 Harriet Sokmensuer, "Ex-County prosecutor Sue Dunning sentenced to year in county jail," *People*, (March 16, 2016).

317 Natalie Thongrit, "Disgusting: New Hampshire Rep. Kyle Tasker arrested for drug possession and intent to sexually assault a minor." *Bipartisan Report*, (March 2, 2016). "1.

318 Phil Fairbanks, "Panepinto gets two months in prison for sexual advances," *The Buffalo News*, (December 15, 2018):"1.

319 Kristine Phillips, "Former Oklahoma state senator admits to child sex trafficking while in office," *The Washington Post*, (November 20, 2017):1.

320 Richard Yates, "Former lawmaker faces at least a year in prison for third offense drunken-driving," *The Morning Call*, March 28, 2018):1.

321 A.J. Perez, "Hector Olivera found guilty of assault, sentenced to jail," *USA Today Sports,* (September 8, 2016):1.

322 Tribune News Service, "Ex-NFL Star Darren Sharper gets 18 years for drugging, raping women." *Chicago Tribune,* (August 18, 2016):1.

323 Richard Severo, "Hedy Lamarr: Sultry Star who reigned in Hollywood:, *The New York Times,* January 20, 2000).

324 Vincent Canby, "Film View-Elizabeth Taylor: Her Life is the Stuff of Movies," *The New York Times,* (March 4, 1986):1.

325 https://www.biography.com/people/marilyn-monroe-9412123, accessed April 10, 2019.

326 https://www.biography.com/people/elvis-presley-9446466, accessed April 10, 2019.

327 Kolodny eet.al. "The prescription opioid and harrowing crisis. A public health approach to addiction." *Annual Review of Public Health,* vol.36, (2015):559-574.

328 Gerhard Falk, End of the Patriarchy. Lanham, Md. Rowman And Littlefield, (2016).

329 Jodi Kantor, "Sexual Misconduct Claims Trail Hollywood Mogul," The New York Times, (October, 2017):A1.

330 Bridget Reed, "Me Too Founder Tarana Buke Voices frustration on Twitter," Vogue, (February 22, 2018): no page.

331 Paul Farhi, "Bill O'Reilly's Fox Career comes to a swift end amidst growing sexual harassment claims," The Washington Post, (April 10, 2017):1.

332 Jodi Guglielmi and Charlotte Triggs, "Matt Lauer turns 61: Inside his quiet life a year after Today show firing," People, (December 31, 2018):1.

333 Michael Cooper, "James Levine's final act at the Met ends in disgrace," The New York Times,, (March 13, 2018):A1.

334 Joyce Chen, "Olivia Munn Among Women Accusing Brett Ratner of Sexual Harassment," Rolling Stone, https://www.rollingstone.com/movies/movie-news/olivia-munn-among-women-accusing-brett-ratner-of-sexual-harassment-128467/, posted November 1, 2017, accessed April 10, 2019.

335 Ronan Farrow, "As Leslie Moonves negotiates exit from CBS, six women raise new harassment claims," The New Yorker, (August 6, 2018).

336 Wayne D. Hall and Michael Farrell, "Reducing the opioid overdose death toll in North America," PLoS Medicine, https://www.ncbi.nlm.nih.gov/pmc/articles/PMC6067703/, posted July 31, 2018, accessed April 10, 2019.

337 L.B. Finer And John B. Philbin, "Trends in ages of key reproductive transitions in the United States, 1951–2010." *Women's Health Issues*, vol.24, no.3 (2014):271-279.

338 J.C. Abma, G.M. Martinez and C.E. Copen, "Sexual activity, contraceptive use and child bearing of teenagers age 15 to 19 in the United States." *NCHS Data Brief No. 209*,(2015).

339 G. M. Martinez, C.E. Copen and J.C. Abma, "Teenagers in the United States: sexual activity, contraceptive use and childbearing," *National Survey of Family Growth, - Vital and Health Statistics*, (2001):Series 23, no.31.

340 John A. Martin, Births: final data for 2015, *National Vital Statistics*, vol.46, no.1 (2015).

341 Washington DC, United States Bureau of the Census, database for single mothers.

342 Federal Register, (March 12, 1997).

343 American Association of University Women Foundation, (1993):5.

344 Centers for Disease Control and Prevention, "Incidence, prevalence and cost of sexually transmitted infections in the United States," Estimate Fact Sheet, (February 2013).

345 Kost, Kay & Maddow-Zone, I. "U.S. teenage pregnancies, births and abortions." *Gutmacher Institute* (2001).

346 Martinez, G. "Teenagers in the United States: sexual activity, contraceptive use and childbearing." *National Survey of Family Growth. Vital Health Statistics*, vol. 23 2011.

347 Ed Richter, "Carlisle baby alive at birth, prosecutor says after teen mom's court," *Dayton Daily News*, (July 2, 2017).

348 Suzanne Russell, "Highland Park teen mom charged with death of newborn baby." *My Central Jersey*, April 15, 2018):1.

349 National Conference of State Legislators, "Not making the grade: academic achievement difficult for parents."(June 11, 2013).

350 Department of Justice, Bureau of Justice Statistics, "Rape and Sexual Victimization among college age females," 1995-2013 (2014).

351 Laura Kerr and Noreen Malone, "The Sex Lives of College Students," *The New Yorker*, (June 28, 2016).

352 William H. Perkins, "Research on women's drinking patterns," *Catalyst*, v.6 (2000):6-7.

353 White, H.R., et.al. "Increases in alcohol and marijuana use during the transition out of high school into emerging adulthood," *Journal of Studies of Alcohol,*, vol. 67, (2000):810-822.

354 John W. LaBrie, Et.al. "Self-consciousness moderates the relationship between perceived norms and drinking in college student addictive behavior." *Addictive Behaviors,* (2008): 393-398.

355 John J Arnett, " Sensation seeking, aggressiveness, and adolescent reckless behavior, *Personality and Individual Differences* (1996): vo.20, no6 : 693- 702.

356 Blake Gumprecht, *The American College Town,* Amherst, MA: University of Massachusetts Press (2009).

357 Arthur Elgart, "This is what it's like to have a sex life in college," *Teen Voice,* (February 20, 2010).

358 Michelle Boba, "How common are alcohol related deaths among college students?" *Share Care* 2010-2019. No date.

359 Karl Menninger, *Man Against Himself,* New York: Harcourt, Brace, & Co. (1938).

360 Zoe Szathmary, "College freshman, 19, dies falling from 20-foot tower on dormitory roof." *The Daily Mail,* (April 5, 2014).

361 Clyde Hughes, "Brogan Dulle found: missing college student's body is discovered," Newsmax, (January 26, 2019).

362 No author," what happened to Ryan Uhre?" Jim Fisher True Crime, November 7 2018):1.

363 No author, "Chico State student killed in the fall from tree in 1 mile recreation area," *Chicago Enterprise Record,* April 3, 20):1.

364 Nick Wilson, "Chico State student to be tried for manslaughter for crash near Avila," *San Louis Obispo Tribune,* January 9, 2012):1.

365 Mark Schachtenhafen, "Friends, others recall Edmund OU student," *The Edmond Press,* (January 11, 2010):1.

366 Howard Pankratz, "CSU student killed on tracks may have been train-hopping," *Denver Post,* (February 5, 2010):1.

367 Eric Italiano, "Death of University of Minnesota student was alcohol related," Tyg Press, https://tygpress.com/post/3508545-1158815-Death-Of-University-Of-Minnesota-Student-Was-Alcohol-Related,-Says-Medical-Examiner, posted January 11, 2019, accessed April 11, 2019.

368 Thomas Weinberg, Gerhard Falk and Ursula Falk, *The American Drug Culture,* Thousand Oaks, CA: Sage, Chapter Seven.

369 Promises Treatment Centers, "How Many Teens Die of Drug Overdose?" https://www.promises.com/resources/overdose/many-teens-die-drug-overdose/, accessed April 11, 2019.

370 Lexi Pandell, "Under the Influence: Alcohol and Drugs." *Daily Nexus*, (May 10, 2010).

371 No author, "Sylvester Graham," Biography.com, https://www.biography.com/people/sylvester-graham-21194545, accessed April 15, 2019.

372 Johannah Cornblatt, "A Brief History of Sex Ed in America," *Newsweek*, (October 27, 2009):1.

373 Ibid.:1.

374 Rachael Low, *History of the British Film, 1918-1929*, New York: George Allen and Unwin. (1971), p.20.

375 Dorothy E Cook, National Film Preservation Foundation" Gift of Life." New York: HW Wilson Company. *Educational Film Catalog*, v.36, (1936), p.152.

376 Kate Blackman and Samantha Scotti, "State policies on sex education in schools," Washington DC: *National Council for State Legislators.* (March 1, 2016):1-2.

377 Ibid.:3.

378 Guttmacher Institute, (2015).

379 Catholic Parents Online, "10 good reasons to oppose public-school sex education," no date, no reference.

380 Russ Pulley, "Discussion in Health Class draws parental complaint," *Kansas City Star "February 2, 1998":1.*

381 Martha Quillen, "Franklin Schools Slice Sex-Ed Chapters out of Health Books" *The News and Observer. (9/27/97):1*

382 Reynolds Holding, "Student's Sex Article Prompts Sad Legal Lesson", *San Francisco Chronicle (July 2, 2000):1*

383 No author, "Diocese will lead classes on abstinence," *Helena Independent Record*, (January 15, 2000):1.

384 No author, "No Sex Please. We're Teens." *Evening Sun*, (February 7, 2000):1.

385 Jill Grossmann "Students fight for Sex Education." *Rocky Mountain News (March 18, 1999).1*

386 Diana Schemo, "Sex Education with Just One Lesson: No Sex." *New York Times (Dec.28,2000):p.A1*

387 Douglas Kirby, "Sexuality and Sex Education At Home and Schools." Adolescent Medicine(October 1999)

388 Priscilla Parbini, Federal Law mandates Abstinence Only Sex Ed," Rethinking Schools (Summer 1998).

389 Alan Guttmacher Institute, "U.S. Teenage Pregnancy Statistics with Comparative Statistics for Women Age Twenty to Twenty Four (2004).

390 Douglas Kirby et.al. "School Based Programs to Reduce Sexual Risky Behavior." Public Health Reports (1994:339)

391 J.E. Darroch, et.al. "Changing Emphasis in Sexual Education in U.S. public secondary schools." *Family Planning Perspectives.v.5 [2000]:204*

392 Jay Ginn and Sara Arber, "Only Connect: Gender Relations and Aging," in Connecting Gender and Aging, Buckingham, PA., Open University Press, 1995, p. 1.

393 U.S. Bureau of the Census, Current Population Reports, ser. P-60 no. 184, Washington, D.C. The United States Government Printing Office, 1993.

394 Edward H. Thompson, Jr., "Older Men as Invisible Men in Contemporary Society," in: Older Men's Lives, Edward H. Thompson, Jr., Editor, Thousand Oaks, Ca., Sage Publications, 1994, pp. 2-5.

395 Gerhard Falk and Ursula Falk, "Sexuality and the Aged," Nursing Outlook, Vol. 28, No. 1, January 1980, pp. 51-55.

396 Thompson, op. cit., p. 12

397 Doris Ingrisch, "Conformity and Resistance as Women Age," in: Connecting Gender and Aging, Buckingham, PA., Open University Press, 1995, p. 54.

398 John C. Macionis, Sociology, Fifth Ed., Englewood Cliffs, N.J., Prentice Hall, 1995, p. 326.

399 Neena L. Chappell and Betty Havens, "Old and Female: Testing the Double Jeopardy Hypothesis," The Sociological Quarterly, Vol. 21, Spring 1980, pp. 157-171.

400 Information Please Almanac, New York, Houghton Mifflin Co., 1996, p. 847.

401 Barbara M. Barer, "Men and Women Aging Differently," The International journal of Aging and Human Development, Vol. 38, No. 1, February 1994, p. 29.

402 C.M. Teuber and I. Rosenwike, "A Portrait of America's Oldest Old," in The Oldest Old, R.M. Suzman, D.P. Willis and K.G. Manton, Eds., New York, Oxford University Press, 1992. See also: B.B. Hess and E.W. Markson, Growing Old in America, Transaction, Inc., New Brunswick, N.J., 1987.

403 William J. Strawbridge, Terry C. Camacho, Richard D. Cohen and George A. Kaplan, "Gender Differences in Factors Associated with Change in Physical Functioning in Old Age etc." The Gerontologist, Vol. 33, No. 5, October 1993, p. 603.

404 William Rakowski and Victor Mor, "The Association of Physical Activity with Mortality among Older Adults in the Longitudinal Study of Aging," journal of Gerontology, Vol. 47, 1992, pp. M122-M129.

405 Kate Bennett and Kevin Morgan, "Aging, Gender and the Organization of Physical Activities," in Aging, Independence and the Life Course," Bristol, PA., Jessica Kingsley, Publishers, 1993.

406 Ibid., Chapter 5.

407 Gerhard Falk and Ursula Falk, op. cit., pp. 51-55.

408 Barer, op. cit., p. 30. See also: U.S. Bureau of the Census, *Money, Income and Poverty Status in the United States*, Washington, D.C., U.S. Government Printing Office, 1989.

409 U.S. Bureau of the Census, "Population Projections of the United States by Age, Sex, Race and Hispanic Origin 1992-2050," *Current Population Reports*, Series P-25, No. 1092, Washington, D.C., Government Printing Office, 1992.

410 Ursula A. Falk, *On Our Own: Independent Living for Older Persons*, Buffalo, N.Y., Prometheus Press, 1989, Chapter 2.

411 Albert M. Matthews and K.H. Brown, "Retirement as a Critical Life Event: the Differential Experiences of Women and Men," *Research on Aging*, Vol. 9, No. 4, 1987, pp. 548-571.

412 Barer, op. cit., pp. 31-33.

413 Ibid., p. 36.

414 Falk, op. cit., p. 21

415 Barer, op. cit., p. 37.

416 Macionis, op. cit., Ch. 10.

417 Karen Hanson and Seymour Wapner, "Transition to Retirement: Gender Differences," *International Journal of Aging and Human Development*, Vol. 39, No. 3, 1994, p. 203.

418 Ibid., p. 204

419 Joseph F. Quinn, "Poverty in the Extremes : The Young and the Old in America," *The Gerontologist*, Vol. 29, No. 6, December 1989, pp. 837-840.

420 Paula I. Dressel, "Gender, Race and Class: Beyond the Feminization of Poverty in Later Life," *The Gerontologist*, Vol. 28, No. 2, April 1988, pp.177-180.

421 Judith A. Levy, "Intersections of Gender and Aging," *The Sociological Quarterly*, Vol. 29, No. 4, 1988, pp. 479-486.

422 Rochelle Jones, *The Other Generation: The New Power of Older People*, Englewood Cliffs, N.J., Prentice Hall, Inc., 1977, p. 175.

423 Elizabeth W. Markson and Beth B. Hess, "Old Women in the City," *Signs*, Vol. 5, No 3, (Supplement) 1980, pp. 127-141.

424 George Herbert Mead, *Mind, Self and Society From the Standpoint of a Social Behavior.* Chicago, University of Chicago Press, 1967.

425 Elisabeth Markson, "Gender Roles and Memory Loss in Old Age: An Exploration of Linkages," International Journal of Aging and Human Development, Vol. 22, No. 3, 1985- 86, pp. 205- 213.

426 Ursula Adler, A Critical Study of the American Nursing Home, Lewiston, N.Y. The Edwin Mellen Press, 1991, p. 5, p. 136, pp. 236-249.

427 Seymour Wapner, Jack Demick, Jose Pedro Redondo, "Cherished Possessions and Adaptation of Older People to Nursing Homes," International Journal of Aging and Human Development, Vol. 31, No. 3, 1990, pp. 221- 222.

428 Jon Lorence, "Age Differences in Work Involvement," *Work and Occupation*, Vol. 14, No. 4, November, 1987, p. 552.

429 Kenneth Solomon and Peggy A. Swabo, "The Work-Oriented Culture : Success and Power in Elderly Men," in *Older Men's Lives*, Edward H. Thompson, Editor, Thousand Oaks, CA., Sage Publications, 1994, pp. 42-64.

430 Edward H. Thompson, op. cit., p. 12.

431 Ibid., p. 228.

432 *Information Please Almanac*, Houghton Mifflin Co., New York, 1996, p. 826.

433 Diana Sainsbury, "Dual Welfare and Sex Segregation of Access to Social Benefits," *Journal of Social Policy*, Vol. 22, January 1993, pp. 69- 93.

434 Judith G. Gonyea, "Making Gender Visible in Public Policy," in *Older Men's Lives*, Edward H. Thompson, Jr., Editor, Thousand Oaks, CA., Sage Publications, 1994, p. 239.

435 U.S. Government General Accounting Office, Elderly Americans: Health, Housing and Nutrition Gaps Between the Poor and Non-poor. Washington, D.C., U.S. Government Printing Office, 1992, p. 171. See also: Gonyea, op. cit., p. 240.

436 Gonyea, op. cit., p. 241.

437 Ibid., p. 246.

438 U.S. Senate Select Committee on Aging, Aging America: Trends and Projections, Washington, U.S. Government Printing Office, 1988.

439 Bureau of Justice Statistics, Cn'minal Victimization in the United States, Washington, D.C., 1991, 1992, 1993 and 1994.

440 James B. Richardson, "Purse Snatch—Robbery's Ugly Stepchild," in *Crime and the Elderly*, Jack Goldsmith, Ed., Lexington, KY, Lexington Books, Inc., 1976.

441 James Alan Fox and Jack Levin, "Homicide Against the Elderly: A Research Note," *Criminology*, Vol. 29, May 1991, pp. 317-327.

442 Georgia M. Barrow and Patricia A. Smith, *Aging, Ageism and Society*, New York, West Publishing Co., 1979, pp. 239-242.

INDEX

B

Babylon 45
Barra, Mary T. 5
behavioral culture 64
Behind the Green Door 49
beliefs and opinions 113
benefit of marriage 62
Bethlehem, Pennsylvania 118
Betty Ford (treatment) Center 120
Biblical prohibition 54
bigamy 70
biological imperatives 127
biological parents 61
Birmingham, Alabama 82
birth control 3, 38, 127, 143, 147
bisexual 57, 58
blood alcohol level 137
Brahmans 91
Bureau of Labor Statistics 7, 11
Byron Police Department 26

C

California law 74
call girls 102
cardiac catheterization 154
career satisfaction 7
caregiver 158
Cast the First Stone 91
Catholic annulment 68
Catholic catechism 68
celebrities 51
Centers for Disease Control 19, 122
chemical companies 88
chemistry 89
Chicago Tribune 59
child as a confidant 159
child marriage 71
child pornography 44
children 74, 162
Child Protective Services 73
children in obscene situations, 47
child support 64
children of same-sex marriages 56
Christianity 54, 73
Christian Puritans 40
Christmas 33
civil lawsuit, 46
Civil War 26

Cleopatra 120
Clinton, President Bill 114
cocaine and heroin 126
codeine, 121
cohabitation 30, 61
college degree 129
college enrollment retention rates 133
college expenses 64
college, staggering amount of debt 22
college students 4, 20, 67, 132, 135
Collins, Chris 115
Colorado Springs, Colorado 24
Columbia Broadcasting System, 125
common-law marriage 30
communication skills 12
competition for power 127
comprehensive sex education 150
Comstock Act 76
Congress 9, 36
Congress Against the Commercial Sexual Exploitation of Children. 98
conspicuous consumption 111
Constitutional Amendments
    First Amendment 46, 47, 148
    10th Amendment 11
    14th Amendment 46, 79, 87
    Second Amendment 52
    26th Amendment 38
contraception 144
Contract with America 36
contract marriage 30
control 3
cost of higher education 34
COYOTE, 97
crime families 69
criminal abortion deaths 77
criminal act 129
criminal indictment 70
criminal mischief 84
criticism 65
culture 3, 29, 113
custodial parent 64
custody of children 66

D

damaged goods 142
Danco laboratories 89
dangerous occupations 23
Dear, Robert Lewis 83

S

sacred occupation, 109
sacred prostitutes 91
Salversan 78
same-sex marriage 34, 37
sanctity of human life 85
Sanderson,Robert 84
San Diego, California 116
Sandy Spring, Georgia 83
Santa Clara, California 150
school curriculum 146
secondary schools 130
self-concept 163
self-induced measures 76
self-preoccupation 163
servicemen 105
sex 3, 29
sex education 44, 141, 143
sex industry 108
sexless 154
sexology 58
sex partners 93
sex roles 153
sex symbol 121
sexual abuse 52, 145
sexual aggression 41
sexual and reproductive behavior 76
sexual assault 124, 131
sexual behavior 99
sexual behavior of students 152
sexual compulsion 60
sexual contact 130
sexual expression 96, 119, 154
sexual functioning 147
sexual gratification 48
sexual harassment 42, 60, 124
sexuality 114
sexual liberation 129
sexually abused 106
sexually transmitted disease 143, 151
sexual maturity 99
sexual misconduct 42
sexual orientation 58
sexual promiscuity 50
sexual relationships 69
sexual revolution 108, 111

sexual solicitation 103
sexual violence 48
sex with strangers, hookups, one night stands 51, 96, 131, 134
sex work 95, 107
Sharper, Darren 119
single mothers 129
single, older women 157
single parent families 35, 128
singles bars, swing parties 109
slaves 37
Slepian, Dr. 81
small community 162
small town colleges 133
small-town residence 133
social aspects of aging 157
social constructionist view 66
social contacts 159
social diseases 110, 143
social honor 79
socially acquired diseases 127
socially disadvantaged 156
Social Register 100
Social Security 28, 98, 161
social work 12
social worth 162
sociological niew 18
Speaker of the House 10
speedball 126
speed dating 36
speeding 16
spontaneous abortions 4
sports "heroes" 119
state brothel 98
status changes 160
status of adulthood 99
status/role of an object 108
status-roles 156
stay-at-home fathers 21
steam engine 89
stepfather or stepmother. 65
stigma associated with retirement 28
stratified subcultures 100
street prostitution 98
student at the small college 134
Students Manual 141
St. Vincent College 136

Printed in the United States
By Bookmasters